Stop and Search

Stop and Search
The Anatomy of a Police Power

Edited by

Rebekah Delsol
Open Society Justice Initiative, London, UK

Michael Shiner
London School of Economics and Political Science, London, UK

Selection, introduction, conclusion and editorial matter © Rebekah Delsol and Michael Shiner 2015
Individual chapters © Respective authors 2015
Foreword © Robert Reiner 2015

All rights reserved. No reproduction, copy or transmission of this publication may be made without written permission.

No portion of this publication may be reproduced, copied or transmitted save with written permission or in accordance with the provisions of the Copyright, Designs and Patents Act 1988, or under the terms of any licence permitting limited copying issued by the Copyright Licensing Agency, Saffron House, 6–10 Kirby Street, London EC1N 8TS.

Any person who does any unauthorized act in relation to this publication may be liable to criminal prosecution and civil claims for damages.

The authors have asserted their rights to be identified as the authors of this work in accordance with the Copyright, Designs and Patents Act 1988.

First published 2015 by
PALGRAVE MACMILLAN

Palgrave Macmillan in the UK is an imprint of Macmillan Publishers Limited, registered in England, company number 785998, of Houndmills, Basingstoke, Hampshire RG21 6XS.

Palgrave Macmillan in the US is a division of St Martin's Press LLC,
175 Fifth Avenue, New York, NY 10010.

Palgrave Macmillan is the global academic imprint of the above companies and has companies and representatives throughout the world.

Palgrave® and Macmillan® are registered trademarks in the United States, the United Kingdom, Europe and other countries.

ISBN 978–1–137–33609–5

This book is printed on paper suitable for recycling and made from fully managed and sustained forest sources. Logging, pulping and manufacturing processes are expected to conform to the environmental regulations of the country of origin.

A catalogue record for this book is available from the British Library.

Library of Congress Cataloging-in-Publication Data
Delsol, Rebekah, author.
  Stop and search : the anatomy of a police power / Rebekah Delsol, Open Society Justice Initiative, London, UK, Michael Shiner, London School of Economics and Political Science, UK.
    pages   cm
  Includes bibliographical references.
  ISBN 978–1–137–33609–5
  1. Searches and seizures—Great Britain.   2. Police power—Great Britain.   3. Searches and seizures.   4. Police power.   I. Shiner, Michael, author.   II. Title.
  KD8338.D45 2015
  345.41'0522—dc23   2014050085

To Elijah and Keziah

Contents

List of Figures and Tables	viii
Foreword by Robert Reiner	x
Acknowledgements	xv
Notes on Contributors	xvi

1	Introduction *Rebekah Delsol and Michael Shiner*	1
2	The Legal Powers and their Limits *Lee Bridges*	9
3	The Politics of the Powers *Michael Shiner and Rebekah Delsol*	31
4	Race Disproportionality and Officer Decision-Making *Paul Quinton*	57
5	Effectiveness *Rebekah Delsol*	79
6	Unintended Consequences *Ben Bradford*	102
7	Counter-Terrorism Policing *Tara Lai Quinlan and Zin Derfoufi*	123
8	Regulation and Reform *Michael Shiner*	146
9	Towards a Transnational and Comparative Approach *Ben Bowling and Estelle Marks*	170
10	Conclusion *Rebekah Delsol and Michael Shiner*	193

References	197
Index	219

Figures and Tables

Figures

3.1 Suspicion-based stop-searches in England and Wales (number) — 33
3.2 Stop-searches under exceptional powers in England and Wales (number) — 37
3.3 Suspicion-based stop-searches by reason in England and Wales, 2012/2013 (percentage) — 42
3.4 Suspicion-based stop-searches for drugs and stolen property in England and Wales (number) — 43
3.5 Suspicion-based stop-searches across England and Wales by police force area, 2012/2013 (rate per 1,000) — 45
5.1 Trends in suspicion-based stop-searches and resultant arrests in England and Wales, 1986–2012/2013 (numbers indexed to 1986) — 88
5.2 Percentage of stop-searches under Section 1 of the Police and Criminal Evidence Act and other legislation resulting in arrest by police force areas in England and Wales, 2012–2013 — 89
6.1 Unfairness damages legitimacy and cooperation — 110
6.2 Trust in police fairness is linked to readiness to use self-help violence — 112
6.3 Trust in police fairness is linked to people's sense of belonging to the UK — 114
7.1 Stop-searches under Section 44 of the Terrorism Act 2000 in England and Wales — 132
7.2 Trends in stop-searches under Section 44 of the Terrorism Act 2000 in England and Wales by ethnic appearance (numbers indexed to 2001/2002) — 134
8.1 An example of a (corporate) regulatory pyramid — 167

Tables

3.1 Suspicion-based stop-searches by self-identified ethnicity in England and Wales (2011/2012) — 50

3.2	Suspicion-based stop-searches by ethnic appearance in England and Wales (1998/1999 to 2011/2012)	51
5.1	Suspicion-based stop-searches and resultant arrests in England and Wales (1986 to 2012/2013)	87
5.2	Section 60 Public Order and Criminal Evidence Act stop-searches and arrests in England and Wales (2000/2001 to 2012/2013)	90
7.1	Section 44 stop-searches by self-identified ethnicity in England and Wales (2008/2009 and 2009/2010)	136
7.2	Schedule 7 examinations by self-identified ethnicity in the UK (percentages)	138
7.3	Stop-searches and resultant arrests under sections 44 and 47A of the Terrorism Act 2000 in England and Wales	140

Foreword

The purposes of policing (when not simply taken for granted) are generally couched in the loftiest of language, as promulgating a general, universal, objectively beneficial good. This was true of Sir Robert Peel's celebrated 1829 instructions to the newly born Metropolitan Police: 'the object to be obtained is the prevention of crime. To this great end every effort of the police is to be directed. The security of person and property, the preservation of the public tranquility, and all the other objects of the police establishment, will thus be better effected than by the detection and punishment of the offender after he has succeeded in committing the crime' (cited in Emsley, 2014: 12). And this remains the nominal purpose today. As Theresa May said at the beginning of the Home Office document initiating the coalition's profound shake-up of policing, 'The mission of the police which was established by Sir Robert Peel as preventing crime and disorder has not fundamentally changed' (Home Office, 2010: 2).

Yet, from the outset, the profane reality of what was described by contemporary critics of Peel's police as the 'New Engine of Power and Authority' contradicted this sanitised agenda. The overwhelming bulk of policing resources and activity has always been devoted to the patrol and surveillance of public space. The benefits and the burdens of policing are borne primarily by those who live out their lives predominantly on the streets and other public places.

The police, for the most part, do not deal with crime in general, but with those offences that are perpetrated by what in the 19th century were dubbed unceremoniously the 'dangerous classes', often, of course, against other working-class people but sometimes against those higher up the social scale too. Police deployment reflected this: they 'guarded St James's by watching St Giles'. The prime targets of both the iron fist and the velvet glove of policing were the crimes and minor disorders of the urban poor, to whom the police acted as 'domestic missionaries'. Peel explicitly recognised this in his policy of recruiting police from those 'who had not the rank, habits or station of gentlemen'. Democratic policing in the 19th century was of the people, by the people, but not primarily for the people.

Policing always has a double aspect. It protects a universally beneficial degree of order that is necessary for any possibility of any coordinated large-scale social existence, but at the same time it reproduces the social inequality and domination that have blighted all societies to date. In Otwin Marenin's striking phrase, the police role encompasses both 'parking tickets and class repression' (Marenin, 1983). The task of legitimating the new policing apparatus was a formidable challenge, accomplished slowly, unevenly and never completely. But within this complex process, the notion that the police are agents of and governed by a fair and – at least in principle – equal 'rule of law' played an essential part.

'Stop and search', the subject of this timely, stimulating and often inspiring collection of papers, is thus at the very heart of the policing process, and the controversies that have always stormed around it. 'Stop and search' (and similar powers with varying names at different times and places) is the outer edge of the state–suspected citizen relationship, the crucial entry point for many, perhaps most, of those who will end up suffering the pains of punishment. As several chapters indicate, the constables who preceded the 1829 creation of the Metropolitan Police Service (MPS) already had highly discretionary powers to handle 'idle and disorderly Persons, and Rogues and Vagabonds' (in the words of the Preamble to the 1824 Vagrancy Act). These powers stretch back over centuries of vagrancy legislation aimed at disciplining the poor and powerless people who were seen as threatening respectable social order, and who have always constituted 'police property' around the world. The 'sus' law (s.4 of the 1824 Act), which conferred wide-ranging stop, search and arrest powers, remained highly controversial until its abolition in 1981. During the century and a half after 1829, many stop and search powers were conferred on particular forces (for example the MPS in 1839) and for a wide range of specific offences (listed in an appendix to the 1981 report of the Royal Commission on Criminal Procedure).

By the time the present major stop and search law (s.1 of the Police and Criminal Evidence Act (PACE) 1984) was passed, the main contours of controversy were already well established in relation to the 'sus' law and the national stop and search power in the 1971 Misuse of Drugs Act. These turned mainly on the huge disproportionality in the use of these powers, especially with regard to ethnicity. There was also concern about the very low rate of success in detecting offences, which indicated that a large number of innocent people were subject to incursions on their liberty on flimsy grounds. The formulation of s.1 of PACE, and the accompanying Code of Practice A, was intended to rectify these problems, specifying that stop and search required 'reasonable suspicion' and indicating a list of stereotypes that did *not* satisfy the requirement. The requirement to complete records of stop and search was the main specific safeguard offered, along with other sections of PACE sanctioning breaches of its procedures and Codes of Practice. These were immediately criticised as inadequate, as they primarily relied on internal police record-keeping and discipline. The list of unacceptable criteria for reasonable suspicion (ethnicity, age, style of dress, etc.) could be cynically interpreted as advice on how to complete acceptable records rather than guidance on what did constitute objectively reasonable grounds.

The chapters of this book document in detail the continuation of these problems despite many reform attempts since 1984, notably in the wake of the 1999 Macpherson Report on the investigation into the murder of Stephen Lawrence. The issues of disproportionality and ineffectiveness are particularly marked in relation to the newer breed of 'suspicionless' stop and search powers introduced by the 1994 Criminal Justice and Public Order Act and the 2000 Terrorism Act (the latter now restricted, though not abolished), with specially negative consequences for police legitimacy. The sources of the powers, the explanation of the disproportionate pattern of their exercise, the reasons why reform has proved so intractable, the poor record of their effectiveness in dealing with crime, the baleful consequences of the rise of new forms of terror and the recurrent appearance of similar problems in other jurisdictions are all thoroughly explored in this excellent volume. The authors are a superb group of scholars and activists, who have produced uniformly clear, authoritative and insightful analyses. Volumes of essays are notoriously often less than the sum of their parts, but this one is an exception. The editors, Rebekah Delsol and Michael Shiner, have done a brilliant job in assembling a collection that provides a coherent, comprehensive, critical yet constructive overview of this topic, which is of pivotal importance for understanding policing and for achieving social justice. It will remain the definitive work on stop and search for a long time to come.

Having said that, I'd like to just offer some hostages to fortune in speculating about the future. The authors document the growing consensus in government and police leadership for reform of stop and search powers since the coalition took office in 2010. They are, on the whole, somewhat sceptical about how far these will succeed, and, I think rightly, foresee the need for organisations like StopWatch to continue their stalwart monitoring and campaigning.

However, I think they are perhaps unduly modest about what has been achieved. This is suggested by comparing the disproportionality of 'reasonable suspicion' stop/searches (unacceptably high as it is) with the spectacular disproportionality of 'suspicionless' searches. The literally paper-thin safeguards afforded by the Codes of Practice make some difference. So, too, does relentless campaigning, as with the now curtailed suspicionless searches.

On the other hand, the history of stop and search also offers serious warnings about the capacity of legal change to regulate police practice. When I conducted my PhD research in the early 1970s in a large urban force, it was one that did not have any general stop and search power. Nonetheless, stops and searches were carried out frequently, with the consent of the suspects. What PACE did in this and other areas of policing was 'authorise and regulate', in David Dixon's evocative phrase (Dixon, 2008). It authorised existing illicit practice and extended common law powers onto a statutory footing, but sought to regulate them by a regime of safeguards of debatable efficacy. The scope for 'voluntary' searches such as the ones I observed in the 1970s remains, even though the Code of Practice says all have to be recorded. In the low-visibility context of street encounters, how is this to be regulated? Even in the event that a complaint is made about an unrecorded search, it will usually be a case of one person's word against a constable's (or several).

The dangers of counter-productive attempts to regulate on-street discretion and 'voluntary' cooperation are indicated further by the unhappy history of 'stop and account'. There is no such power: case law is clear that people are not under a legal obligation to answer a police officer's questions, although, of course, constables are free to ask them and do so frequently, and most people will answer voluntarily. Because of concern that such interventions were as discriminatory as stop and search, Macpherson recommended they should also be recorded, and this was taken up by the Home Office response to his Report. However, the requirement to record 'stop and account' was dropped in 2011, as the chapters in this book make clear. So we are left with a phantom power brought into some kind of formal existence by a now abolished safeguard.

Finally, the chapters in this collection indicate the considerable reforms launched under the coalition (despite the relaxing of recording requirements), in the broader context of a massive shake-up of police governance and conditions of service. They do not offer much by way of explanation of these, and neither can I. The Owl of Minerva flies at dusk, and we may be able to understand the *volte face* in Conservative attitudes to the police when we are looking at them in the rear-view mirror (can't wait). But as a guide to the past and present of police powers to stop and search, and the quest to understand and regulate their operation so as to minimise discrimination and maximise effectiveness and legitimacy, this volume is a superb achievement. It deserves to be a great success.

Robert Reiner
London School of Economics

Acknowledgements

We are very grateful to the Open Society Foundations for funding the Roundtable event that led to this edited collection and to John Jay College of Criminal Justice for hosting it. Particular thanks to Professor Delores Jones-Brown for her organisational skills, her enthusiasm and her all-round indefatigability. You are an example to us all! We are grateful to everybody who attended the event and made for one of the most rewarding experiences either of us has had in our working life. Thanks also to CopWatchNYC and the Malcolm X Grass Roots Movement for the hospitality and for sharing your experiences. It was daunting and inspiring in equal measure. We are honoured that Professor Robert Reiner has written the foreword for this book, especially as he was a teacher and inspiration to us both long before we met him, and continues to be so. We are grateful to Palgrave Macmillan for publishing the book, especially Julia Willan, Harriet Barker and Dominic Walker for their patience and steadfast support. Thanks also to Tony Corbin for editing the manuscript. Finally, we would like to thank everybody at StopWatch for giving up their time and engaging in some much-needed praxis.

Contributors

Ben Bowling is Professor of Criminology and Criminal Justice at King's College London School of Law. His research focuses on practical, political and legal problems in policing and the connections between local and global police power. His recent work includes three books on the themes of fairness, effectiveness and accountability in policing: *Policing the Caribbean* (2011), *Global Policing* (with James Sheptycki, 2012) and *Stop and Search: Police Power in Global Context* (edited with Leanne Weber, 2012).

Ben Bradford is Departmental Lecturer at the Centre for Criminology at the University of Oxford. He specialises in the study of public trust and confidence in the police, the nature of police legitimacy, the impact of personal experience on opinions of the police and other legal authorities, and cross-national comparisons of trust and legitimacy. He has worked with the London Metropolitan Police, the College for Policing and other organisations on various research projects concerned with improving police understanding of public opinions and priorities.

Lee Bridges is Emeritus Professor at the School of Law, University of Warwick. He has a long record of conducting empirical research on aspects of the UK criminal justice system, including the pilot and subsequent evaluation of the provision of custodial legal advice under the Police and Criminal Evidence Act 1984, national evaluations of contracting for criminal legal aid and evaluation of an experimental public defender scheme. He is a joint author of *Standing Accused: The Organisation and Work Practices of Criminal Defence Lawyers in Britain* (1994) and has written regularly on issues of race and criminal justice for the journal *Race & Class*.

Rebekah Delsol coordinates the Open Society Justice Initiative's project on Ethnic Profiling, working with police and impacted communities in various jurisdictions including Hungary, the Netherlands, Spain, the UK and the US. She completed her PhD in the Sociology Department at the University of Warwick, focusing on racial disparities in stop and search.

Zin Derfoufi is a PhD candidate at the University of Warwick. His thesis focuses on the role of the newly elected police and crime commissioners across England and Wales and their impact on police–community relations. He has a background in police–community engagement relating to violent radicalisation and counter-terrorism policing. He acts as a 'critical partner' for a number of cross-governmental programmes set up to counter violent radicalisation and carries out locally based community work around specific counter-terrorism operations and the impact of stop and search.

Estelle Marks graduated with a first-class law degree from King's College London School of Law in 2014 before taking up a scholarship to study for the MSc in criminology at Oxford University. Her research interests are largely focused on civil liberties and the accountability of government. With a keen interest in the relationship between power and the citizen, she is aiming for a career as a lawyer, advising clients on civil actions involving public bodies.

Tara Lai Quinlan is a PhD student in the Department of Sociology at the London School of Economics and Political Science. Her thesis examines counter-terrorism policing in the UK and the US. She recently completed her LLM in criminal law, criminology and criminal justice at King's College London. She is also a licensed New York attorney, and practised law in New York City for seven years before pursuing an academic career.

Paul Quinton is Principal Research Officer at the College of Policing, prior to which he worked at the Home Office and the National Policing Improvement Agency. He has been involved in several studies of stop and search, which formed the basis of his PhD that was completed at the University of Surrey. He and his colleagues received the 2013 Government Social Research Award for Excellence for conducting a randomised controlled trial testing the impact of procedural justice training on officer interactions with the public.

Michael Shiner is Associate Professor in the Department of Social Policy at the London School of Economics and Political Science. He specialises in the study of drugs, drug policy and policing. He has a particular interest in stop and search and was a principal researcher on the evaluation of the national implementation of Recommendation 61 from the Stephen Lawrence Inquiry.

1
Introduction

Rebekah Delsol and Michael Shiner

Stop and search is one of the most common forms of adversarial contact between the police and public, bringing citizens face-to-face with the coercive power of the state. It also provides a visible reminder of what policing is fundamentally about. Although the police 'force' has been repackaged into a 'service', it remains a 'dirty work' occupation (Hughes, 1962) that has to deal with 'inherently contentious situations' as a matter of routine (Reiner, 2010: 253). How officers respond to such situations involves considerable discretion. Whether incidents are treated as crimes is often a matter of judgement, and attending officers may well leave the scene having done little more than listened to the disputants, offered words of advice and, perhaps, 'moved people on' (Sanders et al., 2010). Banton (1964) famously observed that police officers spend far more time 'keeping the peace' than enforcing the law, but the pursuit of peace is often backed up by the threat of force. If conflict escalates or disputants refuse to submit to police authority, officers can invoke their legal powers, and 'no amount of public relations work can entirely abolish the sense that there is something of the dragon in the dragon-slayer' (Bittner, 1970: 6–7). Force or the threat of force remains essential to the police function even though it is typically disguised. According to Manning (2003: 37), the police, in modern welfare states, are 'beneficiaries and guardians of symbolic violence'. Their authority may seem natural and inevitable, yielding instinctive forms of compliance, but it is the product of a carefully cultivated power relationship: 'The police in every society are insulated in some fashion from those they police – by civil laws, traditions, legal conventions such as the common law, civilian review boards, and other modes of accountability' (Manning, 2003: 37).

Somewhat provocatively, perhaps, Klockars (1988: 257) framed the issue in the following terms: 'The only reason to maintain police in

1

modern society is to make available a group of persons with a virtually unrestricted right to use violent and, when necessary, lethal means to bring certain types of situations under control.' This 'fact', he argues, is as fundamentally offensive to the core values of modern society, which seek to eliminate violence as an acceptable means of conducting human affairs, as it is unchangeable. 'To reconcile itself to its police', therefore, 'modern society must wrap it in concealments and circumlocutions that sponsor the appearance that the police are either something other than what they are or are principally engaged in doing something else' (Klockars, 1988: 257). Following Bittner (1970), Klockars suggests that legalisation is probably the most powerful circumlocution currently mystifying the institution and functions of police in modern society. Despite a sizeable body of law covering police behaviour, he argues, courts have little control over what the police actually do. This is due, in part, to the highly selective way in which the police enforce the law and 'the enormous influence on police discretion of such things as suspect demeanour, complainant preferences, and a host of other factors that have nothing to do with "the law"' (Klockars, 1988: 243). Professionalisation is said to be another circumlocution on the grounds that the tasks and situations routinely encountered by the police are too varied and complex 'to be covered by the crude provisions of general bureaucratic regulations' (Klockars, 1988: 246).

Klockars (1988: 240) does not advocate the abolition of the police, noting that 'no one whom it would be safe to have home to dinner argues that modern society could be without police'. Rather, he opposes the 'creation of immodest and romantic aspirations that cannot, in fact, be realized in anything but ersatz terms' (1988: 257). This does not lead him to question the need for regulations governing police conduct, however, and part of his objection to legalisation is that it tends to discourage police accountability to political authorities by creating the impression that courts oversee and control police practice. We might, therefore, be equally wary of having anyone home for dinner who argues that modern society could do without formal regulations governing the ability of the police to use force. To dismiss legal and bureaucratic controls as circumlocutions is, perhaps, to understate their importance and to gloss over the nuances involved in the construction of police legitimacy. It is a characteristic of democratic societies that police are subject to the rule of law; can intervene in the lives of citizens only under limited and carefully controlled circumstances; and are publicly accountable (Marx, 2001). Codifying police powers in this way serves an important normative function, outlining what is expected of police, as well as creating a system through which they may be called to account for misconduct. We cannot assume that changes in regulations and procedures will necessarily translate into changes in practice, but the legal powers that are made available to police are indicative of the political and social context in which they operate. The recent trend has been towards the prioritisation of crime control over 'due process values' and this is a matter of concern 'from a standpoint of principled legality' (Reiner, 2010: 212).

Stop and search is one of the most controversial powers available to police officers in England and Wales. In a recent independent review, Her Majesty's Inspectorate of Constabulary (HMIC, 2013: 2) noted:

> For decades the inappropriate use of these powers, both real and perceived, has tarnished the relationship between constables and the communities they serve, and in doing so has brought into question the very legitimacy of the police service. Thirty years after the riots in Brixton, concerns about how the police use stop and search powers were again raised following the riots in England in August 2011.

The 1981 Brixton 'riots' were a pivotal moment in the history of British policing, which signalled a loss of hard-earned legitimacy. What Reiner (2010: 68) refers to as the 'golden age' of policing rested on a series of disarming policy choices that encouraged a low-profile, legalistic stance built around bureaucratic organisation, the rule of law and the strategy of minimal force. By the 1950s, 'policing by consent' had been achieved to the maximum degree that it is ever possible, and the British police were firmly established as a symbol of national pride. From the late 1950s, the tacit contract between police and public began to fray as social and political changes created a more challenging policing environment. The rise of the Sixties counter-culture and associated protest movements heralded a renewed politicisation of policing. 'A more crucial change', however, 'was the catastrophic deterioration of relations with the black community' as 'a vicious cycle of interaction developed between police stereotyping and black vulnerability to the situations that attract police attention' (Reiner, 2010: 94–5). What happened in Brixton was characterised by the subsequent inquiry led by Lord Scarman (1981: para. 3.110) as 'essentially an outburst of anger and resentment by young black people against the police'. This anger and resentment was attributed, in part, to the adoption of policing priorities and practices that did not command local support and impacted disproportionately on black and minority ethnic communities. Particular criticism was reserved for the heavy-handed use of stop and search in the form of operation 'Swamp 81', which was identified as the immediate trigger of the disorder.

The broader message of the Scarman Report was, in some ways, a familiar one, echoing Reith's (1956: 287–8) insistence that the fundamental principle of policing is 'the process of transmuting crude physical force, which must necessarily be provided in all human communities for securing observance of laws, into the force of public insistence on law observance'. According to Scarman, the functions of the police, which he identified as the prevention of crime, the protection of life and property, and the preservation of public tranquillity, should be pursued with regard to two fundamental principles: namely, 'consent and balance' and 'independence and accountability'. The nub of Scarman's approach was that, where necessary, the maintenance of public tranquillity should be prioritised over law enforcement. This is the opposite of what had been happening in Brixton, and the 'riots' illustrate what can happen when the iron fist forgets about the velvet glove. The solution recommended by Scarman was to rebuild 'consent' using a variety of means, including increased consultation and improved accountability through lay station visitors and independent review of complaints against the police.

Although Scarman's message was not entirely new, it provoked a 'fundamental reorientation of police thinking' (Reiner, 1985: 199). Following the 'riots' and publication of the Inquiry report, several chief constables sought to redirect policing activities in ways that would restore public confidence and relegitimate the force, giving rise to a flurry of 'community policing' initiatives. It was precisely this kind of intervention that Klockars (1988: 258) was so critical of, arguing it was the latest in a long line of circumlocutions: the 'song of community policing', he claimed, like the songs of legalisation, militarisation and professionalisation before it, 'is about some very good things we might gladly wish, but which, sadly, cannot be'.

Since the Brixton 'riots' and their immediate aftermath there have been two 'revolutions' in the development and legitimation of police powers in England and Wales (Reiner, 2010: 207). The first was the introduction of the 1984 Police and Criminal Evidence Act (PACE). For most of its history the legitimacy of the British police had been nourished by the minimisation of its legal powers and the myth of the constable as a 'citizen in uniform' with no special powers beyond the ordinary member of the public. PACE replaced this myth with the principle of a 'fundamental balance' between police powers and procedural safeguards.

An accompanying code of practice was devoted to stop and search and to identifying the circumstances under which such powers can be legally deployed by officers (see Home Office, 2013a). After little more than a decade, the 'fundamental balance' was superseded by a proliferation of police powers which lack balancing safeguards and a whittling away of the due process provisions introduced by PACE. What this meant for stop and search was the rise of 'exceptional' powers that are free of the normal procedural safeguards regulating their use, and the paring back of requirements governing officers' accountability for their use of the powers. Such developments have been justified by claims about the need to rebalance the system in favour of victims due to the threats posed by crime, anti-social behaviour and, more recently, terrorism. This 'shift in legitimatory myths reveals dramatic transformations in the politics of policing and security, and involves deep issues of principle about the relationship between state and citizens in a democratic society' (Reiner, 2010: 208).

It was in the midst of the second, post-PACE, revolution that several contributors to this collection came together to form StopWatch, a coalition of civil society organisations, academics, lawyers, community workers, activists and young people, which campaigns for fair and accountable policing (see http://www.stop-watch.org/). StopWatch works to:

- promote effective, accountable and fair policing;
- inform the public about the use of stop and search;
- develop and share research on stop and search and alternatives;
- organise awareness-raising events and forums;
- provide legal support challenging stop and search.

Since its inception in 2010, StopWatch has led a wide-ranging campaign challenging the disproportionate use of stop and search against people from black and minority ethnic groups, the increased use of exceptional stop and search powers, and the weakening of accountability mechanisms. Collectively, we have carried out and commissioned research, written reports and submitted evidence to various commissions and inquiries; organised seminars and presented papers at conferences; participated in consultations, sat on boards and committees, lobbied politicians and attended parliamentary events; supported legal challenges and signposted people to lawyers for legal advice; organised public hearings, produced factsheets and delivered training; written blogs, placed stories in national newspapers, spoken on the radio and appeared on television; made films, organised a flashmob and produced a play.

Much of this activity lies outside the traditional arena of academia or, indeed, policy work, but can usefully be thought of as an exercise in public criminology in the sense that it represents an explicit attempt to engage in, and shape, political and public debate about a key area of policing. As noted by Loader and Sparks (2011), the crime control climate has become considerably hotter and more volatile in recent times, and, like other criminologists who have made forays into this hostile environment, we have sought to employ 'cooling devices': that is to say, we have responded 'to an emotive and politicized penal field by seeking to reassert the values and institutions that hot penal politics tends to devalue or disregard – legality and justice, scientific evidence and techniques, and bureaucratic rationality' (Loader and Sparks, 2011: 9). In so doing, our aim has been to contribute to 'a better politics of crime and its regulation' through what Loader and Sparks (2011: 117) refer to as 'democratic under-labouring'. While such an approach is committed, first and foremost, to the generation of knowledge, it is said to have most to offer when due attention is also paid to normative aspects of crime and justice. One of StopWatch's principal functions is to inject rigorous criminological knowledge into debates about policing, challenging misinformation and promoting a more evidence-based approach. But this function operates alongside a commitment to ensuring that impacted communities have a voice in the debate (we consider these voices to be a vital source of evidence). In terms of the styles of engagement identified by Loader and Sparks (2011), StopWatch combines the roles of 'scientific expert' and 'social movement theorist/activist'.

Most of the contributors to this collection are members of StopWatch, and many of the chapters were developed for a Roundtable event that took place at John Jay College of Criminal Justice, New York, on 10 and 11 August 2011.[1] The event focused on racial disparities in police-initiated stops in the UK and the US. It began less than a week after the fatal police shooting of black Londoner Mark Duggan, which sparked some of the most serious rioting in recent British history. According to press reports, the riots were 'a sort of revenge' against the police, that were partly fuelled by anger and resentment over stop and search (Prasad, 2011). Despite the best efforts of Lord Scarman and all that followed, it seems the lessons of Brixton have not been learned. What, then, is to be done about stop and search?

The following collection is comprised of eight substantive chapters. Lee Bridges starts things off by reviewing the development of stop and search powers in England and Wales as well as regulations governing their use. His analysis pays particular attention to the role of the Police and Criminal Evidence Act 1984, the impact of the Stephen Lawrence Inquiry and the subsequent weakening of existing regulations through, among other things, the use of 'exceptional' counter-terrorism powers. By way of conclusion, Bridges considers recent moves to reassert regulatory authority over police stop and search activity. The next chapter, by Michael Shiner and Rebekah Delsol, considers how the use of stop and search fits with the broader politics of crime control. Drawing on official statistics, government surveys and observational studies, they argue that stop and search should not be understood as a straightforward response to crime, suggesting that its use has been shaped by the emergence of a more punitive political climate. In developing these claims, Shiner and Delsol examine trends in stop and search, variations between forces, the types of offence that are targeted by police and the characteristics of the people who are stopped and searched. Particular attention is paid to debates about the disproportionate focus on black and minority ethnic groups and the role of police racism. The issue of police racism is examined in more detail by Paul Quinton, who addresses a specific gap in the literature by looking at officer decision-making at a micro level. He begins by identifying several different mechanisms through which ethnic disparities might be produced, before going on to assess them based on the literature and observational fieldwork in several police forces.

Chapters 5 to 7 focus on the impact of stop and search. Rebekah Delsol assesses claims that stop and search provides a 'powerful tool' in the 'fight against crime'. Her analysis is organised around the observation that any judgement about the effectiveness of an intervention should take account of its costs as well as its benefits. In the absence of robust experimental evidence covering England and Wales, the apparent crime-fighting benefits of stop and search are assessed on the basis of arrest rates, the extent to which this activity is intelligence-led and the type of offences that are targeted. Drawing on these indicators, as well as the more general literature, the benefits of stop and search are said to be outweighed by the costs, which include damage to community relations, particularly with black and minority ethnic communities, and loss of trust and confidence in the police. The costs of stop and search are explored further by Ben Bradford, who contrasts the uncertainty surrounding the effectiveness of this tactic with the extensive evidence of its associated harms. Drawing on procedural justice theory, he identifies a series of unintended consequences, arguing that stop and search is likely not only to damage people's sense that the police are fair, but also to undermine police legitimacy, damage cooperation between police and public, encourage a turn towards 'self-help' violence, drag people differentially into the criminal justice system and promote, rather than inhibit, offending. Tara Lai Quinlan and Zin Derfoufi consider the costs and benefits of stop and search in the context of counter-terrorism policing. Using official statistics and the reports produced by the Independent Reviewer of Terrorism Legislation, as well as the broader literature, they argue that counter-terrorism policing, including increased use of 'exceptional' stop and search powers, has been counter-productive, alienating the very communities whose cooperation is most needed to combat the threat of terrorism.

The penultimate chapter, by Michael Shiner, focuses on regulation and reform. Drawing a distinction between conflict and consensus modes of regulation, he argues that the consensus-oriented approach that has been developed in England and Wales has been limited by structural constraints, political barriers and police resistance. While recent developments have continued along familiar lines, it is argued that established approaches have failed to get to grips with an unavoidable central paradox, whereby the police cannot be relied upon to ensure robust regulation themselves, yet are likely to resist and subvert external efforts to this end. As a possible way out of the current impasse, Shiner argues for responsive regulation on the basis that it combines the strengths of conflict and consensus approaches. In the final chapter, Ben Bowling and Estelle Marks consider stop and search in a transnational and comparative context, examining its use by a wide range of different police-like agencies, including domestic police, border guards, customs officers, private security and military officers in policing roles. They also explore the range of purposes for which stop and search is deployed and the main justifications for its use. Having identified particular challenges associated with constraining police powers that are globally connected, Bowling and Marks call for an agenda for transnational and comparative research. Only in this way, they argue, can we hope to ensure such powers are used in ways that are accountable, transparent and fair.

Note

1. For details see http://www.jjay.cuny.edu/centers/race_crime_justice/1935.php [accessed 18 July 2013].

2
The Legal Powers and their Limits
Lee Bridges

This chapter traces the development of the law relating to stop and search within the wider political context. The first section deals briefly with the situation prior to the passage of the Police and Criminal Evidence Act 1984 (PACE), which remains the primary source of the police's legal powers to stop and search. The second section outlines the introduction of national regulations covering stop and search under PACE. The third section discusses developments following publication of the Report of the Stephen Lawrence Inquiry (Macpherson, 1999). The fourth section looks specifically at the use of stop and search in anti-terrorism operations. Finally, several recent developments in respect of stop and search will be described.

Stop and search prior to PACE

Prior to PACE, stop and search powers were contained in a variety of individual pieces of national and local legislation, which in turn led to considerable geographical differences in the use of these powers. Historically, the greatest use of these powers was in London by the Metropolitan Police and in other large conurbations that had significant concentrations of post-World War II immigrants from the former British Commonwealth, particularly the West Indies (Whitfield, 2004). This combination of factors led to a significant politicisation of stop and search (and of policing in general) during the 1960s and 1970s, in particular around the use of the so-called 'sus' laws (under the Vagrancy Act, 1824), which empowered the police to stop, search and arrest 'a suspicious person or reputed thief' being in a public place with the intent to commit a felony (Parliament of the United Kingdom, 1824: 699).

This particular legal provision was eventually repealed on the advice of the Royal Commission on Criminal Procedure which reported in

1981, shortly before the Brixton 'riots' (Leigh, 1981). The 'sus' laws were repealed principally because of concerns about their negative impact on the relationship between the police and the public, particularly with minority ethnic communities (Willis, 1983). In an 'anti-mugging' operation in London, called 'Swamp 81', the Metropolitan Police carried out mass stop-searches of primarily black men in Brixton, and this was identified as one of the key factors triggering the subsequent large-scale riots in the area. Nevertheless, the Scarman Report, which followed the 1981 riots in Brixton and other British cities, emphatically rejected the notion that launching such an operation was indicative of racism in the police beyond the level of individual officers (Scarman, 1981: para. 4.62, 4.63):

> The directions and policy of the Metropolitan Police are not racist. I totally and unequivocally reject the attack made upon the integrity and impartiality of the senior direction of the force. The criticisms lie elsewhere – in errors of judgement, in a lack of imagination and flexibility, but not in a deliberate bias and prejudice.
>
> Such plausibility as this attack has achieved is due, sadly, to the ill-considered, immature and racially prejudiced action of some officers in their dealing on the street with young black people. Racial prejudice does manifest itself occasionally in the behaviour of a few officers on the streets. It may be too easy for some officers, faced with what they must see as the inexorably rising tide of street crime, to lapse into an unthinking assumption that all young black people are potential criminals.

Nor did the Scarman Report recommend any curtailment in the police's legal powers in respect of stop and search.

However, the Royal Commission on Criminal Procedure did acknowledge a need to codify police powers generally, and of stop and search in particular, on a national basis. This report formed the basis of the subsequent passage by a Conservative government of PACE.

PACE and the development of national regulation

PACE was – and remains – the most significant piece of legislation on policing in Britain passed in the post-World War II period. In political terms, it was intended to restore the legitimacy of urban policing, which had suffered a critical loss of public confidence as a result of both miscarriage of justice cases and the recent history of violent confrontations between the police and inner-city communities. Legally, PACE not only codified but strengthened police powers in a number of areas, including arrest and pre-charge detention of suspects and general powers of search. Against this, there were some extensions of rights of suspects, particularly in respect of access to custodial legal advice.

The main way in which PACE sought to 'balance' increases in police powers and regulate them was through the imposition of formal administrative/bureaucratic controls over the exercise of these powers, especially under a national set of Codes of Practice. The Codes of Practice are statutory and violations of them may form the basis of disciplinary proceedings against police officers, formal complaints against the police, and civil legal actions for damages. They may also be taken into account by the criminal courts in interpreting the scope of police powers, but in general there is no exclusionary rule under which evidence obtained in violation of PACE and the Codes of Practice will be strictly excluded from criminal trials.

Legally, PACE established a general power of the police to stop and search a person, vehicle or anything in or on the vehicle in a public place where they have reasonable suspicion that the person is in possession of, or the vehicle contains, stolen goods or prohibited articles. Prohibited articles include offensive weapons, bladed instruments, prohibited fireworks or any article made, adapted or intended for use in burglary, theft, taking a motor vehicle without consent, obtaining property by deception or causing criminal damage. There remain separate powers to stop and search, also subject to reasonable suspicion, for possession of drugs (under the Misuse of Drugs Act, 1971) or firearms (under the Firearms Act, 1968) in a public place and of persons suspected of being terrorists (under the Terrorism Act, 2000). The police also have a general power to stop vehicles, without a requirement of reasonable suspicion, under the Road Traffic Act 1988, although any search following such a stop must be carried out under one of the stop and search powers outlined above.

Reasonable suspicion

In the words of one of the key legal texts on criminal justice, reasonable suspicion is a 'slippery concept' (Sanders et al., 2010: 74). This slipperiness is one the reasons why the concept has proved relatively ineffective as a basis for challenging police practices in this area. There are also other reasons why legal challenges to stop and search may be an ineffective route to enforcing the standard of reasonable suspicion. People who are stopped and searched, but not then arrested, may be reluctant to draw further attention to themselves by challenging the police in this way. Where prohibited items are found, this may be seen as justifying the stop and search in the first place.

On the other hand, the relevant PACE Code of Practice has, following a series of periodic revisions, become increasingly detailed in its guidance to the police as to what does and does not constitute reasonable suspicion. To give a flavour of this, it is worth quoting some key sections of PACE Code A (Home Office, 2013a: 5):

> Reasonable grounds for suspicion depend on the circumstances in each case. There must be an objective basis for that suspicion based on facts, information, and/or intelligence which are relevant to the likelihood of finding an article of a certain kind. Reasonable suspicion can never be supported on the basis of personal factors. It must rely on intelligence or information about, or some specific behaviour by, the person concerned. For example, unless the police have a description of a suspect, a person's physical appearance (including any of the relevant 'protected characteristics' set out in the Equality Act 2010 (see *paragraph 1.1* and *Note 1A*), or the fact that the person is known to have a previous conviction, cannot be used alone or in combination with each other, or in combination with any other factor, as the reason for searching that person. Reasonable suspicion cannot be based on generalisations or stereotypical images of certain groups or categories of people as more likely to be involved in criminal activity.

It is worth noting that the Code was amended in 2009 to reflect concerns that the police had begun to target Muslims in the wake of the terrorist attacks in New York in September 2001 and London in 2005, prompting Sanders et al. (2010: 75) to note: 'It is remarkable that a legislative code of practice directs, in effect, that people should not be stopped just because they are black or Muslim, and is a rare example of the law attempting to take into account the social reality of policing on the streets.'

To continue, the Code goes on to state that (Home Office, 2013a: 5):

> Reasonable suspicion may also exist without specific information or intelligence and on the basis of the behaviour of a person. For example, if an officer encounters someone on the street at night who is obviously trying to hide something, the officer may (depending on

the other surrounding circumstances) base such suspicion on the fact that this kind of behaviour is often linked to stolen or prohibited articles being carried.

However, reasonable suspicion should normally be linked to accurate and current intelligence or information, such as information describing an article being carried, a suspected offender, or a person who has been seen carrying a type of article known to have been stolen recently from premises in the area. Searches based on accurate and current intelligence or information are more likely to be effective. Targeting searches in a particular area at specified crime problems increases their effectiveness and minimises inconvenience to law-abiding members of the public. It also helps in justifying the use of searches both to those who are searched and to the public. This does not however prevent stop and search powers being exercised in other locations where such powers may be exercised and reasonable suspicion exists.

Searches are more likely to be effective, legitimate, and secure public confidence when reasonable suspicion is based on a range of factors. The overall use of these powers is more likely to be effective when up-to-date and accurate intelligence or information is communicated to officers and they are well-informed about local crime patterns.

Again (Home Office, 2013a: 5, 16):

> Where there is reliable information or intelligence that members of a group or gang habitually carry knives unlawfully or weapons or controlled drugs, and wear a distinctive item of clothing or other means of identification to indicate their membership of the group or gang, that distinctive item of clothing or other means of identification may provide reasonable grounds to stop and search a person. (Note 9: Other means of identification might include jewellery, insignias, tattoos or other features which are known to identify members of the particular gang or group.)

This latter provision may be seen as allowing certain forms of group suspicion, the operation of which may extend beyond specific gang members where the identifying item is in fact more widely adopted as part of a local sub-culture.

The Code concludes, on the subject of reasonable suspicion, by noting that (Home Office, 2013a: 6)

An officer who has reasonable grounds for suspicion may detain the person concerned in order to carry out a search. Before carrying out a search the officer may ask questions about the person's behaviour or presence in circumstances which gave rise to the suspicion. As a result of questioning the detained person, the reasonable grounds for suspicion necessary to detain that person may be confirmed or, because of a satisfactory explanation, be eliminated. Questioning may also reveal reasonable grounds to suspect the possession of a different kind of unlawful article from that originally suspected. Reasonable grounds for suspicion however cannot be provided retrospectively by such questioning during a person's detention or by refusal to answer any questions put.

If, as a result of questioning before a search, or other circumstances which come to the attention of the officer, there cease to be reasonable grounds for suspecting that an article is being carried of a kind for which there is a power to stop and search, no search may take place. In the absence of any other lawful power to detain, the person is free to leave at will and must be so informed.

There is no power to stop or detain a person in order to find grounds for a search. Police officers have many encounters with members of the public which do not involve detaining people against their will. If reasonable grounds for suspicion emerge during such an encounter, the officer may search the person, even though no grounds existed when the encounter began. If an officer is detaining someone for the purpose of a search, he or she should inform the person as soon as detention begins.

These last provisions draw attention to what have been referred to as 'voluntary stops', where police officers engage with people on the street and question them without officially detaining them, before going on to conduct a formal stop and search. As we shall see, the practice of searching people on a 'voluntary' basis was prohibited following the Stephen Lawrence Inquiry in the late 1990s, and subsequently the police were required to record 'stops and account' (stops that did not lead to a formal search), although this requirement has been dropped.

Recording of stop and search

This brings us to another feature of PACE regulations, which is the requirement for the police to maintain administrative records relating to a wide range of their activities. On stop and search, PACE originally specified that a record was required to be made, immediately unless not practical to do so, each time a person was stopped under statutory powers (that is, detained) *and* subsequently searched. There was originally no requirement to record stops that did not result in searches. The stop and search record was to include the following items:

- the name and address of the person stopped and searched or, if not known, a description of that person or of the vehicle searched;
- the object of the search;
- the grounds for the search and the power which was used;
- the date and time when it was made;
- the place where it was made;
- whether anything, and if so what, was found;
- whether any, and if so what, injury to a person or damage to property appears to have resulted from the search;
- the identity of the police constable conducting the search.

The Act also required that the person stopped and searched should be entitled to a copy of the record if requested within 12 months of the date of the search.

These statutory requirements were subsequently extended under revisions of the relevant Code of Practice. Most significantly, following passage of the Criminal Justice Act in 1991, which included a requirement that the Home Office publish annual statistics on issues of race and criminal justice, the relevant Code of Practice was amended to require the ethnicity of the person stopped and searched to be recorded. This requirement has now been enshrined in the main statute, but, more importantly, there were significant changes introduced in 2011, which curtailed the recording regime surrounding stop and search (see below).

Theoretically, these recoding requirements can serve a number of purposes. First, they may assist individuals who consider they may have been stopped and searched unreasonably to challenge the police through formal complaints and/or civil claims for damages. Second, statistics derived from such records allow a more general monitoring of the nature, extent and effectiveness of the police's use of their stop and search powers. Third, the data may assist in internal supervision of the use of stop and search within local police areas and even down to individual officer level. For example, it is possible to compare individual officers in terms of their behaviour in stopping and searching members of different ethnic groups and the effectiveness of their stops and searches in leading to arrests.

Stop and search without reasonable suspicion

Perhaps one of the most significant developments in the law governing stop and search in the post-PACE period was the passage of the Criminal Justice and Public Order Act 1994. This Act introduced stop and search powers without the requirement of reasonable suspicion to be used in two circumstances. First, Section 81 amended existing anti-terrorist legislation to allow a senior officer to authorise stops and searches without reasonable suspicion where it was considered 'expedient' to do so in order to prevent acts of terrorism. This power was subsequently revised and incorporated in Section 44 of the Terrorism Act 2000, as discussed below.

Second, Section 60 of the Criminal Justice and Public Order Act 1994 allows a police office of the rank of inspector (a rank that is normally based in a fairly localised area within a particular police force) or higher who reasonably fears serious violence or the carrying of weapons in a particular locality to authorise police officers to search *any* person or vehicle in that locality for weapons over a period of 24 hours. This provision was originally introduced with the aim of combating potential violence associated with specific events, such as hooliganism around football matches, and was later extended to cover 'raves'. However, use of the power has also become associated with anti-knife and gun crime operations, and more generally with combating gang culture in inner cities. In this connection, although each authorisation for the use of the power is time limited, there is provision for a local police superintendent (an officer ranked above an inspector) to renew the authorisation for a further 24 hours, and in practice this has often led to particular areas being subject to stops and searches without reasonable suspicion on a virtually continuous basis.

The Stephen Lawrence Inquiry and its aftermath

Evidence indicates that PACE and the national regulation of stop and search did little to curb its use or the targeting of certain sections of the community (see Chapter 3). On the contrary, in the following decades the recorded use of 'reasonable suspicion' stops and searches rose 10-fold, to over a million a year, with black people being seven times, and Asians two to three times, more likely to be stopped and searched than white people (Miller, 2010). The arrest rate following such searches ranged from just under to just over 10 per cent. The subsequent introduction of Section 60 effectively legitimated the type of mass stop and search operation that had led to the Brixton riots in 1981 and continued to fuel widespread resentment of the police within black communities. Concern over alleged police racism was exacerbated by the murder of a black teenager, Stephen Lawrence, in south London in 1993, and the completely ineffective police investigation that followed. This resulted initially in a failure of the police to bring any prosecutions and eventually to a number of white youths widely believed to be responsible for the murder being acquitted following a private prosecution by Stephen Lawrence's family.[1] These events led the incoming Labour government in 1997 to set up a judicial inquiry into the murder of Stephen Lawrence and the subsequent police investigation.

The Inquiry report, published in 1999, was highly significant in political terms for its endorsement (unlike the earlier Scarman Report) of long-standing claims by the black community that the police are 'institutionally racist' (Macpherson, 1999). This finding was based in large part on the Inquiry's detailed examination of the failings in the original police investigation of Stephen Lawrence's murder. However, at the end of the Inquiry a series of general evidence sessions were held in a number of cities, at which issues relating to stop and search featured prominently. The Inquiry's report identified stop and search as an example of 'institutional racism' in policing.

It is worth quoting, at some length, the Inquiry's conclusions regarding stop and search, particularly its disproportionate use against black and minority ethnic groups (Macpherson, 1999: para. 6.45, 45.8):

> Whilst we acknowledge and recognise the complexity of the issue, and in particular the other factors which can be prayed in aid to explain the disparities, such as demographic mix, school exclusions, unemployment, and recording procedures, there remains, in our judgement, a clear core conclusion of racist stereotyping.
>
> Nobody in the minority ethnic communities believes the complex arguments which are sometimes used to explain the figures as to stop and search are valid... Whilst there are other factors at play we are clear that the perceptions and experiences of the minority communities that discrimination is a major element in the stop and search problem is correct.
>
> It is pointless for the police service to try to justify the disparity in these figures purely or mainly in terms of the other factors which are identified. Attempts to justify the disparity through identification of other factors, whilst not being seen vigorously to address the discrimination which is evident, simply exacerbates the climate of distrust.

18 The Legal Powers and their Limits

Despite the strength of these conclusions, it is perhaps surprising that the first recommendation the Inquiry made in respect of stop and search was that 'the powers of the police under current legislation are required for the prevention and detection of crime and should remain unchanged' (Macpherson, 1999: Recommendation 60). The Inquiry confined itself to proposing a widening and strengthening of the PACE regime for recording and regulating stop and search (Macpherson, 1999: Recommendations 61–3). As well as calling for 'voluntary' or non-statutory searches to be prohibited, it recommended that recording requirements be extended to include statutory and voluntary stops not resulting in searches and the self-defined ethnicity of those stopped. The Inquiry also called for better analysis and use of these records for the purposes of supervising stop and search activities of police officers, and wider publication of the resulting statistics. Although the UK government accepted virtually all of the Inquiry's recommendations in other areas, it did not immediately do so in respect of those relating to stop and search. The PACE Code of Practice was eventually amended to abolish the use of 'voluntary' searches, to require stops that do not lead to searches to be recorded and the 'self-defined' ethnicity of those stopped and searched to be included in the record.

Targeted and 'intelligence-led' stop and search

Even so, the Stephen Lawrence Inquiry's conclusions appear to have had an immediate impact on police stop and search practices, in that it was reported in several areas that rank-and-file officers, resentful of the Inquiry's labelling of the police as 'institutionally racist', effectively decided to boycott the use of stop and search. At the same time, several police forces adopted a policy of a more 'targeted' and 'intelligence-led' use of stop and search, which resulted in some reduction in the overall rate of stops and searches, but also led to even greater ethnic disproportionality in terms of those subject to stop and search (Bowling and Phillips, 2003, 2007; cf Chapter 3). This, in turn, led some to question the nature of the 'intelligence' on which such targeted stop and search was based and whether, in fact, it simply 'institutionalised' and reproduced past racial and ethnic biases in police practices.

Similar criticism arose from a series of research studies on stop and search commissioned by the Home Office following the Stephen Lawrence Inquiry report. One of these studies sought to compare the ethnic composition of those subject to stop and search with that of the population 'available' to be stopped and searched within the areas where, and at the times of day when, police stop and search operations were most frequently carried out (MVA and Miller, 2000). The research used cameras mounted on cars to film the street population, including people in vehicles, in these areas at these particular times of day. Perhaps not surprisingly given the 'self-fulfilling' methodology employed (Equalities and Human Rights Commission, 2010: 52), it was found that the ethnic profiles of those stopped and searched, although disproportionate to the composition of the general population, was not out of line with that of the 'available population'. If anything, white people were said to be stopped and searched more often than their presence in the available population might justify. On this basis, the authors concluded that 'disproportionality [in stop and search] is... a product of structural factors beyond their [the police's] control' (MVA and Miller, 2000: 87). However, as a recent Equality and Human Rights Commission (2010: 57) report on stop and search has noted,

> Street availability is influenced by police decisions where and when to do stops and searches and these decisions heavily influence the people that are 'available' to be stopped and searched. This is compounded by policing that is geared toward street availability.

Other studies in the Home Office series appeared to undermine some of the more common rationales advanced to support the wide-scale use of stop and search. Thus, a finding that stop and search has 'a minor role in detecting offenders for the range of all crimes that they address, and a relatively small role in detecting offenders for such crime that come to the attention of the police' (Miller et al., 2000: 22) seemed to contradict the Stephen Lawrence Inquiry's conclusion that stop and search powers 'are required for the prevention and detection of crime' (Macpherson, 1999: Recommendation 60). The same study questioned the value of stop and search as a more general deterrent to crime (Miller et al., 2000: vi):

> Searches appear to have only a limited direct disruptive effect on crime by intercepting those going out to commit offences... It is not clear to what extent searches undermine criminal activity through the arrest and conviction of prolific offenders. However, it is unlikely that searches make a substantial contribution to undermining drug-markets or drug-related crime in this way, given that drug searches tend to focus on users rather than dealers, and cannabis rather than hard drugs... There is little solid evidence that searches have a deterrent effect on crime.

The impact of the Stephen Lawrence Inquiry on police stop and search practice proved to be relatively short-lived. When, in 2004, the government moved to extend the PACE recording requirements to include 'stop and account', the number of stop-searches had already begun to climb back to the levels found in the mid-1990s, especially when account is taken of the additional searches conducted without reasonable suspicion under Section 60 and anti-terrorism legislation.

Stop and search under anti-terrorism legislation

A major review of UK anti-terrorism law was initiated in 1995, and led eventually to the passage of the Terrorism Act 2000. Section 43 of this Act provides for the police to stop and search any person reasonably suspected of being a terrorist. More importantly, sections 44 to 47 of the same Act empowered senior police officers (at assistant chief constable/commander level) to authorise stop and search without reasonable suspicion of any person or vehicle for articles for use in acts of terrorism where they considered it 'expedient' to do so in order to prevent acts of terrorism. In contrast to Section 60 authorisations, those under the Terrorism Act 2000 had to be confirmed by the home secretary (a central government minister) within 48 hours, but could remain in force for up to 28 days. Like Section 60 authorisations, they could be renewed on a repeated basis. The whole of the Metropolitan Police area in London was continuously subject to such an authorisation for most of the decade after the Act came into force in 2001.

Schedule 7 of the Terrorism Act 2000 also provided a power for a police officer, immigration officer or customs official to stop, search and detain any person entering or leaving the UK for up to nine hours to determine whether s/he is a terrorist. The exercise of this power does not require reasonable suspicion, and people who are stopped are at risk of arrest and criminal conviction for failing to answer any questions or to provide any information requested of them, even though they do not have the 'right' to consult a solicitor unless they are detained. Although not under arrest, those stopped may also be searched (including stripped searched) and have fingerprints and DNA samples taken. Over the decade following the enactment of what is commonly referred to as the Section 44 power, 600,000 persons were stopped and searched under this provision, the vast majority in London. Over half of the 10-year total occurred in just a two-year period between 2007 and 2009. Only a handful of charges for terrorist offences followed from Section 44 stops, and not one Section 44 stop resulted in a conviction for a terrorist offence (Anderson, 2011).

Black and Asian people were very heavily over-represented among those subjected to stop and search under Section 44 (see Chapter 7). However, as the above statistics indicate, once authorised to use them, the police in London came to regard Section 44 powers as having much wider application than to deal with terrorism alone. In particular, they came to be seen as a tactic to be used in controlling protests more generally.

It was just such a use of Section 44 that saw police stop and search two white people on their way to a demonstration against an arms fair in London in 2003, prompting the most significant legal challenge yet to police stop and search powers in the UK. This challenge was based on the grounds that the police and home secretary had acted *ultra vires* in authorising Section 44 stops and searches across the whole of London on a continuous basis, as well as an alleged violation of several articles of the European Convention on Human Rights. These were Articles 5 (right to liberty), 8 (right to a private and family life), 10 (right to freedom of expression) and 11 (right to freedom of peaceful assembly). It is worth noting here that the challenge failed at every level in the British courts, despite the provisions of the European Convention on Human Rights having been incorporated in domestic law under the Human Rights Act 1998.

However, in January 2010 the European Court of Human Rights (2010: 43), in the case of Gillan and Quinton v. the United Kingdom, upheld the challenge and struck down Section 44 of the Terrorism Act 2000 on the grounds that it constituted an interference with the right to respect of private life and that:

> the powers of authorisation and confirmation as well as those of stop and search under sections 44 and 45 of the 2000 Act are neither sufficiently circumscribed nor subject to adequate legal safeguards against abuse. They are not, therefore, 'in accordance with the law' and it follows that there has been a violation of Article 8 of the Convention.

In reaching this conclusion, the court found that 'the safeguards provided by domestic law [in respect of Section 44 stops and searches] have not been demonstrated to constitute a real curb on the wide powers afforded to the executive so as to offer the individual protection against arbitrary interference' (2010: 41). This finding was based on a number of factors:

- Authorisations to use Section 44 stops and searches could be made when a senior officer considered it 'expedient' to prevent an act of

terrorism, rather than 'necessary', and therefore there was no requirement to make any assessment of the proportionality of doing so.
- Although an authorisation required confirmation by the secretary of state, s/he could not alter the geographical area specified and had never refused an authorisation or altered the time period.
- Authorisations were renewable and could cover the whole police force area, which in the UK covers 'extensive regions with a concentrated population' (2010: 42). The lack of a check on authorisations was demonstrated by the fact that the whole of London had been continuously covered by such an authorisation throughout the period the Act had been in force.
- The Act confers a very wide discretion on the individual police officer and effectively does not provide any restriction on his or her decision to stop and search: 'Not only is it unnecessary... to demonstrate the existence of any reasonable suspicion; [the police officer] is not required even subjectively to suspect anything about the person stopped and searched' (2010: 42). While the search must be for articles for use in connection with terrorism, this covers a wide category of items 'commonly carried by people in the streets' and the officer does not have to have grounds for suspecting that the person may be carrying such an article (2010: 42).
- The statistics showed the very wide extent to which the power had been used in practice.
- There 'was a clear risk of arbitrariness in the grant of such a broad discretion and, while the present case did not concern black or Asian applicants, the risk of the discriminatory use of the power against such persons was a real consideration' (2010: 43). There was also a risk of misuse against demonstrators and protestors in breach of Article 10 and/or 11 of the Convention.
- In the absence of any obligation to show reasonable suspicion for a stop and search under Section 44, 'it is unlikely if not impossible to prove that the power was improperly exercised' (2010: 43).

Developments since the 2010 general election

The Gillan decision came just a few months prior to the 2010 general election, which resulted in a coalition government between the Conservative and Liberal Democrat parties taking the place of the previous Labour administration. One of the most immediate effects of the Gillan decision was to put paid to an idea that had been floated by the Conservative Party prior to the election that they would seek to remove the requirement of reasonable suspicion from all stops and searches. Instead, an amended version of the Terrorism Act 2000 power to stop and search without reasonable suspicion, Section 47A, was eventually introduced, in an attempt to meet the objections raised in the Gillan judgement. This, in turn, has called into question the legitimacy of similar powers under both Schedule 7 of the Terrorism Act 2000 and Section 60 of the Criminal Justice and Public Order Act 1994. On the other hand, in the name of 'reducing unnecessary bureaucracy' and saving police time, the new government moved to make significant changes to the PACE Code of Practice governing stops and searches that do require reasonable suspicion as well as those conducted under Section 60.

Changes to stop and search without reasonable suspicion

After the Gillan judgment, the UK government suspended the use of Section 44 stops and searches. However, under a 2011 Remedial Order and subsequent amendment to the Terrorism Act 2000,[2] a revised Section 47A power to stop and search without reasonable suspicion was introduced and a new Code of Practice issued (Home Office, 2011a). The key changes introduced in an attempt to meet the criticisms set out in the Gillan judgement were (Anderson, 2012):

- Authorisations may only be given when a senior officer reasonably suspects that an act of terrorism will take place and considers it is necessary, not merely expedient, to prevent an act of terrorism.
- Authorisations may last for a period no longer than the senior officer considers necessary and for a maximum of 14 days (not 28 days as under the previous provisions).
- The secretary of state may substitute an earlier date or time for the expiry of an authorisation, or a more restricted area or place for the authorisation, when confirming it.
- A senior officer may substitute an earlier time or date or a more restricted area or place, or may cancel an authorisation.
- An officer exercising the stop and search powers may only do so for the purpose of searching for evidence that the person concerned is a terrorist or the vehicle concerned is being used for the purposes of terrorism.

The Code of Practice indicates that authorisations will not normally be given for whole police force areas and that repeat authorisations will not normally be allowed. In fact, as the home secretary has recently confirmed, the new power 'has not been used outside Northern Ireland since it was introduced in March 2011, and there has been no effect on public safety' (May, 2013: 774), which, of course, calls into question why the previous power under Section 44 was so widely (ab)used over the previous decade.

Data relating to the use of Schedule 7 of the Terrorism Act 2000 in ports and airports was first made public in 2010 following a freedom of information request. It has since been published regularly by the Home Office. Recent data shows that 61,145 persons were stopped under Schedule 7 in 2012/2013, and of these 2,277 were detained for over one hour (Anderson, 2013: 97). The majority of those stopped were from ethnic minority groups, including 22 per cent Asians (compared with 8 per cent of the national population), 8 per cent blacks (compared with 3 per cent of the national population), 17 per cent other minority ethnic groups (compared with 1 per cent of the national population) and 11 per cent mixed or not stated (compared with 2 per cent of the national population).[3] These groups were even more heavily represented among those who were stopped for over an hour: 33 per cent Asian, 14 per cent black, 25 per cent other ethnic minorities and 15 per cent from mixed or not stated (Anderson, 2013: 98). In 2011/2012, only 0.03 per cent of Schedule 7 examinations led to an arrest (Anderson, 2013: 100).

A 2011 report by the Equality and Human Rights Commission (EHRC) exploring the impact of counter-terrorism powers on Muslim communities found that Schedule 7 was 'having the single most negative impact on Muslim communities' (Choudhury and Fenwick, 2011: 87). In particular, the intrusive questioning of people over their social, religious and political views; the taking of their fingerprints and DNA; and refusing to await the arrival of a solicitor before conducting the search and questioning, have all created feelings of alienation, being targeted due to religious belief, and a sense in some communities that they are being treated as 'suspect communities'. The report found evidence of some travellers rerouting their journeys to allow them to go through other airports further away where they feel that they are less likely to be targeted for Schedule 7 stops (Choudhury and Fenwick, 2011).

Following a public consultation in 2012 (Home Office, 2012a), the government has introduced changes to Schedule 7 of the Terrorism Act 2000 through the Anti-social Behaviour, Crime and Policing Act 2014. The Act amends the Schedule 7 power, in particular reducing the maximum period for which a person can be detained from nine to six hours, providing a right for detainees held for more than one hour to have access to legal advice, improving supervision of detention decisions, and training for examining officers. There are also a number of legal challenges currently being mounted to the Schedule 7 power, including one by David Miranda, the partner of a journalist writing on information leaked by Edward Snowden about US and UK government mass digital surveillance, who was held for nine hours and had his computer and other electronic equipment seized when transiting through Heathrow Airport in London during August 2013 (Falconer, 2013).

The Gillan case has also raised the issue, which has so far not been addressed publicly by the UK government, of the legality under the European Convention on Human Rights of powers to stop and search without reasonable suspicion under Section 60 of the Criminal Justice and Public Order Act 1994. Indeed, it is notable that authorisations under Section 60, unlike the similar provisions under the Terrorism Act, are solely in the hands of local police, with no requirement of confirmation by the secretary of state or other external authority. As previously noted, there has also been a pattern of virtually continuous authorisation of Section 60 in some areas. These factors, along with the targeting of Section 60 stops and searches at minority ethnic groups, may make it particularly vulnerable to legal challenge on the basis of the considerations set out in the Gillan judgement.[4]

No doubt partially in anticipation of such challenges, the Metropolitan Police in London and those in some other large conurbations, where use of Section 60 has tended to be concentrated, have now adopted internal arrangements whereby authorisations must be made by more senior officers of at least assistant chief constable level. The effect has been similar to that under the revised Terrorism Act 2000, in that the numbers of such authorisations and actual stops and searches under Section 60 have been considerably reduced, although very high levels of ethnic disproportionality in its use have continued and to some extent worsened (Equalities and Human Rights Commission, 2012).

Changes to the PACE Code of Practice

Changes introduced to PACE Code A in 2011 significantly weakened the recording requirements (Home Office, 2011b). The national requirement for the police to record 'stops and account' (that is, stops that do not lead to searches), which had been introduced in response to the Stephen Lawrence Inquiry report in 2004, was dropped. In 2008–2009, there were 2.2 million stop and accounts in England and Wales (Ministry of Justice, 2009), which indicates that there are approximately two such incidents for each stop and search or, to put it another way, that only around one-third of all stops result in a search. With the removal of the national requirement to record stop and account, it was left to each local police force to decide whether to continue such recording in order to meet local public concerns. Most police forces almost immediately decided, often without any meaningful consultation, to drop the recording of stop and account. However, such consultation was carried out in London, which resulted in the Metropolitan Police retaining the requirement to record stop and account (Bridges et al., 2011).

The second change to the Code of Practice was to reduce the amount of information police are required to record in respect of stop and search. Again, it is now left to the discretion of each local police force whether or not to continue recording the name and address of the person stopped and searched, whether any injury or damage resulted from the search, and whether anything was found. As a result, the only uniform information that will be available nationally about stop-searches is the date, time and place of the search, the ethnicity of the person searched, the object of the search, the ground for the search, the power used and the identity of the officer carrying it out. The period for which the police are required to retain stop and search records has also been reduced from a year to three months.

These changes should be seen in the context of the coalition government's wider reform of police governance under the Police Reform and Social Responsibility Act 2011, which introduced directly elected police and crime commissioners for each police force in the country. Although the first elections, held in November 2012, recorded the lowest voter turnout ever for a nationwide election, the introduction of local commissioners can be seen as moving the UK closer to the American model of police governance and to a more localised, and possibly fragmented, system of police accountability. One implication of this would be to shift the political debate on aspects of policing, such as stop and search, away from the national level and down to each local policing area.

Similarly, the curtailment of uniform, national recording requirements for stop and search undermines the ethos behind the Police and Criminal Evidence Act 1984 for the national regulation of police powers and their use. These changes can also be seen as limiting the potential to hold the police to account for stop and search through individual or collective legal action. In particular, with the name of the person stopped and searched being dropped from the records, it will be more difficult to prove that an individual or group has been subject to such action, perhaps on numerous occasions, and that this pattern may constitute discrimination, harassment or victimisation under UK equalities legislation. Similarly, without the recording of injuries or damages caused by the stop and search, it will prove more difficult to mount civil claims for damages. The dropping of the requirement to record the outcome of stop and searches will also render the statistics derived from these records much less useful in evaluating the effectiveness of stop and searches, either internally within the police or by external bodies.

Future directions?

In July 2013, Her Majesty's Inspectorate of Constabulary (HMIC) published a national review of the police's use of their stop and search powers. This review acknowledged much of the political history of stop and search and raised serious concerns about its current use. It found there had been 'a noticeable slippage in the level of attention given to the leadership and supervision of stop and search powers by senior officers since the publication of the Stephen Lawrence Inquiry Report in 1999' (HMIC, 2013: 5).

The main focus of the review was on the effectiveness of stop and search, given that only 9 per cent of stops and searches nationally resulted in an arrest, with the figures for individual police forces ranging from 19 per cent to as low as 3 per cent (HMIC, 2013). It was also noted that, although policing priorities were focused on combating property crime and weapons, almost half of all stops and searches were for drugs, most for low-level possession. However, where police forces targeted the use of stop and search powers at 'crime hotspots' it was found that (HMIC, 2013: 41)

> the resultant arrest rate across the force was lower than in those forces that did not target it in that way. A considerable number of [stop and search] records we reviewed simply had 'crime hotspot' recorded as the grounds. This suggests that where stop and search is targeted to hotspots, officers wrongly believe that this alone provides their reasonable grounds. This leads to the possibility of a high proportion of stops and searches being conducted in a 'crime hotspot' without reasonable grounds.

Overall, in a survey of over 8,700 stop and search records, 27 per cent were found not to contain reasonable grounds for suspicion. Although the report did not take this to be an indication of widespread illegality in the use of stop and search, it did see it as signifying a general lack of proper supervision (HMIC, 2013: 28–9):

> Where we found some supervision of search records, either paper or electronic, this tended to be an administrative check on the completeness of the form (i.e. that all the boxes had been ticked) rather than a check of the legality or appropriateness of the stop and search, or of the quality of the information recorded. The high number of records we reviewed that lacked sufficiently recorded reasonable grounds... indicates that supervisors either did not check the records, or did not understand what was required of them.

Finally, the report found that, following the 2011 changes to the Code of Practice recording requirements outlined above (HMIC, 2013: 8),

> [f]orces had reduced the amount of data collected to reduce bureaucracy, but this had diminished their capability to understand the impact of the use of stop and search powers on crime levels and community confidence.

Indeed, in a barely veiled criticism of these changes, if not of the government's wider policing reforms, the report went on to state that (HMIC, 2013: 41)

> the efforts to reduce unnecessary bureaucracy... resulted in some unintended consequences. Rather than improved processes and better use of technology, forces... simply stopped recording some of the data which we believe is necessary to allow a good assessment of the effectiveness of the power. For instance, too many forces did not record whether a stolen or prohibited item was found – perhaps one of the fundamental factors in testing whether the grounds for suspicion were reasonable. It seems paradoxical that data needed for monitoring is reduced, when forces are increasing complexity by using more than 43 different forms across the 43 forces.

In the light of these findings, the government launched a national consultation on the use of stop and search powers (Home Office, 2013b). In the Home Office statement announcing the consultation, it is clearly implied that, in light of the low proportion of searches leading to arrest, stop and search is currently being over-used, with serious consequences in terms of both police costs and legitimacy (Home Office, 2013c):

when it [stop and search] is over-used, or when people are targeted when they do not need to be, it is a waste of police time and erodes community confidence in the police.

Moreover, in her statement to Parliament on the consultation, Home Secretary Theresa May drew a link between the high rate of use of stop and search and its disproportionate impact on ethnic minorities (May, 2014: 773–4):

> the law is clear that in normal circumstances, stop and search should only ever be used where there is a reasonable suspicion of criminality – and that is how it should be. I am sure we have all been told stories by constituents and members of the public about what it is like to be a young, law-abiding black man who has been stopped and searched by the police on more than one occasion. If anybody thinks it is sustainable to allow that to continue, with all its consequences for public confidence in the police, they need to think again.

Following the consultation, the home secretary made a thinly veiled threat when she told Parliament that primary legislation would be introduced if stop and search was not used more fairly and effectively, but, to date, the government's strategy has been based on a voluntary 'Best Use of Stop and Search Scheme'. The stated aim of this scheme is to promote 'greater transparency' and a more 'strategic' 'intelligence-led' approach, which will 'improve public confidence and trust' (Home Office, 2014a: 2). Under the scheme, forces agree to record a broader range of stop and search outcomes, to provide opportunities for members of the local community to accompany officers on patrol using stop and search, and to introduce a stop and search complaints 'community trigger'. Forces are also expected to reduce the use of Section 60 stop-searches by ensuring they are only used where it is deemed necessary. All 43 territorial police forces in England and Wales have signed up to the scheme (Home Office, 2014c), but it remains to be seen whether it will have the intended effect and, if not, whether significant changes will be made to the law governing stop and search, including possibly some reconsideration of the earlier curtailment of the national recording requirements or steps to ensure that stop and search can only be used where there is a 'reasonable suspicion of criminality' (that is, where the police officer would already have grounds for making an arrest). It will also be interesting to observe whether any future, overall reduction in stop and search is accompanied by a significant lessening in its disproportionate use against ethnic minorities. If not, the law and practice of stop and search will continue to provide a point of tension and potential political conflict between these groups and the police.

Notes

1. In 2011, two of the original defendants were convicted of the murder of Stephen Lawrence. This followed a reinvestigation by the police and the dropping of the traditional 'double jeopardy' bar on reinstituting proceedings against previously acquitted persons where there is substantial new evidence.
2. Enacted by way of the Protection of Freedom Act 2012, which introduced a new Section 47A to the Terrorism Act 2000.
3. Population estimates are based on the 2011 Census (Office for National Statistics, 2012).
4. Section 60 of the Criminal Justice and Public Order Act is currently being challenged through the case of Ann Juliette Roberts v. The Commissioner of the Metropolitan Police and the Secretary of State (see Chapter 3).

3
The Politics of the Powers
Michael Shiner and Rebekah Delsol

Stop and search is a prominent feature of policing, but has not always been so. When the Royal Commission on Criminal Procedure reported in 1981, the law on stop and search was 'confused and incoherent, having developed in an ad hoc manner' based on a patchwork of local and national legislation (Sanders et al., 2010: 72). That there was little transparency about how these powers were deployed is evident from a report that appeared in *The Times* newspaper during the early 1970s, which noted that: 'The Metropolitan Police... stated last week that no statistics were kept on searches because none were requested by the home secretary and the commissioner of police did not feel that they were of sufficient interest or importance' (16 April 1973, quoted by Whitfield, 2009). As well as bringing some much-needed order to police powers of stop and search, the Police and Criminal Evidence Act (PACE) 1984 requires officers to make a record of such encounters, providing the basis for some level of monitoring and scrutiny. Drawing largely on official statistics, this chapter charts the rise of stop and search under PACE and considers fluctuations in the use of some of the different powers. Attention is also given to what the powers are used for and on whom they are used, with a detailed discussion of debates surrounding the disproportionately high rate at which people from black and minority ethnic groups are stopped and searched.

The main argument developed in this chapter is that stop and search should not be understood simply as a narrow policing matter or a straightforward response to crime. Rather, it is argued that the use of such powers is intimately bound up with the broader politics of crime control and the functioning of the nation state. More specifically, increases in stop and search are located within a general 'toughening of crime control' that has its origins in the fragmentation of 'the Keynesian, mixed economy, welfare state consensus' and the rise of 'neoliberalism, individualism and the "risk society"' (Reiner, 2007: 129).

'Reasonable suspicion' powers under PACE

Police officers carry out millions of stops or stop-searches every year, the vast majority of which are not recorded. Section 163 of the Road Traffic Act 1988 is the most widely used stop power and can be deployed by officers without reasonable suspicion and without making a record of the encounter.[1] According to this power, a person driving a motor vehicle or riding a cycle on a road must stop if required to do so by a constable in uniform, and failure to do so constitutes an offence. Vehicle stops have become less common due to 'a complex range of factors, including changes in police tactics, police numbers and the number of vehicles on the roads', but there were still an estimated 5,486,912 vehicle stops in 2010/2011, the vast majority of which did not involve a search (Moon et al., 2011: 22).[2] There are, in addition, approximately two million pedestrian stops per year which fall short of a search. For a brief period, following the Stephen Lawrence Inquiry, police were required to record stops when they asked people to account for themselves (that is, their actions, behaviour, presence in an area or possession of anything) without going on to search them, but this requirement was dropped in 2011 (Ministry of Justice, 2010). In 2008/2009, the last year that records were kept, police carried out 2,211,598 recorded stop and accounts, down from 2,353,918 the previous year.

The number of recorded stop-searches carried out under PACE or related legislation requiring 'reasonable suspicion' has increased sharply since recording began in the mid-1980s (see Figure 3.1). Improved recording practices account for part of this increase, but only the smaller part. Comparisons between police records and responses to the British Crime Survey indicate that the proportion of searches recorded by officers increased from 40 per cent in 1987 to 75 per cent in 1999/2000 (Sanders et al., 2010). Even when we allow for improved recording practices, the number of stop-searches almost quadrupled during this period. The upsurge in stop and search activity cannot simply be explained as a function of increased crime, not least because it continued after 1995, when the crime rate was falling (Newburn, 2007). There is, moreover, no straightforward relationship between crime levels in police force areas and rates of stop and search, as some forces with high crime rates make relatively little use of these powers (Miller et al., 2000). It follows that

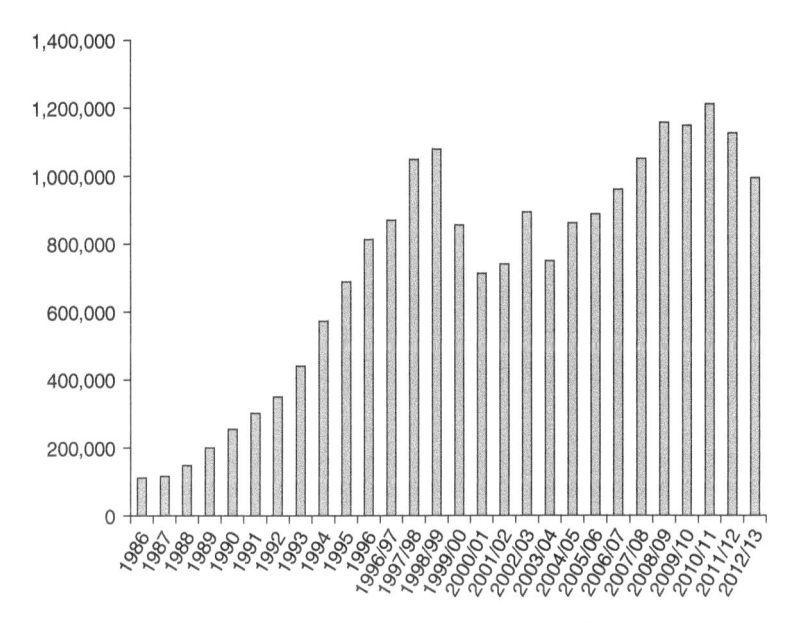

Figure 3.1 Suspicion-based stop-searches in England and Wales (number)
Source: Sanders et al. (2010); Home Office (2009a); and Home Office (2014b).

'trends in the recorded use of stop-search do not appear to be driven by the amount of reasonably suspicious behaviour taking place but rather by police policies and practices' (Sanders, et al., 2010: 77).

This is not to suggest that stop and search is entirely disconnected from crime, but rather that the connections are complex, indirect and mediated by a range of other factors. Dramatic increases in crime during the post-war period have given rise to an increasingly punitive, security-oriented approach to crime control (Garland, 2001), which may involve a 'lagged response to rising crime (among other things)' (Newburn, 2007: 452). Anxieties about crime began to be exploited during the 1970s when the Conservative Party attacked the then Labour government's record and offered an alternative politics of 'law and order' (Reiner, 2007). After winning the 1979 general election, Margaret Thatcher cemented her alliance with the police by improving their pay and increasing recruitment. In return, the police were expected to manage 'the brute consequences of economic recession' and sharpening social inequalities (Reiner, 1985: 210; see also Fielding, 1991). Subsequent increases in stop and search accelerated during the course of the 1990s as the social and political climate became even more conducive to tough policing methods. While the continued dominance of free-market economic policies exacerbated an already turbulent situation (Reiner, 2010), the murder of two-year-old James Bulger in 1993 triggered a pronounced shift in the politics of crime control (Garland, 2001). With the two main political parties seeking to out-tough one another on crime, a new political consensus was forged, prompting 'a step change' involving 'a rather sharp accentuation of a trend towards harder crime control' (Reiner, 2007: 118; see also Newburn, 2007).

High crime rates have also created incentives for the police to engage in stop and search because doing so provides a means through which they can be seen to be dealing with the problem. The 'remorseless rise of recorded crime from the mid-1950s to the early 1990s' challenged the cherished image of the police as an effective law enforcement service, contributing to a sharp decline in public confidence (Reiner, 2010: 108). Evidence that traditional police tactics are largely ineffective in reducing crime has given rise to a range of innovative approaches, including various 'hard cop' tactics that rest on the assumption that policing has been unduly constrained by civil liberties, human rights and 'political correctness' (Reiner, 2010). Aggressive patrol and the use of stop and search came to prominence during the 1990s and early 2000s with the rise of 'zero-tolerance policing', due largely to contested claims that this approach was responsible for the crime drop in New York City (Reiner, 2010; see also Eterno and Silverman, 2012). While several British forces experimented with such an approach, the most explicit attempt to introduce it was undertaken by Detective Superintendent Ray Mallon in Hartlepool, earning him the moniker 'Robocop' (Jones and Newburn, 2007). When Mallon resigned from his post in 2002, after pleading guilty to 14 disciplinary charges (Tran, 2008), Cleveland had the highest rate of stop and search in the country (Home Office, 2004a). Traces of zero-tolerance can also be seen in the 'total policing' model implemented by Bernard Hogan-Howe as part of his 'total war on crime' when he was chief constable of Merseyside (Godfrey, 2011). When Hogan-Howe left in 2009, Merseyside had one of the highest rates of stop and search in the country, second only to the Metropolitan Police Service (Ministry of Justice, 2010).

Why, then, did the use of stop and search dip so sharply at the end of the 1990s, and why has it been falling more recently? These reversals further illustrate the importance of broader political influences. Echoing the findings of the Scarman Report into the 1981 Brixton 'riots' (Scarman, 1981), the Inquiry into matters arising from the death of Stephen Lawrence, which reported in 1999, highlighted a loss of trust and confidence in the police among black and minority ethnic communities and the implications it had for policing by consent (Macpherson, 1999: para. 46.38):

> The public and the Police Services of the United Kingdom are justifiably proud of the tradition of an unarmed police service which polices with the consent of the public... [But] our view [is] that at present the confidence and trust of the minority ethnic communities is at a low ebb. Such lack of confidence threatens the ability of the Police Services to police by consent in all areas of their work.

As well as identifying serious failings in the investigation of Lawrence's murder, which it attributed to 'a combination of professional incompetence, institutional racism and a failure of leadership by senior officers' (1999: para. 46.1), the Inquiry identified a general problem of institutional racism 'both in the Metropolitan Police Service and in other Police Services and other institutions countrywide' (1999: para. 6.39). A series of public hearings produced 'inescapable evidence' of a lack of trust between the police and minority ethnic communities (1999: para. 45.6), with stop and search being singled out as an almost universal area of complaint.

The Inquiry's detailed recommendations led to 'the most extensive programmes of reform in the history of the relationship between the police and ethnic minority communities' (Bowling and Phillips, 2003: 546). All its recommendations were implemented, creating something of a siege mentality within the police service and a sense of collective, organisational trauma (Shiner, 2010). The psychological vulnerabilities associated with these developments were laid bare by Sir Paul Condon, the outgoing commissioner of the Metropolitan Police Service. Amid claims that crime was increasing due to demoralised officers disengaging from the use of stop and search for fear of being branded racist, Sir Paul declared that officers were 'grieving' for the loss of the force's reputation, claiming that some were so traumatised they could 'no longer function as human beings': the whole business, he said, had been a 'tragedy' for the police service (Riddell, 2000). While the reduction in stop and search activity from 1999/2000 reflected this initial sense of disorientation, subsequent increases were indicative of a police service pushing back and reasserting its authority. Bolstered by a backlash against the Lawrence Inquiry led by Conservative politicians and news media, the police mounted a successful rear-guard action against what they widely perceived to be an attack on the integrity of the service (Shiner, 2010; see also McLaughlin, 2007). Psychological defences translated into patterns of organisational resistance, blunting some of the key reforms that emerged out of the Inquiry's recommendations, including those relating to police stops (Shiner, 2010).

Police stop and search activity increased steadily following the initial dip that accompanied the publication of the Lawrence Inquiry report, peaking in 2010/2011. Since then there has been a fairly sharp decline, with the number of suspicion-based searches falling by almost a fifth (18 per cent) in two years (2014b). This reduction has not been evenly spread and several large urban forces, including the Metropolitan Police Service, Greater Manchester and Merseyside Police, have reported reductions of approximately a third (32 per cent in each case). Even greater reductions have been reported by Thames Valley, Cheshire and Leicestershire Police (46 per cent, 66 per cent and 76 per cent respectively). The overall decline in stop and search activity is partly a function of falling police numbers due to austerity measures – police officer strength fell by 10 per cent across England and Wales from March 2010 to March 2013 (Home Office, 2010a, 2013e). The reduction in stop and search activity has been greater than the reduction in police numbers, however, and forces that reported the most striking reductions in stop and search did not experience particularly sharp falls in police numbers: police strength fell by 10 per cent or less in the Metropolitan Police Service, Thames Valley and Leicestershire Police.

External pressures have played a key role in the recent reduction in stop and search activity. Following the riots of August 2011, which were partly attributed to anger and resentment over the use of stop and search, police have come under renewed pressure to moderate their tactics (Riots, Communities and Victims Panel, 2011). Within less than six months of the riots the home secretary, Theresa May, had announced there would be an official review of stop and search, prompting the commissioner of the Metropolitan Police Service, Sir Bernard Hogan-Howe, to unveil a plan to dramatically cut the use of the powers in London (Davenport, 2012; see also Chapter 8). Two of the forces where stop and search fell particularly sharply – Leicestershire and Thames Valley Police – were singled out by the Equality and Human Rights Commission (2010, 2012) as having especially problematic patterns of use, and implemented an agreed plan of action after facing legal compliance action. The Metropolitan Police Service avoided such action by agreeing to implement a programme for securing best practice. Two other forces that were singled out, but avoided formal compliance action, reported increases in the use of suspicion-based searches between 2010/2011 and 2012/2013 – Dorset (by 13 per cent) and West Midlands (by 65 per cent).

The rise and fall of 'exceptional' powers

The rise and fall of stop and search activity has also been evident in the use of 'exceptional' powers that do not require 'reasonable suspicion'. Section 60 of the Criminal Justice and Public Order Act 1994 and Section 44 of the Terrorism Act 2000 are very different in terms of their ostensible target, but their use has followed a remarkably similar trajectory. The number of stop-searches carried out under these powers increased sharply as part of the general reassertion of police authority following the Lawrence Inquiry, before falling away dramatically in the context of legal challenges (see Figure 3.2).

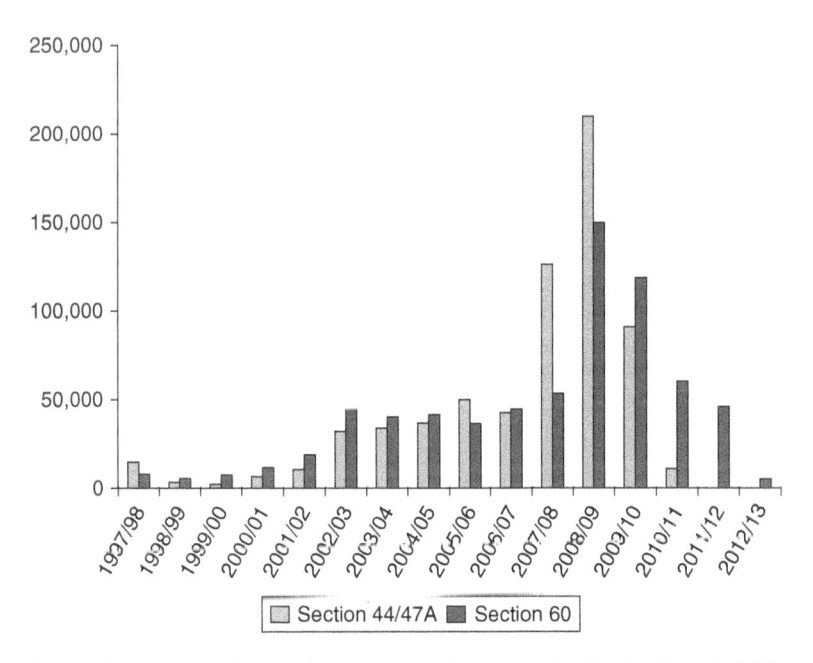

Figure 3.2 Stop-searches under exceptional powers in England and Wales (number)

Note: Section 60 refers to the Criminal Justice and Public Order Act 1994 and Section 44 to the Terrorism Act 2000. Figures shown for Section 44 prior to 2001/2002 refer to Sections 13A and 13B of the Prevention of Terrorism (Temporary Provisions) Act 1989, which were repealed under the Terrorism Act 2000.
Source: Home Office (2009a, 2014).

Although Section 44 of the Terrorism Act was exempt from the usual requirement for 'reasonable suspicion', it could only be used when specifically authorised by the home secretary. In practice, a series of rolling authorisations were issued, which meant Section 44 was actively in place across London for the best part of a decade (Sander et al., 2010). The number of searches conducted under this power increased sharply during the first three years it was in place. After a period of relative stability (despite the London bombings in July 2005) the numbers then quadrupled in just two years, from 2006/2007 to 2008/2009. With the vast majority of these searches being carried out in London, 'the capital's police' had, 'with the connivance of the Home Secretary and the domestic courts, turned an apparently exceptional power into a routine one' (Sanders et al., 2010: 86).

Section 44 proved controversial well before the 2008/2009 spike in its use and was repeatedly criticised by Lord Carlile, the then independent reviewer of terrorism legislation. In 2005, amid reports that the power was being deployed against people who would normally be regarded as protesters rather than terrorists, and that it had been used to search a group of train-spotters at a station included on a Home Office list of possible terrorist targets, Lord Carlile insisted the number of searches could be cut by half 'without significant risk to the public or detriment to policing' (Johnson, 2005). A few years later, Lord Carlile endorsed complaints from professional and amateur photographers that counter-terrorism powers were being used to threaten them with prosecution if they took photographs of officers, while also expressing frustration that Section 44 was being used unnecessarily on people who are 'so obviously far from any known terrorism profile that, realistically, there is not the slightest possibility of him/her being a terrorist, and no other feature to justify the stop' (Travis, 2009; see Carlile, 2009, 2010; see also Chapter 7). The use of Section 44 on journalists and protesters at an arms fair in the Docklands area of east London in September 2003 led to its eventual demise. A legal challenge was bought by two of the people who were stopped and searched at the event, Pennie Quinton and Kevin Gillan, eventually making its way through the domestic courts to the European Court of Human Rights (2010), which ruled that Section 44 was unlawful and incompatible with the right to respect for private life under Article 8 of the Convention on Human Rights. As a result, Section 44 was treated as repealed from March 2011, when it was replaced by Section 47A, which provides a more tightly circumscribed stop and search power that has, at the time of writing, not been used in England and Wales and has been used only once in Northern Ireland (Anderson, 2013; Home Office, 2013f).

Section 60 of the Criminal Justice and Public Order Act aims to tackle the threat of imminent violence and was originally introduced to help deal with football hooliganism (Delsol, 2010). Procedurally it is similar to Section 44 in the sense that it is exempt from the usual requirement for reasonable suspicion and can only be used with prior authorisation. Authorisation of Section 60 is an internal police matter, however, and there is no requirement for external scrutiny or confirmation. As the power was originally framed, an officer of the rank of superintendent or above may authorise its use in a given area for a period of up to 24 hours if s/he 'reasonably believes' that incidents involving serious violence may take place and it is expedient to do so to prevent their occurrence. Section 60 was amended by the Knives Act 1997, the Crime and Disorder Act 1998 and the Serious Crime Act 2007, which reduced the rank of the authorising officer to inspector or above and allowed the initial 24-hour authorisation to be extended for a further 24 hours.

Use of Section 60, much like use of Section 44, increased in two main waves. After the amendments introduced by the Knives Act 1997 and the Crime and Disorder Act 1998 came into force, the number of Section 60 searches more than quadrupled in just four years. There then followed a period of relative stability, before the number of searches almost trebled again in one year following the introduction of the Serious Crime Act 2007. This spike reinforced concerns that the power was being used to respond to a far wider range of incidents than originally intended (Delsol, 2010), including low-level disorder (Sanders and Young, 2007), and that police were circumventing the time restrictions by rotating authorisations around the same area (FitzGerald, 2010a).

The upsurge in Section 60 searches following the Serious Crime Act 2007 was due almost entirely to the Metropolitan Police Service, which launched Operation Blunt 2 in May 2008 with a view to preventing the killing of young people using weapons (Metropolitan Police Authority, 2008). A month later the Home Office launched its Tackling Knives Action Plan (TKAP), which aimed to reduce serious violence and related homicides, paying particular attention to stabbings among young people (Ward et al., 2011). Shortly after the launch of these initiatives, London witnessed four separate murders on a single day in July 2008. Although widely reported, this 'spate' of murders was not indicative of a growing problem, as the number of homicides in the capital during 2008 remained broadly in line with what had been happening over the previous three years (Spiegelhalter and Barnett, 2009: 8). As such, the massive growth in Section 60 searches was neither an objective nor a proportionate response to increases in serious violence, and, once again, factors other than crime seem to have been crucial in shaping police tactics.

In a further parallel with Section 44, use of Section 60 declined sharply in the midst of mounting external pressure and a looming legal challenge. As part of its response to a Home Office consultation about stop and search, StopWatch (2010) expressed serious concerns about the way Section 60 was being deployed, particularly the extent to which it was being used disproportionately on people from black and minority ethnic groups (see below). The submission called for an independent review into the use of Section 60 as well as the introduction of effective safeguards, including external monitoring and supervision. StopWatch also engaged in a public awareness campaign highlighting the misus of the power (see Townsend, 2010, 2012; Akwagyiram, 2012), and provided ongoing support for a legal challenge. Coming off the back of StopWatch's concerns about Section 60, the legal challenge arose out of a stop and search conducted on Ann Roberts in Haringey, north London, during September 2010 (Dodd, 2011; StopWatch, 2013). Officers stopped Roberts, a 37-year-old African Caribbean woman with no previous convictions, under Section 60, claiming she was holding onto her bag in a suspicious way in an area that was a 'hotspot' for gang violence and the possession of knives. Roberts asked to be searched in a police station, rather than in public, in order to avoid being seen by the young people with whom she worked as a special needs assistant, but her request was refused and a struggle ensued, during which she was restrained on the floor and handcuffed. After being detained in a local police station, Roberts was cautioned for obstruction. The legal challenge proceeded on the basis that there are insufficient safeguards limiting officers' discretion in the use of Section 60, leading to a risk of arbitrariness and discrimination (StopWatch, 2013). Having been turned down by the High Court and the Court of Appeal, the case looks set to go to the European Court (*The Guardian*, 2014a).

On the day that permission was granted for the original Section 60 challenge to proceed to the High Court, the deputy commissioner of the Metropolitan Police Service, Craig Mackey (2012), wrote to all chief constables and commissioners informing them about the challenge, noting: 'Since the successful challenge was made in the European Courts on the "no suspicion" powers of Stop and Search contained within Section 44 Terrorism Act 2000, the potential for a similar scrutiny of Section 60 powers has always been anticipated.' In an apparent attempt to pre-empt the challenge, he went on to announce significant reforms to the use of Section 60, including the introduction of a target to halve the number of authorisations (Dodd, 2012). According to the recent review carried out by Her Majesty's Inspectorate of Constabulary (2013: 41), the Metropolitan Police Service had reduced its use of Section 60 by almost 90 per cent 'with no associated impact on violent crime rates'. Following the publication of the HMIC report, Theresa May, the home secretary, announced that stop and search needs to be scaled back, noting particular concerns about the use of Section 60, including the extent to which black people are disproportionately stopped and searched (Travis, 2013a).

What are the police looking for?

Stop and search is primarily an investigative power used for the purposes of crime detection or prevention (Lustgarten, 2002), enabling 'officers to allay or confirm suspicions about individuals without exercising their power of arrest' (Home Office, 2013a: 4). According to the PACE Code of Practice, an 'officer must not search a person, even with his or her consent, where no power to search is applicable' (2013a: 4). Most stop and search powers require that officers have reasonable grounds for suspecting they will find stolen or prohibited articles, although what is counted as a 'prohibited article' is fairly wide-ranging. While officers may search for drugs under the Misuse of Drugs Act 1971, PACE defines a prohibited article as either an offensive weapon or an article intended for use in burglary, theft, taking vehicles or fraud (Sanders et al., 2010).

We might expect stop and search to be dominated by the investigation of 'volume crime' such as domestic and non-domestic burglary, including theft of and from vehicles. Looking for stolen property and items that may be used to facilitate a theft or burglary are among the most common reasons officers give for stopping and searching people, accounting for slightly more than a third of all suspicion-based searches (see Figure 3.3). By far and away the most common reason for a search, however, is drugs, which account for slightly more than half of all such searches. Given that cannabis possession accounts for around 70 per cent of police-recorded drug offences (Home Office, 2012c), we would estimate that slightly more than one-third of suspicion-based searches are for suspected cannabis possession.

It is only fairly recently that drugs have come to dominate stop and search in the way they have, and this development has not been driven by increases in use. During the late 1990s, when drug use was peaking in England and Wales (Home Office, 2012d), approximately a third

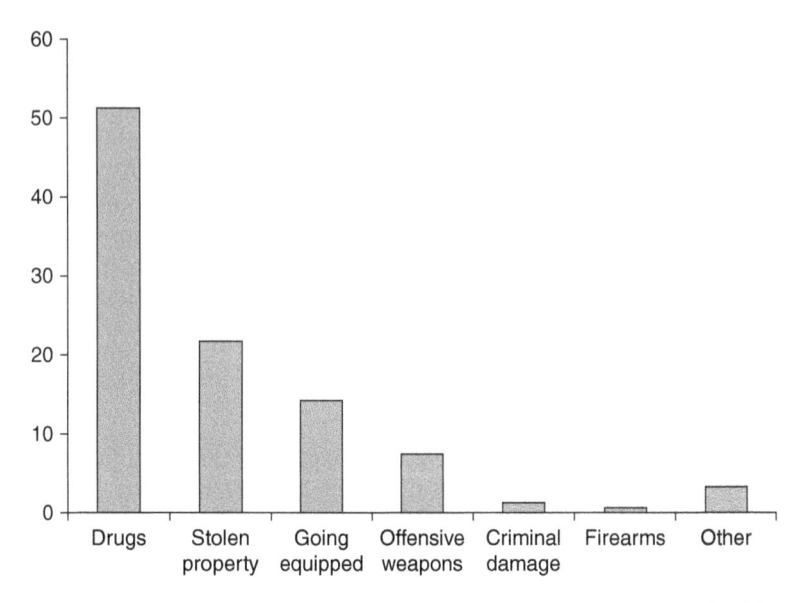

Figure 3.3 Suspicion-based stop-searches by reason in England and Wales, 2012/2013 (percentage)
Note: 'Going equipped' refers to carrying any item designed for use in carrying out a theft or burglary.
Source: Home Office (2014b).

of suspicion-based stop-searches were for drugs (Home Office, 2009a). While rates of drug use have fallen since then (Home Office, 2013g), the number of stop-searches for drugs has more than doubled (see Figure 3.4). The greater focus on drugs has primarily come at the expense of searches for stolen property, which have gone from accounting for two-fifths to one-fifth of suspicion-based searches.

Rather than being a function of increased drug offending, the expansion of stop and search for drugs appears to have been the unintended consequence of a target-driven culture that rewards officers for targeting minor drug offences. While the distorting effects of police performance targets have been well documented (Flanegan, 2007; Sergeant, 2008; Morgan and Newburn, 2012; Padfield et al., 2012), the introduction of cannabis street warnings in 2003 provided officers with a quick way of clearing up offences or securing 'sanctioned detections' (Eastwood et al., 2013). Police-recorded offences where there is no specific identifiable victim, including drug use, increased annually from 2002/2003, peaking in 2007/2008, but this was an artificial trend that reflected 'changes in police workload and activity rather than in levels of criminality'

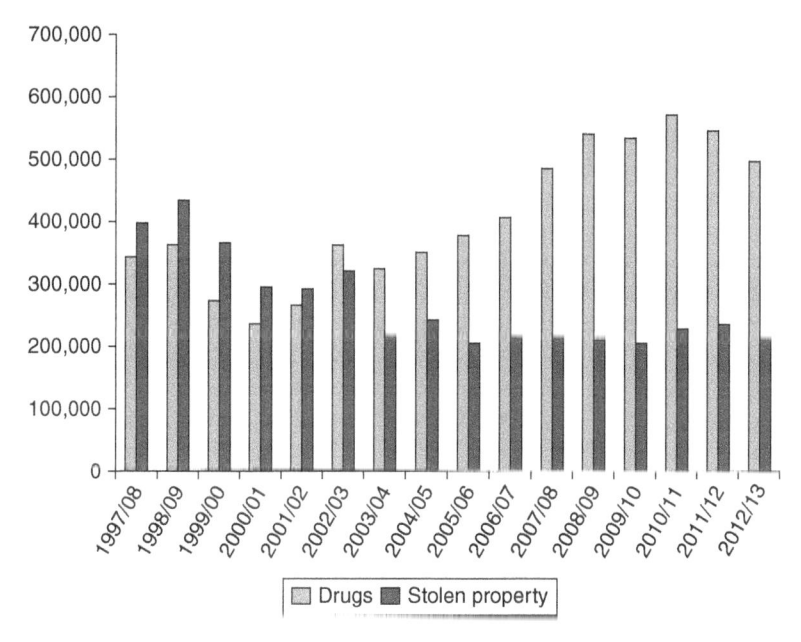

Figure 3.4 Suspicion-based stop-searches for drugs and stolen property in England and Wales (number)
Source: Home Office (2009a, 2014b).

(Office for National Statistics, 2013a: 16). The number of cannabis possession offences recorded annually by the police almost doubled between 2004/2005 and 20011/2012 (Home Office, 2012c), while rates of self-reported use were falling (Home Office, 2013g).

Variations between forces

Policing takes a range of different styles based on various 'hard', 'good' and 'smart' tactics (Reiner, 2010: 155) that have significant implications for the use of stop and search. Recent research in four basic command units from three police forces across England and Wales found markedly different styles of policing: some teams and officers were highly proactive, while others were more reactive; and some tended to engage with the public on the basis of a 'rule of law' style, while others tended to be more adversarial (May et al., 2010). The adversarial style was found to be particularly prevalent within certain teams in one of the police force areas, which was described as a 'busy inner-city area, where the relationship between the police and young black people was shaped by a history of friction, dating back at least to the early 1980s' (2010: 40). This style was said to have been adopted by two teams of specialist officers whose remit was to disrupt the illegal activities of young people and to be seen to take command of the local area, but not by the local neighbourhood policing team, which took a more consensual, responsive approach to policing.

Use of stop and search varies sharply across England and Wales, and does so in ways that are suggestive of markedly different policing styles. Stop and search is heavily concentrated in London, which accounts for 15 per cent of the population (according to the 2011 Census), but more than a third of suspicion-based searches (Home Office, 2012b, 2014b). Use of 'exceptional' powers has been even more heavily concentrated in the capital: the Metropolitan Police carried out 94 per cent of Section 44 stop-searches and 76 per cent of Section 60 stop-searches when use of these powers was at its height (Home Office, 2010b). Previous analysis reported by Miller et al. (2000) found suspicion-based stop and search was used at very different rates by similar forces, and that such differences were unrelated to patterns of offending. This remains so. As was the case a decade ago, Cleveland, the Metropolitan Police and Dyfed Powys are among the biggest users of suspicion-based searches, while Essex continues to make little use of such powers (see Figure 3.5). More detailed analysis, updating and extending that reported by Miller et al. (2000), found a modest association between stop and search and crime rates, which disappeared in a multi-level regression model, indicating that there are characteristics in the different force areas that explain the cross-sectional association, the most likely being the different contexts, policies and police cultures (Bradford, 2013). Illustrating the importance of policy and culture, use of suspicion-based stop and search fell by two-thirds in Cleveland between 2002/2003 and 2003/2004 (Home Office, 2004b) following the appointment of a new chief constable who reoriented the force away from the practices associated with its earlier commitment to 'zero-tolerance' policing, which had given rise to 'a culture of stopping and searching' (Equalities and Human Rights Commission, 2010: 73). This proved to be a temporary reversal, however, as Cleveland has subsequently gone back to having the highest rate of stop and search in the country.

Who gets stopped and searched?

Police are routinely called on to deal with the messy business of social conflict, much of which is bound up with the stresses and strains

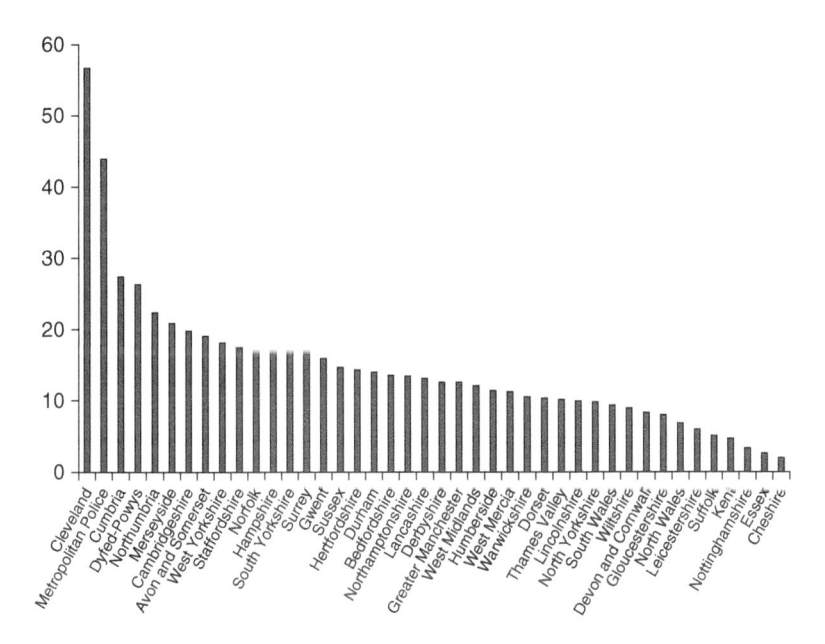

Figure 3.5 Suspicion-based stop-searches across England and Wales by police force area, 2012/2013 (rate per 1,000)
Note: The City of London force has been excluded from this figure on the grounds that the very marked differences between the resident population and the transitional population render the results unreliable.
Source: Home Office (2014b).

emanating from wider social and economic pressures (Reiner, 1985, 2010; Fielding, 1991). A good deal of police time is spent on those who are marginalised in various ways, and the sociology of policing has long been concerned with the potential for discrimination. In *Police and People in London*, Smith and Grey (1985) observed that the requirement for 'reasonable suspicion' had little effect on police decision-making and documented the non-random nature of police stops. Drawing on the results of a public survey, they identified several groups that were many more times likely to have been stopped than others: namely, young people; men, especially those who were unemployed or from lower social classes; and black people. While noting that these differences might reflect patterns of offending, the authors concluded that their findings 'would fit very well with the idea that there is an "underclass" of people who, among other things, are often in trouble with the police' (1985: 114).

Concerns about discrimination have persisted despite the introduction of tighter regulations seeking to ensure that stop and search is based on objective decision-making (see chapters 2 and 4). According to Sanders and Young (2007: 85), research evidence 'shows that very large numbers of stop-search decisions are based on crude stereotypes, and that PACE made little difference to this'. Officers are often unclear about what constitutes 'reasonable grounds' and do not meet this requirement in a substantial number of cases (FitzGerald, 1999; Quinton et al., 2000; Shiner, 2006; HMIC, 2013). The implications for operational decision-making are evident from recent observational studies. According to May et al. (2010: 39), stop and search tends to be enthusiastically embraced by officers who favour an adversarial style of policing geared towards demonstrating 'control of the streets'. This style, they note, was prevalent in 'high crime areas' and tended to focus on the same small group of people who challenged police authority. While adversarial tactics were often said to be adopted in the context of tense, conflictual encounters, the authors also observed that, where offending is, or is believed to be, concentrated among particular groups, these groups tend to 'attract differential police treatment' (2010: 39). A dynamic of mutual antagonism was identified between police and a group of young, mainly black, teenagers who were suspected of being criminally active or engaged in gang activity. Members of this group were subject to 'rigorous enforcement', including targeted stop and search, in what the authors interpreted as an attempt by the police to demonstrate who was in control of the streets. Complementary statistical analysis showed that, proportionately, black, Asian and mixed-race young people were considerably more likely than white young people to have been arrested as a result of proactive police work. Black youth, in particular, were found to be over-represented among arrests for robbery and drugs.

Similar themes are discussed in Loftus's (2009) recent ethnography of policing. While noting that explicitly racist language has been more or less eliminated from the police vocabulary, Loftus maintains that 'police culture continues to impact adversely on minority groups in ways identified in earlier research' (2009: 127; see also Foster et al., 2005). Officers continue to display an ongoing antipathy towards minority groups and retain enduring stereotypes about the involvement of minority ethnic men in crime: young black Caribbean men are particularly associated with drugs and burglary, public order offences, prostitution, gangs and guns. While the actual drug raids Loftus observed were invariably of houses belonging to white people, she notes, 'the assumption that minority ethnic males were responsible for drugs crime could result in stop and search powers being used against this group' (2009: 144). The practical implications of such stereotypical associations were, nonetheless, 'contradictory and uneven' because some officers, it was claimed, avoided proactive encounters with minority ethnic groups for fear of recriminations from the police organisation (2009: 155). Loftus also warns against overstating the 'ethnic component' of police suspicion, arguing that social class is an underlying factor that shapes police discourse and practice towards minority groups. Signs of 'roughness' precipitated police suspicion and, 'to this end, the *white* residuum also became targeted' (2009: 157, original emphasis).

The non-random nature of police-initiated stops has been confirmed by various self-report surveys. Drawing on a booster sample of minority ethnic respondents, the 2000 British Crime Survey pointed to significant ethnic differences: proportionately more young black men than young white men had been stopped by the police on foot (32 per cent compared with 21 per cent) or in a vehicle (39 per cent compared with 25 per cent) (Clancy et al., 2001). For foot stops, however, these differences appeared not to be directly attributable to ethnicity. When other, significant, variables were taken into account – being aged under 25, being male, going out regularly after dark, not owning a car and being unemployed – ethnicity did not help to distinguish those who had been stopped from those who had not. Many of the same variables were predictive of vehicle stops, but they did not entirely explain ethnic differences in this regard. While the analysis pointed to a pattern of indirect discrimination in relation to foot stops, the results for vehicle stops were consistent with 'a degree of direct racial discrimination' (Sanders et al., 2010: 86).

More recently, the Edinburgh Study of Youth Transitions and Crime has reported particularly high rates of adversarial contact with police among young, low-status males from deprived neighbourhoods who frequently spend time in public space and have a history of prior contact with the police (McAra and McVie, 2005). While offending histories were also found to be predictive of such contact, they did not over-ride these other influences. Initial police contact was most readily explained by 'persistent serious offending and a complex inter-relationship between low socio-economic status and hanging around on the street', whereby less affluent young people who 'hang around' are more likely to have contact than those from more advantaged backgrounds (2005: 26). Later contact with police was predicted by having had prior personal contact or vicarious contact through friends, low social class and persistent serious offending, as well as other risky and street-based behaviours. Prior personal contact was a particularly powerful predictor. Such findings, the authors argue, are indicative of 'a disciplinary model of policing' that focuses on 'a permanent suspect population' and has the potential to amplify levels of police contact and levels of offending among certain sectors of the youth population (2005: 26). This pattern of policing, they note, cannot be justified by the results: fewer than a fifth of the young people who had experienced adversarial police contact at age 15 were charged with an offence.

Similar results have been reported on the basis of the Offending Crime and Justice Survey, covering young people in England and Wales. Detailed multivariate analysis provided further evidence that police-initiated stops focus on the 'usual suspects' who have had prior contact with the police and whose friends have had prior contact with the police (Medina Ariza, 2013). Such factors, it is noted, appear to be better predictors than respondents' own self-reported offending behaviour, indicating that 'who you hang out with' seems to matter more 'than what you do' (2013: 219). In contrast to the Edinburgh study, which was unable to assess ethnic differences because of the small number of respondents from minority groups (McAra and McVie, 2005), the Offending Crime and Justice Survey confirms that young people from black and minority groups are stopped by the police at a higher rate than whites (see also Singer, 2013). Even when self-reported offending and other relevant variables, including presence on the street, were taken into account, ethnicity still mattered: indeed, it seemed to matter more than self-reported offending behaviour (Medina Ariza, 2013). All minority ethnic groups exhibited a higher risk of being stopped and searched than the white group, and this effect was particularly marked for black young people: controlling for other factors, black young people were more than four times as likely as white young people to have been subject to such an intervention. The analysis was less clear about the impact of ethnicity on other, less intrusive, forms of police-initiated contact and found that it did not have a direct effect on the likelihood of having been stopped without being searched.

Regulations governing the use of stop and search include a particular focus on ethnicity and require that any apparently disproportionate use of the powers can be identified and investigated (Home Office, 2013a). Police records are regularly collated and published by the Home Office and Ministry of Justice, showing how the number of stop-searches per 1,000 population varies between groups. Such comparisons have highlighted consistent ethnic differences, indicating that black people are subject to suspicion-based stop-searches at around five to six times the rate of white people and Asians are stopped and searched at approximately twice the rate of whites (Miller, 2010). Even starker differences are evident in relation to the exceptional powers, especially Section 60, which has been used to stop and search black people at more than 20 times the rate of white people (Equalities and Human Rights Commission, 2012; StopWatch, 2012; see Chapter 7 for a discussion of Section 44).

Ethnic differences are typically assessed on the basis of broad categories that obscure some important variations between specific groups. A more detailed classification shows that all black groups experience relatively high rates of stop and search compared with whites, but that black Caribbeans are stopped and searched at almost twice the rate of black Africans (see Table 3.1). While Indian people are stopped and searched at a similar rate to white British people, Bangladeshis and Pakistanis are stopped and searched at more than three and two times the rate of the white British group, respectively. This may be indicative of a particular focus on Muslim communities (the vast majority of Pakistanis and Bangladeshis are Muslim, while Indians are spread more evenly across a range of religions; see Heath and Martin, 2013), though it may also reflect vulnerabilities associated with other socio-demographic differences: Pakistanis and Bangladeshis are subject to particularly high levels of deprivation (Hills et al., 2010), while Bangladeshis are heavily concentrated in London (Office for National Statistics, 2012), where the overall rate of stop and search is high. Within both white and black categories, those classified as 'other' are subject to high rates of stop and search. This may be because 'other' includes particular groups that are susceptible to high levels of police attention – white 'other' includes gypsies and Irish travellers, who are subject to widespread stereotypes about involvement in criminal activity (see Cemlyn et al., 2009). Among black communities, 'other' may include young people who do not readily identify with their family country of origin and members of relatively recent migrant communities, who may be susceptible to police attention because of their youthful age structure and patterns of residence (the 'other' groups tend to include a proportionately large number of people living in London).

Ethnic differences appear to have become more marked since the late 1990s. Miller (2010: 968) found overall levels of disproportionality for suspicion-based searches did not improve between 1996/1997 and 2007/2008, noting that the 'relative chances of people' from black and Asian groups 'being searched, compared to whites have apparently

Table 3.1 Suspicion-based stop-searches by self-identified ethnicity in England and Wales (2011/2012)

	Rate per 1,000	Disproportionality Ratios
White	16	1.0
Black	86	5.5
Asian	30	1.9
Mixed	27	1.7
Other	15	1.0
White		
British	15	1.0
Irish	17	1.1
Other	33	2.3
Black		
African	54	3.6
Caribbean	101	6.9
Other	170	11.5
Asian		
Bangladeshi	48	3.3
Indian	16	1.1
Pakistani	33	2.2
Other	41	2.8
Mixed		
African	20	1.3
Asian	8	0.6
Caribbean	36	2.4
Other	39	2.7
Other		
Chinese	5	0.4
Other	23	1.5

Notes: (1) Disproportionality ratios are calculated by dividing the rate per 1,000 for a minority group by the rate per 1,000 for the white group or, in the case of the more detailed classification, the white British group.
(2) For the purposes of presentation, the number of stop-searches has been rounded to the nearest whole number.
(3) Stop and search rates were calculated using figures published by the Ministry of Justice (2013) and population estimates based on the 2011 Census (Office for National Statistics, 2012).
(4) The rates per 1,000 for the broader ethnic categories are slightly different from those reported by the Ministry of Justice (2013) because population estimates have not been adjusted to exclude children younger than 10 years of age (this was not possible using the available estimates because they are not broken down by age).

increased'. Technical difficulties in estimating the size of the various ethnic populations have since become apparent (PEEGS Team, 2011a, 2011b), which mean it is not possible to provide reliable year-on-year comparisons. Nonetheless, the longer-term trend can still be assessed by comparing relatively short time-frames around the 2001 and 2011 Census (population changes across England and Wales over the short term are likely to be minor). Such comparisons indicate that black/white disproportionality dipped during the immediate aftermath of the Lawrence Inquiry, but then increased quickly, surpassing previous levels (Table 3.2). The publication of the Inquiry report in February 1999 was followed by a marked reduction in the rate of stop and search for both black and white people: a reduction that was maintained for white people, but not black people. When the stop and search rate for black people increased markedly during 2001/2002, disproportionality also increased and appears to have been more than maintained during the subsequent period. This increase in black/white disproportionality was accompanied by the emergence of a focus on Asian people, especially Muslim groups (see above), which became more marked during

Table 3.2 Suspicion-based stop-searches by ethnic appearance in England and Wales (1998/1999 to 2011/2012)

	1998/1999	1999/2000	2000/2001	2001/2002	2010/2011	2011/2012
Rate per 1,000						
White	21	17	14	14	17	16
Black	74	52	54	67	91	79
Asian	24	17	16	20	32	29
Other	19	14	12	15	17	16
Disproportionality Ratios						
White	1.0	1.0	1.0	1.0	1.0	1.0
Black	3.6	3.1	4.0	4.9	5.3	5.0
Asian	1.1	1.0	1.2	1.5	1.8	1.8
Other	0.9	0.9	0.9	1.1	1.0	1.0

Notes: (1) The analysis presented here is based on ethnic appearance or officer-identified ethnicity because this was the published format for the earlier period (the classification of ethnic appearance is based on broad ethnic groups).
(2) Disproportionality ratios are calculated by dividing the rate per 1,000 for a minority group by the rate per 1,000 for the white group.
(3) For the purposes of presentation, the number of stop-searches has been rounded to the nearest whole number.
(4) Stop and search rates were calculated using figures published by the Home Office (1999, 2002) and Ministry of Justice (2013). Rates for the earlier period are based on population estimates from the 2001 Census (Home Office, 2004b), while figures for the later period are based on population estimates from the 2011 Census (Office for National Statistics, 2012).

the course of the decade. Over the long term, then, the primary police response to the concerns raised by the Lawrence Inquiry about institutional racism and the use of stop and search seems to have been one of resistance and defiance (see Shiner, 2010).

Evidence that people from black and minority ethnic groups are stopped and searched at disproportionately high rates has been sharply contested, not least by the police themselves (Delsol and Shiner, 2006; Shiner, 2010). This controversy has been fuelled by a tendency, on both sides, to treat disproportionality as a direct index of police racism. The Ministry of Justice (2013: 9) provided some much-needed clarification when it noted that the 'identification of differences should not be equated with discrimination, as there are many reasons why apparent disparities may exist'. Such differences remain important, however, 'because they illustrate the experience of different ethnic groups irrespective of the reasons that may explain any disparities' (Home Office, 2009b: 26–7). While other factors are, no doubt, significant,[3] it is implausible to suppose that police biases are not part of the causal mix. Various studies have found that 'race' features prominently in officers' thinking (HMIC, 1999; Shiner, 2010) and have identified enduring stereotypes that are reinforced through differential treatment of minority groups (Loftus, 2009; see also May et al., 2010). There is, moreover, a wealth of social-psychological research which shows that stereotypes are common among the general population and result from basic cognitive functions (Wilson et al., 2004; Dovidio et al., 2005). Many people, it seems, harbour unconscious racial biases that operate independently of conscious beliefs, so those who are not consciously prejudiced tend to operate on the basis of stereotypes when acting automatically (Harris, 2007). To claim policing is free of racial bias under such circumstances represents a form of denial, rooted in fantasies of omnipotence (Shiner, 2010).

Two principal arguments are used to explain disproportionality in ways that do not implicate police decision-making: one based on levels of offending and the other based on the 'available population' (Delsol and Shiner, 2006; Bowling and Phillips, 2007; Shiner, 2010). The claim that black and minority ethnic groups are subject to disproportionately high rates of stop and search because of their patterns of offending rests on the assumption that members of these groups offend at a higher rate than whites or, at least, are more likely to commit the kinds of offences that attract police attention. Such claims have long proved controversial and tend to polarise opinion (see Lea and Young, 1984; Gilroy, 1987). Although differences in offending and differences in enforcement are often treated as competing explanations, it does not necessarily follow that they work in isolation from one another. The over-representation of black people in arrest statistics, for example, has been attributed to a 'vicious cycle of interaction' between 'police stereotyping and black vulnerability to the situations that attract police attention' (Reiner, 2010: 95; see also Smith, 1997).

Official criminal justice statistics, including arrest rates, are a poor indicator of offending rates because they are partly a product of differential enforcement and potential biases in decision-making (Bowling and Phillips, 2007; May et al., 2010). More reliable evidence comes from self-report studies, which produce data that appear to be 'acceptably valid and reliable for most research purposes' (Thornberry and Krohn, 2000: 33). A series of self-report surveys in England and Wales has consistently found that black and minority ethnic groups offend at a similar or lower rate than whites (Graham and Bowling, 1995; Flood-Page et al., 2000; Sharp and Budd, 2005). This helps to explain the finding, noted above, that self-reported offending does not account for ethnic differences in police contact. Nor do people from black and minority ethnic groups appear to be prone to types of offending that attract police attention. According to the Offending, Crime and Justice Survey, for example, relatively few black and Asian people commit serious offences (Sharp and Budd, 2005). Repeated surveys have also shown that black and minority ethnic groups tend to use drugs at a lower rate than whites, and yet drug-related stop and search is particularly disproportionate in its focus on these groups (Eastwood et al., 2013).

Claims that disproportionality may be explained by the available population have greater face validity, but remain controversial and have been described as a 'smokescreen' by the National Black Police Association (see Metropolitan Police Authority, 2004). Although widely cited as an explanation for apparent ethnic differences, the evidence on the available population is fairly limited. Only two published British studies have attempted to assess the ethnicity of those 'who use public places *where* and *when* stops or searches are carried out' and compared the results with those who are stopped and searched (MVA and Miller, 2000: 9; see also Waddington et al., 2004). Both studies concluded that people from black and minority ethnic groups are more available in these areas and that this greater availability goes a long way towards explaining why they are stopped and searched at a higher rate than would be expected based on their numbers in the residential population. Leaving aside the methodological difficulties of determining the ethnic composition of the available population in what may be busy thoroughfares, these studies are limited in several important respects. The largest study, conducted by MVA and Miller (2000), was 'conducted at an unusual point in time and space' (Sanders and Young, 2007: 84). Fieldwork was carried out from July 1999 to May 2000, just after the Lawrence Inquiry report was published, when levels of disproportionality were relatively low (see Table 3.2). Taken together, moreover, the two studies cover a handful of tightly defined localised areas with relatively high rates of stop and search, which means the results cannot be generalised to the country as a whole with any degree of confidence.

MVA and Miller (2000: 87) make it clear that their study 'did not give a clean bill of health to the police use of stops and searches', noting instances when people from minority ethnic backgrounds were stopped and searched more often than would be expected from the available population. Nor does availability readily explain why levels of disproportionality are more marked in relation to stop and search than less invasive stops that fall short of a search – when figures were last published, black/white disproportionality for stop and search was more than twice that for stop and account (Bridges et al., 2011). This difference reflects the greater rate at which police proceed to search black people once they have stopped them (Sanders and Young, 2007) and clearly implicates police decision-making as a driver of disproportionality. Crucially, the conditions in which stop and account and stop and search are undertaken are the same with regard to the available population and relative rates of offending within the various ethnic groups. Given that these factors are, in effect, held constant, they cannot explain why disproportionality is higher for stop and search than for stop and account.

The focus on the available population arguably involves a degree of conceptual confusion. Both British studies were designed to assess possible biases emanating from street-level decision-making. While such decisions are a potentially significant source of discrimination, they are not the only, nor necessarily the most important, consideration. The Lawrence Inquiry identified ethnic disparities in stop and search as evidence of *institutional racism*, which recognises that discriminatory outcomes may occur in the absence of individually biased decision-making due to organisational policies and practices (see Macpherson, 1999). Viewed from this perspective, the nature of the available population is partly a function of organisational decisions about where and when to conduct stop and search. To the extent that stop and search is concentrated in neighbourhoods with large minority ethnic populations, members of these groups are bound to be more 'available'. As a general explanation for disproportionality, then, the available population is 'self-fulfilling' (Equalities and Human Rights Commission, 2010: 52) and simply exchanges one problem – discrimination at the level of the individual – for another – discrimination at the level of the neighbourhood (Bowling and Phillips, 2007). While some forces direct stop and search activity to crime hotspots using carefully constructed maps, the vast majority do not (HMIC, 2013). In the absence of such a systematic approach, recent analysis has shown that stop and search tends to be clustered in hotspots that are 'hotter' than would be predicted from crime levels and in areas with relatively large black and minority ethnic communities (Chainey and Macdonald, 2012). As a result, members of these communities tend to be stopped and searched at a heightened rate. MVA and Miller (2000) found similar evidence of stop and search being targeted at areas with disproportionate numbers of black and minority ethnic residents, but where local crime rates did not appear to justify such attention. Insisting that their research should not be seen as an 'excuse' for the police to turn attention away from the potential role of discrimination, they recommended that forces 'should continue to compile measures of disproportionality based on residential figures' because 'these figures remain an important indicator of the actual experience of different ethnic groups within police force areas' (2000: 88).

Conclusion

Stop and search illustrates the gap that often exists between legal rules and police practice. While legal justifications focus on crime-fighting applications, the actual link with crime is, at best, imprecise: trends in stop and search do not follow crime trends; variations between forces do not map onto crime patterns; and factors other than offending help to explain who is and who is not stopped and searched. None of this makes stop and search unusual. Public debates are routinely based on the misapprehension that policing is primarily about crime-fighting, when the 'core mandate of policing, historically and in terms of concrete demands placed upon the police, is the more diffuse one of order maintenance' (Reiner, 2010: 208). This mandate is tightly bound up with the wider structure of racial and class disadvantage, drawing attention to the activities of the young 'street' population, economically marginalised minority ethnic communities and other elements of the 'underclass' that make up 'police property' (Reiner, 2010: 208). As social divisions have deepened and inequality has widened, it is unsurprising that police have made greater use of the formal powers available to them and have come to rely on more punitive modes of social control. Rather than providing a straightforward response to crime, sharp increases in the use of stop and search since the introduction of PACE represent an immediate police response to the growing stresses and strains associated with the fragmentation of the welfare state and the pursuit of neo-liberal policies (Reiner, 2010). While offering little as a crime-fighting tactic (see Chapter 5), stop and search provides police with a flexible and highly visible means of dealing with their 'property', enabling them to contain and, where necessary, criminalise, those who threaten, or are perceived to threaten, the social order. In this sense, stop and search is both structured by, and contributes to, broader processes of social exclusion (see Chapter 6).

Notes

1. See http://www.legislation.gov.uk/ukpga/1988/52/section/163/enacted [accessed 10 June 2013].
2. The British Crime Survey (BCS) indicates that, over the last decade or so, approximately 10 per cent of adults in England and Wales were stopped in a vehicle by police per year, down from 16 per cent in 1991 (Moon et al., 2011). Applying recent estimates to the general adult population in England and Wales as recorded by the 2011 Census indicates that there were slightly fewer than 5,500,000 vehicle stops in 2010/2011. Allowance has been made for multiple stops – of the BCS respondents who had been stopped in a vehicle, 74 per cent had been stopped once, 16 per cent had been stopped twice and 9 per cent had been stopped three times or more (for the purposes of the calculation it was assumed that those in this group had been stopped three times).
3. Most black and minority ethnic groups are concentrated in London (Office for National Statistics, 2012), for example, which makes them susceptible to the relatively high rates of stop and search that are evident within the capital. Even within London, however, black and minority ethnic groups are stopped and searched at a higher rate than the white group (Equalities and Human Rights Commission, 2010).

4
Race Disproportionality and Officer Decision-Making

Paul Quinton

Every two years, the publication of official data for the police service provokes a debate about the extent to which people from black and minority ethnic (BME) groups are stopped and searched compared with white people, and whether any disparities are fair. The most recent figures – which compare stop and search records with the resident population – showed that black people were six times more likely, and Asians twice as likely, to be searched than white people (Ministry of Justice, 2013). These data are important because they tell us about the public's exposure to, and experience of, police-initiated encounters regardless of the reasons for that contact. However, the police have become locked into a public debate that is fixed on the headline figures, rather than using the statistics as a prompt for more detailed investigation into the nature, causes and consequences of disproportionality. On one side of the debate, the position has been taken that these disparities are unquestionable proof of racism. The police, on the other side, have tended to explain the issue away with reference to a range of possible hypotheses, such as biased police recording and differential offending rates (Delsol and Shiner, 2006; Shiner, 2010).

Debates that focus solely on the official statistics can only ever be limited in scope because they present a partial picture and lack explanatory power. While racial differences in stop and search rates point towards the *possibility* of discrimination, they cannot provide concrete evidence of its existence as they tell us nothing about how or why the disparities arise (Bowling and Phillips, 2002). Even in the absence of discrimination, disproportionality should still be regarded as a problem because of the number of innocent people who will be brought into unnecessary contact with the police,[1] and its resulting effect on the legitimacy of the police (Jackson et al., 2012a) and differential entry into the criminal justice system (May et al., 2010).

The Stephen Lawrence Inquiry (Macpherson, 1999) concluded that the police service was institutionally racist partly because of the countrywide disparities in the stop and search figures. Overall, in defining institutional racism as the 'collective failure of an organisation to provide an appropriate and professional service to people because of their colour, culture, or ethnic origin', the Inquiry highlighted how the unreflective and ordinary working practices of the police resulted in discriminatory outcomes (Macpherson, 1999: para. 6.34). While indirect organisational and social processes were seen to affect stop and search (citing the specific influence of demographic mix, school exclusions, unemployment and police recording practices), the Inquiry concluded that disproportionality resulted from racist stereotyping. Foster et al. (2005) argued that the Inquiry's notion of institutional racism was problematic in that it simultaneously highlighted and conflated conscious and unconscious discrimination at both individual and organisational levels, which led to anger and defensiveness across the service in the mistaken belief that the Inquiry said overt racism was widespread among officers (see also Shiner, 2010). Given these complexities, to what extent does disproportionality result from officer decision-making or factors outside the control of the police? Furthermore, as previous research has suggested that officers use cognitive 'rules-of-thumb' to decide whether to initiate contact with a suspect (Quinton, 2011), to what extent does racist stereotyping contribute to disproportionality?

This chapter aims to build a picture of police decision-making and its effect on disproportionality by drawing together insights from the relevant literature and fieldwork I was involved in, which explored police stop and search practices (see Bland et al., 2000a; Quinton and Olagundoye, 2004). The ethnographic research – which was carried out in response to the Lawrence Inquiry – was conducted in 10 study sites in the early 2000s.[2] It consisted of interviews with 198 police officers and observations of over 565 hours of police patrol, during which 281 police-initiated encounters were observed (including 58 searches, 191 stops and 32 other traffic encounters). The study methods inevitably affected the behaviour of those being observed and cannot provide access to hidden thought processes, but, nevertheless, enabled the social world inhabited by police officers to be better understood through their action and talk. The time that has elapsed since the fieldwork means that the findings may not reflect current practices, though their consistency with other studies suggests that they remain relevant (such as Rubinstein, 1973; May et al., 2010).

The chapter is divided into three parts. The first part seeks to place officer decision-making in context. It will be argued that structural, legal and organisational factors can have a significant effect on disproportionality overall, and that the extent to which different groups use public space is likely to be particularly important. Nevertheless, it will be shown that these factors do not determine the outcome, and that officers remain active agents within this process. The second part examines the extent to which disproportionality results from information provided by the public. It will be argued that, while suspect descriptions provided by crime victims are likely to be biased, their effect on disproportionality is probably small overall and will vary according to how reactive the police are to calls for service. Suspect descriptions, however, will be shown to have a more indirect effect on disproportionality in terms of fostering stereotypes and how they are used by officers to initiate an encounter. The third part looks more directly at police decision-making. It will be argued that, while the use of racist language has largely disappeared from policing, stereotyping remains central to practice. However, while officers appear to have heightened suspicions about black people in particular – which probably is one of the main contributing factors to disproportionality overall – examples of individual racism are very limited.

Reference is made throughout the chapter to Reiner's (2010: 10) typology of discrimination, a process he describes as resulting in 'some social categories being over-represented as targets of police action even when legally relevant variables (especially the pattern of offending) are held constant'. Reiner highlighted six types of discrimination. 'Categorical discrimination' – the most direct form of discrimination – was said to occur when a person was treated differently by virtue of being a member of a particular racial or ethnic group. 'Statistical discrimination' occurs when differential treatment results from a group being stereotyped as being, say, more criminal than another with no evidential basis. 'Transmitted discrimination' takes place when police action simply responds neutrally to, and replicates, wider social prejudice. 'Interactional discrimination' is said to occur when a person is treated differently as a result of their non-criminal behaviour during an encounter. 'Situational discrimination' describes how a racial or ethnic group is subject to police targeting as a result of the socio-economic position or lifestyle of its members. Finally, Reiner defined 'institutionalized discrimination' in terms of the differential treatment of a group that resulted from universally framed policies or practices interacting with wider structural bias.

The role of structural and legal influences

One criticism levelled at early ethnographies (such as Rubinstein, 1973) was that, while they described police practices in the here-and-now, they failed to explain why these practices occurred (Grimshaw and Jefferson, 1987). Because they were committed to observational methods and eschewed the idea of social structure, ethnographers tended not to discuss the conditions in which police action took place that simultaneously enabled and constrained behaviour (Rock, 1979). These early studies, for example, often talked about how the police used the law as a resource, but failed to recognise how it also situated police discretion (see Dixon, 1997). It has been argued, therefore, that a more systemic perspective is required in order to take into account broader organisational, legal and social influences on decision-making (Hawkins, 2003).

Structure, 'availability' and targeting

The works of MVA and Miller (2000) and Waddington et al. (2004) are important in broadening our understanding of officers' decision-making in relation to stop and search. They examined the basis upon which police actions were judged to be disproportionate. As different social groups were likely to use public spaces in different ways, they suggested it would be more meaningful to compare the people searched by the police with those people in the places where searches are carried out rather than with local residents. Such comparisons might provide a better assessment of bias in individual officer decision-making, on the basis that decisions to initiate encounters will be constrained by the pool of people 'available' to be searched.

The two studies used similar methods to profile the visible characteristics of the people in the places where stop and search was concentrated. Systematic observations were carried out in these locations to emulate what officers would see on patrol. Both studies found significantly higher proportions of people from BME groups in the street populations than in the residential population. White people were more likely to be searched, and Asian people less likely, relative to the 'available' population, while the picture for black people was mixed. In other words, there did not appear to be any systematic bias in officer decision-making against people from BME groups. Notably, both studies showed that young men – irrespective of their race – were most over-represented in stop and search based on the 'available' population.

These studies concluded that the disparities in stop and search could not be explained solely by racist decision-making by individual officers. They did not deny that people from BME groups were most exposed to stop and search, but suggested that the reasons for this problem might rest elsewhere. Certainly, the 'supply side factors' that might explain why some groups are more likely to be present in public places where searches are most used by the police are very likely to be subject to racial and ethnic bias (MVA and Miller, 2000; Waddington et al., 2004; Bowling and Phillips, 2007). Reiner (2010) refers to this process as situational discrimination, in which the socio-economic status of a group exposes its members to police targeting. For example, the extent to which a person is 'available' to be policed will undoubtedly be affected by wider structural factors (such as unemployment and school exclusion), which may themselves be biased and result from discrimination. Moreover, because 'availability' is predicated on an officer and a suspect being present in the same place, the police inevitably have a role in determining which groups are 'available' because of how they use stop and search (Bowling and Phillips, 2007). The National Black Police Association, as a result, labelled the idea of 'availability' as a smokescreen for discrimination (Metropolitan Police Authority, 2004). While the collective actions of individual officers in the here-and-now help shape who is 'available' to be searched at any given time, the historical choices of the police to prioritise street crimes over other offences and target particular neighbourhoods rather than others will also have a bearing.

To what extent, then, do the police decide to target their activities towards high-crime areas, and with what effect? Chainey and Macdonald (2012) recently examined these issues in five UK police forces. They found that police search activity was clustered geographically and was not spread randomly. While there was some overlap between these clusters and crime hotspots, the relationship was not perfect, which suggested stop and search was not consistently well targeted against crime. Moreover, stop and search may have been over-used in some cases, because it was more concentrated than the underlying crime rate and did not translate into higher arrest rates. Importantly, the search hotspots tended to have higher levels of deprivation and higher proportions of BME residents than the surrounding areas, which would suggest that the geographic targeting of stop and search – which did not always correspond with crime – was likely to contribute towards disproportionality.

What is not clear from this study is why stop and search should be clustered in such a way. It seems plausible that these hotspots are a product of the routine activities of frontline officers – a reflection of their cumulative decisions. My own fieldwork suggested that stop and search was mainly left to the discretion of officers and was not a highly directed activity. There were no indications that senior officers made strategic decisions about where and when stop and search was to be targeted, and then communicated their instructions down the hierarchy. Officers were routinely given briefings about where recent crimes had occurred and who was thought to be responsible, but this information did not appear to result in stop and search being targeted in a proactive way. Studies have also shown that officer knowledge about crime hotspots is not always accurate (Ratcliffe and McCullagh, 2001), and they tend to recall and use intelligence which supports their prior knowledge about who is involved in crime (Chainey and Macdonald, 2012). The observations showed that officers did not restrict their attention to crime hotspots or active offenders, and tended to react to a wide range of cues in their immediate environment based on their expectations of what was 'normal'. As Rubinstein (1973) noted, officers had to develop sophisticated territorial knowledge in order to identify particular people and behaviours as suspicious. This raises the possibility that the way officers categorise some places as 'trouble spots' might be racialised, meaning stereotyping might operate more at a neighbourhood level. In relation to drugs, Murji (1997) has argued that particular locations symbolically become 'dangerous places' because of their perceived crime levels and high proportion of black residents. For example, officers described the 'bottom end' of Chapeltown as a particularly difficult and dangerous place to police, and it is defined by them largely by its ethnic diversity, robbery and drugs problem, and the presence of 'Yardie gangs' and firearms.

The legal context and officer decision-making

How, then, should the relative contribution of wider structural factors towards disproportionality in stop and search be weighed up? Miller's (2010) study examining the impact of increased levels of monitoring and accountability around stop and search after the Lawrence Inquiry offers some valuable insights. Miller's time series analysis suggested that levels of disproportionality significantly improved outside London after the Lawrence reforms were introduced in 2002/2003. However, when London was included in the analysis, disproportionality worsened over time and appeared to be unaffected by the changes. The reforms seemed to have a differential impact across the country. While substantial downward trends were observed in most areas, disproportionality increased in the three largest forces. The barriers to implementing change in large organisations were cited as possible reasons for the reforms not having a consistent impact. Importantly, however, the differential effect of the reforms, coupled with the evidence that disproportionality could be reduced, prompted Miller to conclude that 'historical patterns of disproportionality were probably not rooted in structural factors alone' (2010: 970) and that biased officer decision-making was likely to have contributed, in part, to the problem.

Miller's argument is strengthened somewhat when disproportionality is compared for different types of police-initiated encounter. Official data suggested that disproportionality in 'stop and account' was less marked than in 'stop and search'. In the last year national data were available (2008/2009), 15 per cent of searches were of black people compared with only 7 per cent of stops. While still disproportionate, the disparities for these less intrusive encounters were significantly lower. Stop and account is subject to the requirement for 'reasonable suspicion', and observations suggested that police suspicions for these different types of encounter were developed in similar ways. As noted by other commentators, 'Given that these factors are, in effect, held constant they cannot explain why disproportionality is so much higher for stop and search than for stop and account' (Bridges et al., 2011: 20). The effect of social structure on racial disparities in stop and search is, therefore, unlikely to be deterministic, suggesting that officer decision-making also contributes to the problem (see also Sanders and Young, 2007; Shiner, 2010).

By demonstrating a reduction in disproportionality in many forces, Miller's (2010) study showed, conversely, that officer decision-making could be affected by the wider social, legal and organisational context. Officers who were interviewed during my own fieldwork talked about how the Lawrence reforms made them 'think twice' about carrying out a stop or search (see Bland et al., 2000a). Furthermore, officers tended to think the Inquiry's claims about the police being institutionally racist were unfair, and were reportedly 'afraid' to use stop and search because they 'feared being branded a racist' (see also Foster et al., 2005). The heightened political and social discourse around stop and search at the time seemed to result in some officers actively choosing to be constrained by the rules (or their understanding of them, which varied). Many officers were mistakenly of the view that the law had been *tightened* and that they needed to have *stronger* grounds to search someone, even though there had been no change in the way reasonable suspicion had been defined. It is likely that this effect was short-lived, however, given that the number of recorded searches increased after an initial dip, and the police response to the Inquiry became more defensive (see Chapter 3; Shiner, 2010).

While the legal framework around stop and search may have little inhibitory effect on officer behaviour (Delsol and Shiner, 2006; Sanders and Young, 2007; Quinton, 2011; see also Chapter 2), it nevertheless provides context for officer decision-making. Certainly, officers varied in their understanding of what constituted reasonable suspicion, and the grounds for many observed encounters probably did not reach this legal standard. However, reasonable suspicion appeared to act as some sort of constraint. When this legal threshold was not in place, stop and search was conducted on a much more speculative basis. As Quinton (2011) previously noted, when officers were authorised under Section 60 of the Criminal Justice and Public Order Act 1994 to search anybody in a defined area without reasonable suspicion, they tended to act on very low levels of suspicion and often with a view to disciplining people for disorderly behaviour. When the legal context was more enabling and afforded officers more latitude, there was arguably greater scope for stop and search to be biased and based on stereotypes. In one example observed during a Section 60 operation, officers were seen searching three young black men after receiving a call about a fight. It was unclear, however, whether they had been involved in the incident, as they did not appear agitated. Furthermore, a comment by one officer afterwards pointed to the searches being more about reasserting his authority: 'They were staring me out, so I decided to search them' (Leicester/N4).

Summing up

The research on 'availability' suggests that situational discrimination plays a significant role in explaining levels of disproportionality. Even if individual decisions to stop and search are unbiased, they may cumulatively produce a discriminatory outcome because they reflect and compound wider social inequalities. However, while structural conditions provide an important backdrop and probably make a sizeable contribution to the problem, they do not *determine* this outcome, as the police are active agents in the process: officers make decisions that shape who is available to be policed. Decisions to focus stop and search activity in hotspots with a high proportion of BME residents are likely to contribute to disproportionality in ways that cannot necessarily be justified in terms of levels of crime in these places. Furthermore, the evidence that disproportionality can be reduced (Miller, 2010) suggests that officer decision-making is a contributory factor, although police behaviour will also be influenced by the more immediate legal and organisational environment in which they operate.

The role of information from the public

In addition to the wider influences on police practice, decisions to stop and search will be more immediately situated by the flow of information about crime. Research has highlighted that the police's role in responding to calls for service from the public could have a significant impact on disproportionality (Young, 1994; FitzGerald, 1999b). Reiner (2010: 161) referred to this process as transmitted discrimination, which occurs 'when the police act as a passive conveyor belt for wider social prejudices'. This section looks at the extent to which stop and search is carried out in reaction to calls from the public and whether that process might be biased. The way officers used suspect descriptions when deciding to stop and search members of the public is then described in detail.

Calls from the public

Studies by Young (1994) and FitzGerald (1999b) pointed out that the flow of information from the public about who was involved in crime had a crucial role in shaping the overall ethnic profile of those stopped and searched. FitzGerald (1999b) went so far as to predict that, if officer discretion was severely curtailed and suspect descriptions had a stronger influence on stop and search, disproportionality would increase because of the proportion of suspects described by victims as black. She noted that 'the pattern of searches tends to reflect the rate at which different groups are reported to the police as having been involved in crime' (1999b: 43). In other words, the disparities in stop and search are partly a product of the biased information provided by victims – or, as one officer put it in an interview, 'We're just the agents of the public, but we get the grief' (Leicester/21/R1). In theory, this could result from either biased public reporting of crime or differential involvement in particular types of crime.

My own fieldwork – possibly because much of it was conducted outside London – presented a slightly different picture. Calls from the public were less central to officers' decisions to stop and search, but, nevertheless, seemed to make an important contribution to disproportionality. Overall, the observations suggested that 'fire brigade' policing – where the police largely respond to calls – was more typical in London than elsewhere. Also, the observations indicated that a large majority of calls did not result in a suspect description being dispatched over the radio. When they did, the calls tended to involve a disturbance or dispute which required immediate action. It was also generally the case that the suspects were present at the scene, meaning that the officers could immediately take steps to keep the peace. In these situations, searches were not carried out.

Police data also indicated that calls for service could not always explain overall levels of disproportionality. Fitzgerald (1999b: 40) found that 70 per cent of all searches in the Metropolitan Police were 'low discretion' in that they were 'undertaken by officers in direct response to some trigger from a third party' rather than being 'initiated solely on the basis of officers' judgments about people's behaviours or actions'. The term 'reactive' provides a better label for these encounters, as it does not underplay the extent to which officers are active agents in the process. Even when responding to emergencies, officers still have considerable discretion over whether to respond, what information to draw on and how to handle the situation. The proportion of reactive encounters in Central Leicester – the only study site to have comparable data – was notably lower than in London, with 38 per cent of searches resulting from a call for service.[3] Moreover, calls prompted a higher proportion of searches for white people (40 per cent) than for Asian and black people (36 per cent and 35 per cent, respectively). Thus, it is important not to overstate the impact of so-called low-discretion encounters in some forces, where officer proactivity might have greater relevance.

Young's (1994) argument is slightly different from FitzGerald's. He pointed out that, while most police work was reactive to public demand, the effect for stop and search was limited because of its more proactive nature. Nevertheless, he argued that stop and search decisions were informed by, and flowed from, information about suspects provided by the public. He suggested that police had reasonably accurate knowledge about robbery suspects because of the contact between victim and perpetrator. This knowledge was, however, thought to be racialised because 'street robbery is a crime which typically has a high proportion of black offenders' (1994: 38). This bias, coupled with limited knowledge about suspects for non-contact crime types and a propensity for the police to focus on groups likely to produce the greatest 'yield', was seen to result in the stereotyping of black people. Smith (1997) has also noted that black people are subject to proactive law enforcement because of the higher rates of arrest for robbery for this group.

While Young's suggestion that black people are more likely to be involved in street robbery may not be widely supported by empirical research on offending (see Bowling and Phillips, 2002), his overall argument is borne out to some extent by the British Crime Survey and my own fieldwork. Clancy et al. (2001) used British Crime Survey data to examine how victims described the ethnicity of the perpetrator who committed the crime against them. They showed that only a small proportion of burglary and vehicle crime victims could provide details about the offender compared with those who experienced a crime involving face-to-face contact, such as robbery. Moreover, a significantly higher proportion of offenders were described as black by victims of 'muggings' than for burglary (31 per cent compared with 3 per cent).

It is possible that similar patterns were evident during my own fieldwork, although the small numbers involved mean only tentative conclusions are possible. During the interviews, robbery was said by officers to be the crime type most likely to generate suspect descriptions, and was mentioned by a majority of respondents. Moreover, officers tended to associate young black men with street robbery. Seven calls for service were also observed out of the dozens that the police responded to during the fieldwork (a large proportion of which were not crime-related). Five of the calls included some information about suspects involved – the number, their perceived race and, occasionally, a general clothing description. The suspects were described as black in four out of five incidents. It is possible, therefore, that the profile of the incidents could have been biased and supported generalised suspicions about black people. Only one call contained sufficient information that would have enabled officers to have searched a specific person.

> The suspect is identified as IC3 [black] youth (17–20) on a red mountain bike that appeared to be sprayed. He is described as wearing blue baggy jeans and a denim jacket.
>
> (Hackney/L1)

Overall, the direct impact of calls for service on disproportionality is probably variable across England and Wales, and likely to depend on the extent to which the police are organised to be reactive towards public demand. In many cases, stop and search was observed to be used by officers proactively and unrelated to any particular incident, suggesting that the effect of calls for service is likely to be small overall. The effect of racial biases in suspect descriptions may, nevertheless, be important in its indirect effect on police practices.

Suspect descriptions as a resource

While calls for service situated police decisions in a general sense, I observed that suspect descriptions were an important resource that enabled officers to initiate encounters. The extent to which people were thought to resemble suspect descriptions was found to be central to police decision-making, and there was some evidence that such descriptions were used to support generalised suspicions about particular ethnic groups.

Officers invariably initiated an encounter when they attended an incident and identified people whose appearance matched the descriptions of those reportedly involved. Officers usually assumed that the person at the scene was involved in the incident, sometimes to the extent that they responded uncritically to the information they were given without forming an independent view of the situation (as required in law). Nevertheless, even when responding to emergencies, it was clear from the observations that officers made active decisions about whether and how quickly to respond, how closely or not somebody matches a description, whether to stop them and how to initiate contact. In one example, an officer was observed searching an area for a black male following an emergency call about a stabbing. He explained how he would decide whether to stop a person, and then possibly carry out a search, based on a range of subtle behavioural signals as well as information from the detailed suspect description that was provided.

> I'd stop anyone that was close [to the description] – you'd just want to find out who they are and if they answer to the name of [xxxx] then you have more grounds for a search.[4] You also look out for other things – whether they have blood on them. Of course they might not have blood but you'd look for it ... For this person, I'd look for whether they are breathing heavily or are sweating. They might have been running or doing physical exertion ... You look at their mannerisms – are they nervous? And is that because this is the first time they have been stopped by the police or something else.
>
> (Hounslow/L1)

Responding to a call for service was not seen to be automatic or straightforward, because officers had to interpret and apply the information given to them. Overall, they tended to be fairly critical of the quality of suspect descriptions: '[They are] not very accurate [and] vary a lot' (Ipswich/18/R2). Descriptions that were vague or lacked specific detail meant officers had considerable latitude over whether to initiate contact and with whom. Furthermore, this latitude was sometimes seen to increase over time: 'Most give reasonable descriptions at the scene [which are] useful for five minutes afterwards near the scene' (Leicester/3/R1). There was a suggestion that some officers would place less emphasis on some of the more specific elements of the description as time went by (such as particular items of clothing). Generally, officers appeared to downplay some specific details from suspect description in favour of the information that supported their own working knowledge, which could have supported suspicions based on generalisations and stereotypes.

> The [descriptions] we've got at the moment are probably between 16 and 20. White, slim-build, wearing dark clothing, baseball caps, certain types of clothing we're looking for as well and certain types of vehicles that may be used... If we see somebody who we think is round the area about the right time, wearing a baseball cap or the right age then, without a doubt we will give him a stop and turn him over.
>
> (Bournville/5)

When officers did focus on specific elements of a suspect description, the process was sometimes focused on race: 'Colour tends to be pretty correct' (Leicester/1/R1). As Rubinstein (1973) previously noted, officers regarded the suspect's reported race to be the most reliable part of a description. The following incident was particularly notable in this respect, as the officers' response was framed only by the race of the suspects rather than, say, their gender or attire.

> A call comes in about a robbery. Two IC3 [black] males in blue hooded jackets near the Tesco's. We speed to the area, and [the officer] says they will do an area search: 'We will look to stop any IC3s'.
>
> (Bournville/N1)

Some officers were more willing than others to carry out stop and search on limited information, despite the possibility they could be stopping innocent people and contributing to disproportionality. Others were more cautious and were observed not to initiate encounters even when a person matched the description along racial lines. The reliance on vague suspect descriptions and the focus on race, nevertheless, were likely to have resulted in officers initiating unnecessary contact with people based on low levels of suspicion.

Summing up

The impact of calls from the public on disproportionality may vary locally depending on the policing model in place, but is unlikely to be a driving force behind the problem at a national level. Nevertheless, public information may have a more subtle effect on policing, in the sense that the profile of suspect descriptions might be biased and shape police knowledge about who the offenders are. The way officers use suspect descriptions as a resource is likely to be important, but, again, is unlikely to be the main cause of racial disparities in stop and search. Rather than having low discretion, officers were seen to have considerable latitude in the way they interpreted and applied the information given to them. By relying on race more than other aspects of a suspect description, officers were liable to stop and search people unnecessarily and exacerbate racial disparities.

Police attitudes and decisions to stop and search

This final section looks at whether race played more of a direct role in police decisions to stop and search. In general, when officers were observed carrying out a stop and search they drew on a series of rules-of-thumb, derived from their experiential knowledge, rather than surveying the material facts around them and weighing up the likelihood of finding a prohibited item on the person (see Quinton, 2011). These typifications were found to be central to police practice and were seen to help officers make sense of what was happening and what action to take. To what extent, though, did officers hold negative stereotypes about people from BME groups, and did they affect police activity? This section explores the attitudes of the police towards different racial and ethnic groups. Examples are then discussed where race appeared to be more central to decisions to stop and search.

Attitudes and stereotypes

Studies conducted during the 1980s noted that it was 'normal, automatic, habitual' for racist language to be used in the police (Smith and Gray, 1985: 391). People from ethnic minorities were 'usually described in derogatory terms – "coon", "nig-nog", "spade", "black", "razor blade", "wog", "animal"' (Holdaway, 1983: 66). In line with other recent research (Foster et al., 2005), my fieldwork revealed that explicit racist language had virtually disappeared.[5] Officers were usually careful about how they talked about different groups, though this was not always the case for gypsies: ' "Fucking gypsies" says [the officer] making a spitting noise' (Ipswich/L3). In some sites, they were referred to as 'gyppos', 'pikeys' and 'do-as-you-likeys'. Despite the general absence of racist language, officers were heard very occasionally to make insulting comments along racial lines.

> [The officer] noticed some lads with Afro-style hair. She said she couldn't understand them growing it like that as it looked like a 'microphone'.
>
> (Hackney/L3)

Despite this important change in the use of racist language, it remains possible that race-based stereotypes informed police thinking and behaviour. Smith and Gray's (1985: 406) ethnographic work in London found that police action in the early 1980s stemmed from 'a tendency to assume that black people have committed crimes and that whoever has committed a crime must be black'. Reiner (2010) suggested that statistical discrimination – differential treatment based on a police stereotype that they are more likely to get a 'result' from certain groups – is undoubtedly a tacit feature of stop and search. In this sense, stereotypes have a functional quality in that they are used to reduce 'cognitive uncertainties' (Glassner, 1980) by placing people into fixed categories which prevent the need for differentiated thinking (Schutz, 1970).

During the interviews, officers were specifically asked about ethnic differences in offending. A very small number gave the impression that black people were *more* criminal than white people, because the incidents they often associated with white people were non-criminal in nature (such as anti-social behaviour). One officer went so far as to say that these differences were determined by race: '[It's an] in-built thing – understanding violence will get you things' (Hounslow/2/15). Another officer revealed deeply racist attitudes when asked about different groups (previously quoted by Quinton, 2011):

> Afro Caribbeans commit street robbery ... Up-town, most Nigerians commit fraud. [They come from] a corrupt country. [We get] lots of indecency from Kosovans. They think they are the dog's bollocks when it comes to looks. Somalians come from the most violent country in the world. [We] shouldn't be surprised when [they're] violent over here....
>
> (Greenwich/23/R2)

A more recent study which looked, in part, at the policing of young people found similar views in relation to why stop and search might be disproportionate: 'They [black teenagers] commit more crimes' (cited in May et al., 2010: 60).

The majority of officers in my own fieldwork discussed race and crime in more cautious terms and took care to contextualise their views. Many respondents were concerned about their comments being taken out of context and wanted to underline that their views were based on recent experience or intelligence. Some also said that racial differences in offending varied by area and were due to other factors (such as deprivation). They tended to talk about offending patterns across different groups, but did not suggest one group was inherently more criminal than another: 'Offenders are from all walks of life' (Ipswich/2/6). Nonetheless, offending patterns were often seen in racial terms. Overall, it was common for officers to talk about black men in relation to street robbery and drugs: 'Whenever a robbery comes in, 90 per cent [of the time] you'll be thinking it's a black male because of the description and because you know who does robbery in the past' (Leicester/2/21). More recent research has shown that officers link young black teenagers with gang activities (May et al., 2010). White people were generally seen to be involved in a wider range of crimes – usually public order, burglary and vehicle crime. Negative stereotypes about Asians were much less common (though much of the fieldwork was carried out before widespread concerns about Islamist terrorism). The observations suggested that some linked young Asian men with drug use: 'If you stop them you are likely to find a spliff' (Leicester/N2). Strong negative views were expressed about gypsies in one of the sites, who, some said, 'are responsible [for] a lot of vehicle crime, burglary' (Ipswich/25/R2).

It is beyond the scope of this chapter to review the research on the involvement of different ethnic groups in crime; suffice it to say that these studies are likely to present only a partial picture due to a range of methodological issues (see Bowling and Phillips, 2002). Self-report studies, nevertheless, have found similar levels of offending among white and black respondents (Graham and Bowling, 1995; Hales et al., 2009). In respect of the crimes often associated with black people, there is also evidence to suggest officers may have overstated the relationship. Home Office research has shown, for example, that involvement in robbery is influenced more by socio-economic factors than by ethnicity (Smith, 2003), and that drug use is lower among black young people than their white or mixed-race peers (Aust and Smith, 2003).

Heightened suspicions and race

Unpicking the role played by race in individual decisions to stop or search during the fieldwork was difficult because of its implicit nature in the decision-making process and officers' guardedness in front of researchers. While many of the observed encounters involved people from BME groups, other signals were usually present that were also relevant to the officer's decision to initiate contact. It was impossible to tell, though, whether or not officers became sensitised to these other signals because of the perceived race of the person.

To add to this complex picture, many of the other prompts for officer suspicions were likely to be racialised (see Quinton, 2011). The police focus on known offenders, for example, could exacerbate racial disparities already present in the criminal justice system. Similarly, the general targeting of young people – particularly those wearing clothes associated with street culture – will adversely affect people from BME groups due to their younger age profile (Office for National Statistics, 2013b).

Despite these analytical challenges, race appeared to hold some tacit meaning for officers. In one encounter, a question posed by an officer to his colleague potentially revealed a shared assumption about the involvement of different ethnic groups in crime (Ipswich/L1). After a stop involving three young people (one black, two white), an officer said he recognised one of the teenagers. His colleague asked who he was referring to: 'The black one?' In so doing and not asking about the white teenagers, he potentially revealed an underlying prejudice. This was all the more notable because of the general tendency observed among police officers to place a lot of value on remembering criminals. Officers tended to think that anyone they remembered by face must have been an offender.

Previous research has pointed towards officers having a heightened sense of suspicion towards black people (Holdaway, 1983; Smith and Gray, 1985; FitzGerald and Sibbitt, 1997). There were a few examples from the observations where race was seen to act as a prompt for police action. In these examples, the presence and role of other signals in the decision-making process was, at best, ambiguous. Although the officers in the following example did not end up carrying out a search, there was a sense in which their suspicions were drawing on racial cues.

> [The officers] share a joke which involves them saying 'I is the Babylon' in a Jamaican accent. [One of them] also comments that there are going to be a lot of robberies tonight because there are people in the streets getting 'pissed up'. I think this comment may

have been made because we just drove past two black men who were hanging about by a fence not too far from a pub.

(Hackney/N3)

The clearest example of what seemed to be direct discrimination was observed in Leicester (see also Quinton, 2011). Race appeared to be central to the decision to carry out the stop because it was referred to – using racist language – in the build up to the encounter. Notably, the research did not identify any other reason for stopping that particular vehicle apart from the perceived race of the driver. Moreover, the encounter took place during a quiet night shift when the officers were 'looking for action'.

Follow blue Fiesta. 'Rasta man, worth a look', says [xxxx]. Four in car. One white woman, the others – black men all drinking. Have quick word with the driver: 'Where are you going? Where have you been? Have you been drinking?'... The sergeant jokes that they have to fill in the form because of [the researcher], but they don't.

(Leicester/L4/7)

This encounter may have formed part of a wider pattern of behaviour. Earlier that evening, the same officers stopped four young black men in a car because of a traffic offence. While race played more of an ambiguous role in that encounter, there was a suggestion of selective enforcement. The officer said 'it was "lucky" they had gone through the red light because he was going to stop them anyway' (Leicester/L4/5).

While race may have heightened police suspicions, it did not appear to affect the nature and flow of encounters to any great extent after officers had decided to make contact (though an observer effect is possible). There was no evidence to indicate that black people were more likely to act in a way that would have been found in 'contempt of cop' or to be subject to interactional discrimination in the sense that they received a noticeably different outcome as a result of their behaviour towards the police (see Reiner, 2010). Overall, and in line with earlier studies (Reiss, 1971; Smith and Gray, 1985; Norris et al., 1992), encounters with people from BME groups were generally well-handled, fairly relaxed and broadly similar to those involving white people. Officers were observed to be 'brusque or authoritarian' in 3 out of the 51 encounters involving black or Asian people (none were 'hostile or provocative'). As Smith (1997: 753) has previously noted about observational studies:

'The collective hostility of the police and black people towards each other does not seem to be expressed at the micro-level of individual encounters.'

The perspective of those stopped and searched by the police should, of course, not be ignored, and recent studies have highlighted a strong view that the police adopt an adversarial approach and show a lack of respect during stop and search encounters (see May et al., 2010; Lewis et al., 2011). Despite most of the encounters during my own fieldwork being well-handled, there was one example where a suspect was handled in a more violent way, possibly because he was black. Two officers were observed to stop and question two drunks – an old white man and a young black man – who were reportedly staggering around on a busy main road. During the encounter, the black man remained calm and polite. One of the officers repeatedly barked instructions to the white man because he failed to listen, and held him back at one point for approaching the observer. The two men were told to go their separate ways, but they failed to comply. While the more aggressive officer eventually lost his cool with both men, his reaction to the black man was much more hostile for no apparent reason.

> The black man then starts to wander back in the [opposite] direction. [The officer] runs up to him and pins him against the wall. He is being pointed at aggressively, held with his chest, and being talked at sternly. I don't hear exactly. I am surprised when [the officer] pushes the man's chin back firmly – rather like a slap. He is then pushed in the direction he has to walk off in.
>
> (Hackney/N2)

While the uniqueness of the incident precludes firm conclusions, race may have influenced the officer's behaviour. It is perhaps notable that this encounter took place in Hackney, because the policing style was more overtly confrontational there than in the other areas. Hackney officers were more inclined than those elsewhere to stress a 'them-and-us' mentality and to view the police as an 'occupying force', possibly because of longstanding tensions between the police and the community. Several situations were observed in which the police were antagonistic towards people from the local black community, including an example where an officer used language that drew attention to the perceived status of the police as a racist oppressor: 'We are the Babylon' (Hackney/N3).

Summing up

The fieldwork demonstrated that typifications were central to police practice. While the general disappearance of racist language represents a major change, there was some evidence that officers continued to stereotype people from BME groups in ways that overstate their involvement in crime. Race certainly appeared to hold some shared, tacit meaning for officers, and there was some evidence of heightened suspicions towards black people, particularly in relation to types of crime against which stop and search might be targeted. Being black was certainly something that was observed to prompt suspicions, despite encounters not always being initiated and other signals often being present that could have explained officers' interest. Many of these other signals – age, clothing, respectability – could result in suspicions falling on people from BME groups. Overall, the reliance on stereotyping as the primary way in which the police develop their suspicions is likely to be one of the main causes of disproportionality, alongside the effect of structural factors. Identifying examples where a person's race was the *sole* reason for a stop and search was difficult, though race appeared pivotal in a small number of encounters. The observations suggested that the effect of categorical discrimination on racial disparities is likely to be fairly small, though the presence of the observers will have changed the way some officers behaved. As Reiner (2010) noted, it is hard for observational studies to isolate the effect of race. Once initiated, though, encounters with people from BME groups were generally well-handled and on a par with those involving white people. Nevertheless, examples of antagonism towards young black men were observed. Thus, while there was some evidence of interactional discrimination, its effect was unlikely to be widespread.

Conclusion

The evidence presented in this chapter suggests that disproportionality in stop and search is a complex social phenomenon which is very likely to have multiple causes. Trying to isolate and explain how much each of these causes contributes to the overall problem is likely to be an impossible and frustrating process. Examining the way officers decide when and how to conduct stop and search – rather than examining the headline statistics – helps to develop a better understanding of some of the underlying issues, but can only tell part of the story. The approach adopted in this chapter has shown that officer decision-making is generally informed by stereotyping (often in the form of statistical discrimination). Officers appeared to have heightened suspicions about young black men in particular, whom they often associated with street robbery and drug use – an association that seems to overstate their involvement in crime. In addition, officers were seen to develop generalised suspicions from suspect descriptions, which could have resulted in people from BME groups being unnecessarily stopped and searched because of their race. However, it was difficult to identify specific examples of encounters that were based on categorical discrimination – where race was the only reason for contact. As Reiner notes, 'it is hard to pinpoint [categorical discrimination] as a separate factor from the overall context of encounters' (2010: 171). While individual racism will inevitably play a role – particularly when researchers are not around – its overall contribution is likely to be fairly small, given how rarely clear-cut examples were observed.

The role of officer decision-making in disproportionality is probably best understood when a more systemic perspective is taken. Police practice does not occur in a vacuum and will be shaped by wider structural inequalities. Bias and discrimination in other areas of life will undoubtedly affect the 'opportunities' that people from different social groups have to be the subject of police attention. Disproportionality is likely, therefore, to be significantly shaped by situational and institutionalised discrimination. The police, nevertheless, have agency and determine where their attention is focused. While stop and search at an individual level may not be routinely biased, the everyday decisions made by police officers about where to patrol and when to take action will, collectively, affect which groups are most likely to be stopped and searched. Moreover, the evidence that disproportionality can be reduced through reform (Miller, 2010) warns us not to overstate the importance of wider structural factors. There are also likely to be more local influences on police practice. Certainly, the specific legal and organisational setting in which officers operated appeared to influence how ready they were to use stop and search, their threshold for action and their willingness to work within the rules. The complexity of these issues ultimately points to disproportionality being a product of a range of processes, including indirect and institutionalised forms of discrimination.

Disproportionality is, in itself, an issue that the police should take seriously because it is one that has far-reaching implications. Over time, disproportionality has been shown to undermine trust in the police among BME groups. Skogan (2006) has shown that contact with the police has an asymmetrical effect on feelings of trust. While positive contact tends to have a small positive effect on trust, negative contact has a strong detrimental effect. Exposure to stop and search is, therefore, likely to be significant. Policing that is perceived to be procedurally and distributively unfair is very likely to undermine the legitimacy of the police. If it is demonstrated to people that they are not valued and that society's rules do not apply to them, they will be less inclined to obey the law and cooperate with the police (Tyler, 2006a; Jackson et al., 2012). In other words, disproportionality could be criminogenic. Given that its causes are complex and multifaceted, a range of interventions are likely to be required if a reduction in disproportionality is to be sustained. Indeed, disproportionality will be more of an intractable problem for the police because they are not its sole cause. There is evidence that effective steps can be taken nationally (Miller, 2010) and locally, such as in Cleveland (see Equalities and Human Rights Commission, 2010), but more work needs to be done to understand how this problem can be addressed.

Notes

1. With fewer than one in ten searches resulting in arrest (Home Office, 2013).
2. The sites included: Leicestershire (Central Leicester); Merseyside (Sefton); the Metropolitan Police (Greenwich, Hackney and Hounslow); North Wales (Wrexham); Nottinghamshire (South Notts); Suffolk (Ipswich); West Midlands (Bournville); and West Yorkshire (Chapeltown).
3. $N = 1,043$ (November 1999–May 2000).
4. It was not clear from the quote whether the officer felt he had sufficient grounds for a search before initiating contact. Officers have no power to detain a person to build grounds, though police practice varied on this point.
5. It is possible that some officers have simply become more cautious in the presence of researchers.

5
Effectiveness
Rebekah Delsol

Stop and search epitomises the *discretionary non-negotiable coercive powers* available to police officers to investigate crime (Bowling and Weber, 2012). Originally introduced in England and Wales during the early 19th century to combat vagrancy and loitering by suspected people, stop and search has become a routine feature of police responses to a variety of problems. The effectiveness of this tactic is largely taken for granted and has been subject to little critical scrutiny. Police officers, in particular, have an almost mythical belief in its efficacy, insisting that the 'use of stop and search is a powerful tool to combat violence and weapons' (Metropolitan Police Service, 2014). Such a view has been shared by successive governments which have granted the police a series of new stop and search powers, progressively extending the level of intrusion while scaling back procedural safeguards. Successive policing ministers and home secretaries have repeated the mantra that stop and search is effective and provides an important tool in the fight against crime. While more critical than her predecessors, home secretary Theresa May (2013: 773–4) has maintained that stop and search 'is an important power' in the police's 'daily fight against crime' and 'is especially important in relation to combating gangs, knife crime and drug offences'.

Claims about the effectiveness of stop and search emphasise the assumed crime-fighting benefits, while ignoring potential costs. This selective focus is at odds with the available evidence. The police do not routinely use research evidence to inform their crime-fighting practices (Karn, 2013), and this is certainly the case with stop and search. Surprisingly little research has been conducted into the effectiveness of stop and search, and that which has been carried out offers little support for claims that it provides a 'powerful tool' in the fight against crime. Assumptions that stop and search is effective have also obscured the need to look for more effective alternatives. The paucity of evidence on the effectiveness of stop and search contrasts with a growing body of evidence that identifies significant costs in terms of reduced public trust and confidence (see Chapter 6). As one of the most common forms of adversarial contact with the public, stop and search has the potential to do considerable damage to police–community relations and, by extension, the legitimacy of the police. Described as 'the most glaring example of police abuse of power' (Bowling and Phillips, 2002: 138), stop and search has been a particular source of tension between police and ethnic minority communities (Bowling and Phillips, 2007) and has been implicated as a trigger of public disorder in 1981, 1985 and 2011 (Bowling and Phillips, 2002; Riots, Communities and Victims Panel, 2011).

This chapter is organised around the claim that the effectiveness of stop and search should not be assessed solely in relation to potential crime-fighting benefits, but must also take account of potential costs. It begins by exploring the intended effects or purpose of stop and search and by considering the processes through which it might be thought to operate. In the absence of experimental or quasi-experimental evidence covering the UK, the discussion focuses on three possible indicators of effectiveness: arrest rates; the extent to which stop and search is intelligence-led; and the types of offences that are targeted. The chapter then goes on to consider the costs of stop and search as well as possible alternatives.

Setting the parameters of effectiveness

Establishing whether stop and search is effective depends on what *effects* or *purpose* it is intended to have. Although there is considerable confusion in police practice and public discussions about the purpose of stop and search, it is, in fact, quite clearly defined in law. Police powers of stop and search are granted by various pieces of legislation that are regulated by the Police and Criminal Evidence Act (PACE) 1984 Code of Practice A. The vast majority of stop-searches are carried out under the auspices of PACE 1984 (Section 1) and the Misuse of Drugs Act 1971 (Section 23). These searches should reach a threshold of reasonable suspicion: an objective and articulable requirement that does not rely on stereotyping and generalisations (see Chapter 2).

Different kinds of stop and search power have different functions in law, though claims about effectiveness regularly conflate the mechanisms through which they are thought to operate, mixing up detection and deterrence, and claiming success in both areas with little evidence.

Stop and search is primarily an investigative power, used for the purposes of crime detection and prevention in relation to specific individuals at a specific time (Lustgarten, 2002). PACE searches are founded on the principle that an officer must reasonably suspect that individuals have carried out a crime or are in the process of doing so (Home Office, 2013a). Conducting a search on the street enables officers to confirm or eliminate their suspicions, avoiding the need for arrest. The primary purpose is to detect prohibited articles or stolen property, which indicate that an individual has been, or is preparing to be, involved in crimes such as theft, burglary and robbery. There are entire domains of criminal behaviour, including domestic violence, that will not be discovered through stop and search. In terms of their underlying assumptions, suspicion-based searches draw on more general ideas about the mechanisms through which law enforcement is expected to operate. Such interventions may be thought to work on the basis of detection and incapacitation – intercepting (would-be) offenders, preventing them from offending and/or potentially leading to them being taken off the streets to prevent future crime.

Exceptional stop and search powers that are not subject to the requirement for reasonable suspicion are legally justified in terms of prevention and deterrence of crime. These powers include Section 163 of the Road Traffic Act 1988 (stop power only); Section 60 of the Criminal Justice and Public Order Act 1994 (covering offensive weapons); Sections 14 and 64 of the Criminal Justice and Public Order Act 1994 (covering raves and trespassory assemblies); Sections 44 to 47a of the Terrorism Act 2000 (covering articles for use in terrorist activities); Schedule 7 of the Terrorism Act 2000 (providing for examinations in ports and airports for terrorist activities); and Section 4 of PACE (which allows road checks in relation to indictable offences). Although most stop-searches take place under Section 1 of PACE, Sanders and Young argue (2007: 76) that 'so many stop-searches may now take place without reasonable suspicion that the police are left with the ability to stop-search almost whenever they want'. While Section 60 and Section 44 have been 'sold' politically as a means of tackling serious violence and terrorism, they have actually been used as a resource for responding to low-level crime and disorder where no other power is available (Rowe, 2004; Sanders and Young, 2007; Delsol, 2010).

The legal justification of prevention or deterrence rests on the idea that potential offenders may 'think twice' about committing an offence given the possibility of being stopped and searched by police. As one officer put it: 'If active criminals know that they can't go out without being searched that tends to put a damper on their activities' (quoted by Fitzgerald, 1999: 24). According to Sampson and Cohen (1988), proactive policing, in the form of police stop and search or visible enforcement against minor offences, may be perceived by potential offenders as indicating a change in the risk of apprehension. Von Hirsch et al. (1999) distinguish two types of deterrence: 'general deterrence', which might occur when a potential offender does not commit a crime because of the possibility of being apprehended and punished; and 'marginal deterrence', when a potential offender might adapt his or her offending behaviour due to police activity and the likelihood of being detected. A third category of 'focused deterrence' refers to interventions that are targeted at locations, specific types of offending or criminal groups and might result in displacing offending behaviour or disrupting the operation of criminal groups (Felbab-Brown, 2013). The mechanisms through which deterrence might be thought to work in the context of stop and search powers are, therefore, two-fold: we might expect would-be offenders not to commit a crime for fear of being apprehended or to change their pattern of offending to escape apprehension. Stop and search may also play a preventative role by generating intelligence that is used subsequently in the detection or disruption of crime. Although suspicion-based stop and search cannot be legally justified in this way, intelligence may be seen as an 'added value' outcome (Miller et al., 2000).

The potential crime-fighting benefits of stop and search provide a useful starting point for discussions of effectiveness, but are only part of what needs to be considered. According to Lacey (1988), any assessment of the effectiveness of the law must consider the costs or harms of an intervention alongside its benefits. Inefficiencies, she notes, may arise where difficulties are experienced in enforcement or detection; where the law is ineffective; if costs outweigh the benefits; or if a less costly means of enforcement is available. Applying this framework to stop and search poses a number of questions. Is stop and search effective in terms of its stated aims? Do the benefits outweigh the costs? And are there other, less intrusive, interventions that might produce similar results with fewer costs? Our ability to answer these questions is limited by the available evidence. Ideally, we would be able to draw on experimental or quasi-experimental studies that measure the impact of stop and search on crime, but, to date, there are no published studies of this kind covering the UK. In the absence of experimental evidence, three indicators will be used to get some sense of the likely effects of stop and search: arrest rates; the extent to which stop and search is intelligence-led; and the types of crimes that are targeted.

Evidence on the effectiveness of stop and search

Several American studies have used experimental designs to assess different police tactics, including the use of 'stop and frisk'. Such studies have examined the concentrated use of stop and search to target small geographic areas with high crime rates – an approach commonly known as 'hotspot' policing (Braga et al., 2012). Used in this way, there is evidence that stop and search may have some impact on crime. A randomised controlled experiment of problem-oriented policing interventions in New Jersey, including 'aggressive order maintenance' approaches such as stop and frisk, found reductions in recorded crime and calls for service across all the 12 treatment sites without causing displacement to surrounding areas (Braga et al., 1999). However, the study failed to identify how stop and frisk was used and how it contributed to crime reductions across the hotspot areas reviewed. Another randomised controlled trial, in Philadelphia, found that targeted foot patrols in violent crime hotspots can significantly reduce violent crime (Ratcliff et al., 2011). Areas that received over 90 hours of foot patrol per week during a 12-week period experienced a 23 per cent reduction in violent crime compared with control areas. Officers were not given specific orders on policing styles within the patrol areas, and observations revealed that these differed greatly; however, pedestrian stops increased by 64 per cent in the treatment areas compared with 1 per cent in the control areas. The authors concluded that officers tended to be proactive in the treatment areas, conducting more stops and arrests and intervening in more disturbances and incidents. Without a measure of informal community contacts and problem-solving, however, it is difficult to isolate the precise impact of these formal activities.

The most systematic analysis of the effectiveness of stop and search in England and Wales was undertaken by Miller et al. in 2000 on behalf of the Home Office. Their analysis drew on Home Office statistics, existing literature, interviews with over 100 officers and 340 hours' observation of police officers at work. The study found that stop and search seems to have a minor role in detecting offenders for the range of crimes that it appears to address, and a relatively small role in detecting offenders for all crimes that come to the attention of the police. Overall, it was estimated 'that searches reduce the number of "disruptable" crimes by just 0.2%' (Miller et al., 2000: 28). Based on an analysis of the British Crime Survey, the authors found that for every arrest generated by stop and search there were 106 crimes that might, in theory, have been detectable. Similarly, for every 26 offences recorded by the police there was one arrest from stop and search. A comparison of force clear-up rates and search arrest rates found there was 'no statistically significant association' between them (2000: 22). Some forces had high arrest rates from stop and search, but low overall clear-up rates, while other forces had low arrest rates from stop and search, but higher overall clear-up rates. For some police forces, however, stop and search made a substantial contribution to arrests for certain offences, such as those relating to drugs.

To test the deterrent effect of stop and search, Miller et al. (2000) compared trends in its use with trends in crime. Such comparisons produced 'little solid evidence that searches have a deterrent effect on crime' (2000: vi). Further analysis of data from the Metropolitan Police Service found no strong or consistent correlation between searches and crime levels a month later. The authors concluded that 'claiming a relationship between total crime and the number of searches seems untenable' (2000: 33), though they did note that searches *may* have deterrence or displacement effects when used intensively in particular locations over a short period of time.

The effectiveness of stop and search under Section 60 of the Criminal Justice and Public Order Act 1994 was recently assessed as part of a broader quasi-experimental evaluation of the government's anti-knife crime action plan. Under Section 60, an inspector or higher-ranked officer who reasonably believes that incidents involving serious violence or the carrying of weapons may take place in a particular locality may authorise uniformed officers to search any person or vehicle in that locality for a period of up to 24 hours. Although the legislation restricts such stop-searches to a specific time and place, individual officers are not required to have reasonable suspicion in order to search somebody (see Chapter 2). Amendments introduced by the Knives Act 1997 and the Crime and Disorder Act 1998 saw the number of Section 60 stop-searches increase by 20 times or 2,000 per cent over the next decade (see Chapter 3). The sharp increase in the numbers of Section 60 searches appears to have been accelerated by anti-knife crime initiatives such as Operation Blunt 2, a pan-London anti-knife operation introduced in May 2008, and the Home Office's Tackling Knives and Serious Youth Violence Action Programme (TKAP), launched in June 2008 (Home Office, 2011c). These initiatives sought to prevent the killing of young people and relied heavily on the application of Section 60 powers in high-risk areas as well as other tactics including the use of airport-style metal detectors ('knife arches').

The evaluation of TKAP included police forces that made most use of Section 60 searches and found no measurable impact on levels of knife crime. The evaluation of the first phase of the programme, from

2008 to 2009, did find that increases in the number of 'TKAP stop-searches' across all 10 areas had been accompanied by reductions in various forms of violent offending among young people, though there was evidence of increased offending among older groups (Ward and Diamond, 2009). The initial findings were considered 'encouraging' and prompted the conclusion that 'TKAP may well have contributed to a decline in some measures and persisting reductions in others' (Ward and Diamond, 2009: 1). When the second phase of TKAP was evaluated using a quasi-experimental methodology, however, the analysis pointed to a different conclusion. Trends in knife crime in the TKAP forces were compared with trends in other forces not involved in the programme. Homicide data pointed to reductions in the number of victims and principal suspects in the target age group across England and Wales, but these reductions were not proportionately greater in areas participating in the TKAP initiative than in non-TKAP areas. While hospital admissions for assault involving the target age group also declined, these reductions were only evident in the non-TKAP areas. The authors concluded (Ward et al., 2011: 24):

> These findings provide encouraging evidence that serious youth violence declined across the country in recent years. However, given that the reductions were not specific to or consistently greater in the TKAP areas, and taking into account the methodological limitations described above, it is impossible to directly attribute reductions in the TKAP areas to Phase II activities.

A similar conclusion is supported by the findings of an evaluation of the use of Section 60 in London after the introduction of Operation Blunt 2 (FitzGerald, 2010a). A comparison of London boroughs during this period found there to be no direct relationship between the use of Section 60 searches and the extent of police-recorded knife crime (FitzGerald, 2010a). Among the 11 boroughs with the highest knife crime figures, the biggest fall of 25 per cent between 2008/2009 and 2009/2010 was in Islington, which had the second fewest Section 60 searches. Southwark, by contrast, experienced an 8.6 per cent rise in knife crime despite having the second highest use of Section 60 searches (FitzGerald, 2010a).

Arrest rates

In the absence of robust experimental data, arrest rates provide a useful proxy measure for the effectiveness of stop and search. Arrest rates, showing the proportion of stop-searches that result in an arrest for a notifiable offence, are published annually by the Home Office. Using arrest rates as an indicator of effectiveness has a number of problems, as they have the potential to both exaggerate and underestimate success. Arrest is an intermediate outcome which may exaggerate the impact of stop and search because it takes no account of attrition. Not all arrests result in further legal action, and police forces do not systematically monitor the proportion of search arrests that lead to charge or conviction, though previous studies suggest that a significant proportion do not (Phillips and Brown, 1998; FitzGerald, 1999a). The arrest rate also includes arrests arising from stop and search encounters where no stolen or prohibited articles are found; for example, where a computer check reveals that the person is already wanted for an offence or where the encounter itself triggers an angry reaction by the person searched, leading to an arrest for a public order offence. On the other hand, arrest rates arguably underestimate the effectiveness of stop and search because they take no account of other sanctions. Some forces have begun to use 'positive outcome' rates that include fixed penalty notices (FPNs), penalty notices for disorder (PNDs) and cannabis warnings. Other forces use 'hit' rates as a measure, which includes all articles found and confiscated as a result of stop and search (Her Majesty's Inspectorate of Constabulary, 2013). The use of either positive outcome or hit rates is not standardised across forces, however, which means it is not possible to make systematic comparisons.

Even allowing for these problems, arrest rates provide a useful means of assessing the likely impact of stop and search in the absence of more reliable indicators. For stop and search to be effective, we would logically expect high arrest rates. Detection and incapacitation depend on identifying and arresting offenders, taking them off the street and preventing them from committing further offences. Deterrence also requires high arrest rates, as offenders must consider the risk of apprehension to be a tangible one and adjust their behaviour accordingly. Arrest rates provide little evidence to support the proposition that stop and search is effective at detecting or preventing crime. Arrest rates are low and have declined over the last two decades, suggesting that stop and search has a very limited role in identifying offenders and taking them off the streets. In 2012–2013, the police recorded 1,006,187 PACE Section 1 stop-searches across England and Wales, only 10 per cent of which led to an arrest (Home Office, 2014b). While official figures do not provide arrest outcomes, previous studies estimate that between half (FitzGerald, 1999) and one-third (Phillips and Brown, 1998) of search arrests do not result in a caution, charge or conviction. On this basis we would estimate that as few as 5 per cent of PACE searches proceed beyond arrest.

Stop and search activity has increased substantially since monitoring began in 1986 and has continued to do so since 1995 despite a sharp drop in the crime rate (see Table 5.1). The number of arrests has also increased, but this increase has been more modest (see Table 5.1

Table 5.1 Suspicion-based stop-searches and resultant arrests in England and Wales (1986 to 2012/2013)

Year	Stop-searches	Arrests	Arrest Rate (%)
1986	109,800	18,900	17.2
1987	118,300	19,600	16.6
1988	149,600	23,700	15.8
1989	202,800	32,800	16.2
1990	256,900	39,200	15.3
1991	303,800	46,200	15.2
1992	351,700	48,700	13.8
1993	442,800	55,900	12.6
1994	576,000	70,300	12.2
1995	690,300	81,000	11.7
1996	814,500	87,700	10.8
1996/1997	871,500	91,106	10.5
1997/1998	1,050,700	108,700	10.3
1998/1999	1,080,700	121,300	11.2
1999/2000	857,200	108,500	12.7
2000/2001	714,100	95,400	13.4
2001/2002	741,000	98,700	13.3
2002/2003	895,300	114,300	12.8
2003/2004	749,400	95,100	12.7
2004/2005	861,500	95,800	11.1
2005/2006	888,700	102,700	11.6
2006/2007	962,900	111,100	11.5
2007/2008	1,053,000	120,400	11.4
2008/2009	1,159,400	113,300	9.8
2009/2010	1,095,000	99,800	9.1
2010/2011	1,156,300	106,700	9.2
2011/2012	1,096,000	103,000	9.4
2012/2013	970,400	100,300	10.3

Note: All figures have been rounded to the nearest 100. Due to inconsistencies in recording procedures, data from three forces were excluded from the figures for 2009/2010 to 2012/2013. As a result, these figures are incomplete and are not directly comparable with those for earlier years.
Source: Sanders and Young (2007); Home Office (2009a, 2014b).

88 Effectiveness

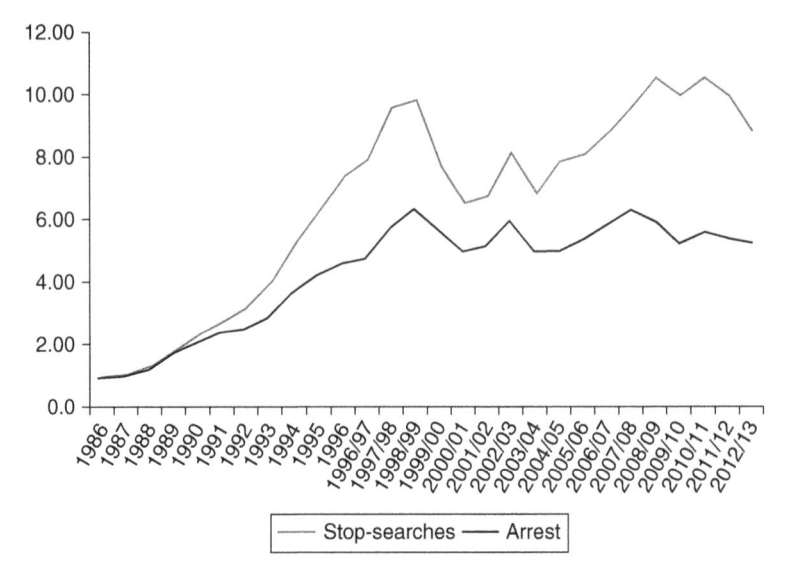

Figure 5.1 Trends in suspicion-based stop-searches and resultant arrests in England and Wales, 1986–2012/2013 (numbers indexed to 1986)
Source: Home Office (2009a, 2013, 2014b).

and Figure 5.1). Over the period as a whole, the arrest *rate* has fallen fairly steadily, almost halving from a high of 17 per cent in 1986 to a low of 9 per cent in 2009/2010. A falling arrest rate in the context of more stop and search, but less crime, suggests there has been a shift in police behaviour, with stop and search being applied at a lower threshold of suspicion: poorer grounds result in more innocent people being searched and proportionately fewer arrests. The decline in the arrest rate may partly be a function of improved recording practices as more unsuccessful searches are recorded, but it remains likely that the requirement for reasonable suspicion is less stringently observed as the number of searches increases. When the number of searches fell after the publication of the Stephen Lawrence Inquiry report in 1999, the arrest rate increased slightly, suggesting a degree of rule-tightening.

The proportion of stop-searches that yield an arrest varies sharply between forces (see Figure 5.2). In 2012/2013, City of London Police had the highest arrest rate at 20 per cent, while Cambridgeshire reported the lowest rate at just 1.5 per cent. Substantial variations are also evident when forces are compared with their nearest 'force family relatives' – the most similar forces based on key social and economic variables.

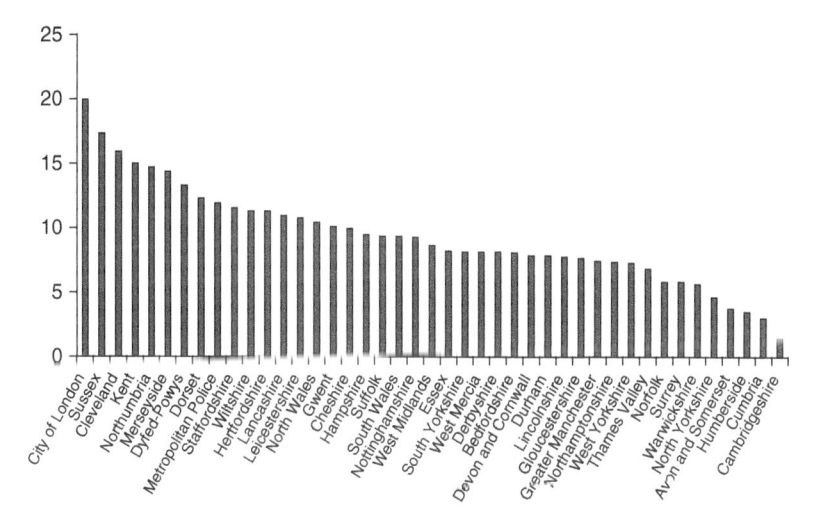

Figure 5.2 Percentage of stop-searches under Section 1 of the Police and Criminal Evidence Act and other legislation resulting in arrest by police force areas in England and Wales, 2012–2013
Source: Home Office (2014b).

Of the searches undertaken by Kent Police, for example, 15 per cent resulted in arrest compared with 8 per cent of those undertaken by Essex police. Such marked differences between broadly similar forces suggest significant differences in approach.

The arrest rate for exceptional powers is low even by the modest standards of conventional suspicion-based powers. Over the last decade or so, the arrest rate for Section 60 searches has rarely exceeded 5 per cent per year, while the arrest rate for Section 44 has been even lower (see Table 5.2 and Chapter 7 for discussion of Section 44). Overall arrest rates arguably exaggerate the efficacy of these powers because relatively few of the arrests made are for the targeted offences: during each of the last 10 years, no more than 1 per cent of Section 60 searches have resulted in arrests for possession of a weapon. The low arrest rate for Section 60 stop-searches is sometimes cited as evidence that these searches provide an effective deterrent (see Shiner, 2012). According to this argument, potential offenders stop carrying weapons for fear of being caught. Such claims might be plausible if the arrest rate had fallen sharply after a large number of arrests had been made, but no such pattern is evident. In the absence of such a spike, it is unclear why potential offenders would be motivated to change their behaviour and stop carrying weapons.

Table 5.2 Section 60 Public Order and Criminal Evidence Act stop-searches and arrests in England and Wales (2000/2001 to 2012/2013)

Year	Stop and Searches	Persons Found Carrying Offensive Weapons or Dangerous Instruments (%)	Arrests for Offensive Weapons (%)	Arrests for Other Reasons (%)	All Arrests (%)
2000/2001	11,330	3.2	2.7	3.6	6.4
2001/2002	18,900	7.2	1.1	2.6	3.6
2002/2003	44,398	3.5	0.8	4.8	5.6
2003/2004	40,436	1.4	0.7	3.1	3.8
2004/2005	41,611	0.7	0.6	2.3	2.9
2005/2006	36,276	1.5	0.5	4.2	4.7
2006/2007	44,707	1.6	0.6	3.1	3.6
2007/2008	53,501	1.4	0.6	3.3	3.9
2008/2009	150,174	0.8	0.4	2.5	2.8
2009/2010	118,446	0.7	0.3	2.1	2.4
2010/2011	60,230	0.8	0.4	1.9	2.3
2011/2012	45,696	0.5	0.4	2.3	2.7
2012/2013	4,912	1.3	1.0	4.4	5.4

Source: Home Office (2011c, 2014b).

Mirroring the pattern identified above in relation to suspicion-based searches, the arrest rate for Section 60 searches has tended to fall over the last decade or so as the number of searches has increased, suggesting a less discerning use of the power. According to a Home Office evaluation of initiatives tackling homicide (Brookman and Maguire, 2003: 33–4),

> Considering that the search powers in question should be used only where a specific threat of violence is present, these 'hit rates' are surprisingly low, and suggest that police actions alone are unlikely to have a huge impact on the carrying of knives.

The role of intelligence

There has been little formal evaluation of the role that intelligence plays in targeting stop and search, reflecting the lack of independent evaluation of the impact of intelligence-led policing more generally (Maguire, 2008; Karn, 2013). If stop and search is to be effective, we might expect it to be intelligence-led: that is to say, we would expect it to be carefully targeted in terms of place (in areas where crime is taking place), time (when crime is taking place) and people (at individuals who are committing crime or at least behaving suspiciously). Intelligence-led policing aims to reduce crime by collecting relevant and reliable information to provide a clear and accurate picture of the most pressing current and future crime problems, prioritising and planning targeted responses to them, evaluating the outcomes, and feeding this knowledge and experience back for future responses (Ratcliffe, 2008). Research has shown that, where officers work in an intelligence-led way and have stronger grounds for suspicion, stop-searches are more likely to result in arrest (Miller et al., 2000). In general, however, arrest rates (or hit rates) show that officer suspicion is falsified in the vast majority of cases, suggesting that the bar for reasonable suspicion is being set too low. According to Bowling (2007: 26),

> Evidence from the UK is that of every 100 recorded searches 'on suspicion', about 88 are fruitless; that is, they do not result in an arrest for the behaviour suspected or for any other reason. The research evidence suggests that the targeting of the power is woefully inaccurate. The basis for 'reasonable suspicion' often turns out to be absent, and there appears to be limits to the skill of the police officer in distinguishing the person who is actually involved in crime from those for whom a generalized suspicion exists in the police lexicon – urban males wearing hooded sweatshirts, for example.

A review conducted by Chainey and Macdonald (2012) on behalf of the Home Office found that patterns of stop and search are often not consistent with an intelligence-led approach. This review was based on in-depth interviews with operational officers from two case study police forces as well as statistical and geographical analysis of search records from a further five case study sites. Confirming previous research (e.g. Miller et al., 2000), the analysis identified substantial variations in stop and search rates across the five sites which could not be explained by underlying crime rates. Overall, there was little relationship between the volume of crime and the volume of searches over time, and searches did not track crime levels in the way that would be expected with an intelligence-led approach. Across the study sites, searches were geographically clustered into hotspots, but the clustering could not always be explained by the volume of crime in these areas. Search hotspots often seemed 'hotter' than would be predicted from the level of crime in the area, and did not necessarily produce a high arrest rate. Search hotspots sometimes appeared in places where recorded crime problems were low, but were not evident in other areas with high crime rates. Based on the case study sites, it was reported that the search hotspots tended to have a higher than average proportion of residents from black and minority ethnic groups, and this concentration often translated into higher rates of stop and search for such groups. There was, moreover, no consistent relationship in the study sites between the ethnic profile of the suspect descriptions reported by victims and witnesses, and the profile of those searched by the police.

Research into police decision-making has found that officers are often unclear about what constitutes 'reasonable grounds' and do not meet this requirement in a large number of cases (FitzGerald, 1999; Quinton et al., 2000; Shiner, 2006; Sanders and Young, 2007). Her Majesty's Inspectorate of Constabulary (2013: 8) recently reported that slightly more than a quarter of the 8,783 search records it reviewed did not 'include sufficient grounds to justify the lawful use of the power'. Extrapolating from this figure, it follows that as many as 300,000 stop and searches may be conducted without reasonable grounds each year, rendering them unlawful and probably ineffective. Even where grounds are provided, they may be based on little more than assumptions and generalisations. According to Chainey and Macdonald (2012), the officers they interviewed claimed to value intelligence, but displayed a loose definition of what it involved that included low-grade information and often did not think about its reliability, highlighting 'the potential for officers to conduct searches based on comparatively weak information' (2012: 19). There was also some evidence that officers were selective in what they considered to be relevant from intelligence briefings, prioritising and retaining specific pieces of intelligence about 'known offenders' they were already familiar with, while excluding newer information that was not in line with their experience: 'With some officers indicating they largely focused on the intelligence that supported their pre-existing knowledge and experience, there may have been potential for stop and search to be targeted towards a subgroup of offenders who had a longstanding relationship with the police, and for that targeting possibly to be self-perpetuating' (2012: 58).

In the absence of specific intelligence, police decisions about whom to stop and search may be based on crude stereotypes about the kinds of people who commit crime (FitzGerald, 1999; Quinton et al., 2000). During a group discussion reported by Shiner (2006: 54), officers described how they targeted 'the criminal fraternity' and 'known' offenders, noting: 'I'm sure sociologists, liberal types, would say that we're employing stereotypes to make those decisions, well yes, and it works. That's how we catch criminals.' 'Bottom-enders', 'hoodies' and 'junkies' were singled out as targets and were sharply distinguished from those the police said they left alone – the latter being characterised as 'normal members of the community', 'everyday law-abiding citizens', 'Joe average who's driving home from work', 'Mrs Bloggs with her two children' and 'ladies going with shopping bags'.

Seriousness of offences

Claims that stop and search is effective are typically made in relation to serious offences involving violence and weapons, but such claims are misleading because relatively few searches target this type of offence or lead to arrests for them. Fewer than 1 in 10 suspicion-based searches are for weapons, including only 1 per cent for firearms (Home Office, 2014b). Drugs provide the most common reason for stop and search, accounting for slightly more than half of all suspicion-based searches. Although the police are not required to record the type of drug they are looking for or whether the suspected offence relates to possession or supply, it is clear that the vast majority of drug searches target minor possession offences. While cannabis possession accounts for around 80 per cent of police-recorded drug offences (Home Office, 2012c), Her Majesty's Inspectorate of Constabulary (2013: 25) confirmed that 'the vast majority' of drug searches 'are for low-level possession offences'. After drugs, stolen property and 'going equipped' provide the next most common reasons for a search, accounting for slightly more than a third of suspicion-based searches (Home Office, 2014b). Concerns about the amount of attention being given to relatively minor offences were acknowledged by the Commissioner of the Metropolitan Police Service, Bernard Hogan-Howe, in January 2012 when he announced that officers would be told to focus less on stopping people for small amounts of cannabis, and focus instead on those suspected of violent offences and carrying weapons (Davenport, 2012).

Arrests resulting from stop and search are also dominated by less serious offences. Of arrests made as a result of suspicion-based stop-searches in 2012/2013, 1 per cent were for firearms and 11 per cent were for other weapons (Home Office, 2014b). Most arrests were made for drugs or stolen property (41 per cent and 28 per cent, respectively). The focus on drugs is unlikely to have a substantial effect on crime, not least because many drug users are not deterred by the threat of stop and search, but merely move their activities elsewhere (Ream et al., 2010) or purchase more drugs immediately after the search if any are seized (Werb et al., 2008). Even if levels of use are reduced, there is little evidence to show that reducing cannabis possession will reduce violence or any other crime (Harcourt, 2004). While FitzGerald (1999) found that over three-quarters of drug arrests were for cannabis possession, Miller et al. (2000: 45) concluded that the focus on minor drug offences – mainly cannabis possession – means it is 'unlikely that searches make a substantial contribution to undermining drug markets or drug-related crime'. There is also some evidence that cracking down on drug markets may be counter-productive, with violence increasing after markets have been disrupted as potential dealers compete for the territory (Weisburg and Eck, 2004).

The costs of stop and search

Stop and search comes at a cost, not just for those who are subject to such interventions, but also for the police, the criminal justice system and the communities they serve. The range of costs involved has been illustrated by Bernard Harcourt in his discussion of the 'ratchet effect' associated with law enforcement in the US. According to Harcourt (2004: 1279), a ratchet effect 'occurs when racial profiling produces a supervised population disproportionate to the distribution of offending by racial group'. He elaborates (2004: 1329):

> The ratchet effect disproportionately distributes criminal records and criminal justice contacts, with numerous secondary implications. Disproportionate criminal supervision and incarceration reduces work opportunities, breaks down families and communities, and disrupts education. It contributes to the exaggerated general perception in the public imagination and among police officers of 'black criminality.'... This in turn further undermines the ability of African-Americans to obtain employment or pursue educational opportunities. It has a delegitimizing effect on the criminal justice system that may encourage disaffected youth to commit crime. It may also corrode police-community relations, hampering law enforcement efforts as minority community members become less willing to report crime, to testify, and to convict. And, to make matters worse, a feedback mechanism aggravates these tendencies. Given the paucity of reliable information on natural offending rates, the police may rely on their own prior arrest and supervision statistics in deciding how to allocate resources. This, in turn, accelerates the imbalance in the

prison population and the growing correlation between race and criminality.

The impact of stop and search in England and Wales weighs heavily on black and minority ethnic communities. Home Office data routinely show that black people are stopped and searched at more than five times the rate of whites, while Asian people are stopped and searched at roughly twice the rate of whites (see Chapter 3; Miller, 2010). This pattern of over-policing helps to produce ethnic disparities at later stages of the criminal justice system that cannot be explained by differences in rates of offending (Eastwood et al., 2013; see also May et al., 2010). Such differences have given rise to longstanding concerns about the role of police prejudice and racial discrimination (Bowling and Phillips, 2007; see also Chapter 3). According to the American Psychological Association (2001), the effects of racial profiling on victims can include post-traumatic stress disorder and other forms of stress-related disorders as well as perceptions of race-related threats. Similar effects were identified by a recent study of the 'human cost' of stop and search in England and Wales, with two interviewees – both men from black and minority ethnic groups – describing the effects in the following ways (StopWatch and the Open Society Justice Initiative, 2013: 4, 20):

> The impact it had on me was huge, huge; and it was negative. I felt that I needed a shower after. I felt really inadequate, I felt dirty. You're looked at a certain way, you are treated a certain way, as if you are actually guilty.
>
> The impact of being stopped and searched on regular occasions is that, in a sense, it reinforces the view that you have, that you are being criminalized because of the way you look or the beliefs you have. It creates that fear, and it creates that anxiety.

Another study, focusing on young people from various minority ethnic communities in the West Midlands, found their experiences were characterised by hostility, lack of confidence in the police and a mistrust of authority (Sharp and Atherton, 2007). Noting parallels between parts of Britain and the US, the authors describe how 'an element of "over-exposure" to the police result[ed], in the young people... simply discounting the police as a suitable agency to deal with crimes that might be committed against them, or their families' (2007: 753). Stop and search was identified as a particular grievance among the young people who felt that the police abuse their powers and target youths from black and other minority ethnic groups without reasonable suspicion. These misgivings impacted on the strategies the young people employed 'in all their interactions with the police': 'Theirs is a strategy that excludes the police – a service that does not inspire trust and confidence, and which is staffed by people who are viewed as racist' (2007: 746, 753).

The damage stop and search does to trust and confidence in the police has been well documented over many years. Following the Brixton 'riots' in 1981, Lord Scarman (1981: para. 4.11) identified a 'policing dilemma', the essence of which is 'how to cope with a rising level of crime – and particularly street robbery (in the colloquial phrase "mugging") – while retaining the confidence of all sections of the community, especially the ethnic minority groups'. In an attempt to resolve this dilemma, Scarman (1981: para. 4.55) drew on 'two well-known principles of policing a free society' – 'consent and balance', and 'independence and accountability'. The principle of consent and balance means that 'if the police are to secure the assent of the community which they need to support their operation, they must strike an acceptable balance between the three elements of their function': preventing crime, protecting life and property, and preserving public tranquillity (1981: para. 4.56). In order to strike this balance, Scarman (1981: para. 4.57–4.58) argued, it has 'long been recognised by the police themselves' that the duty to maintain order may come into conflict with the duty to enforce the law, in which case 'the priority must be given to the former'. The second 'basic principle' of independence and accountability requires that police operate 'not only within the law but with the support of the community as a whole' – something that demands accountability and effective consultative machinery (1981: para. 4.60).

Scarman (1981: para. 4.67) was clear that the police were partly responsible for what happened in Brixton, pointing specifically to the strain stop and search had placed on community relations in the lead up to the 'riots':

> I do not doubt that harassment does occur. Stop and search operations in particular require courtesy and carefully controlled behaviour by the police to those stopped, which I am certain is sometimes lacking... Whether justified or not, many in Brixton believe that the police routinely abuse their powers and mistreat alleged offenders. The belief here is as important as the fact.

Particular criticisms were made of Swamp 81, a 'saturation operation', which made extensive use of stop and search and 'contributed to the great increase in tension' during the 'days immediately preceding the disorders' (1981: para. 4.43). Police made 943 stops in less than a week as part of the operation, leading to 118 arrests and charges against 75 people, only one of which was for robbery – the ostensible target of the operation. While noting that hard policing is often necessary, Scarman concluded that Swamp 81 had been 'a serious mistake', insisting: 'when a community becomes resentful and restless and there is widespread loss of confidence in the police, the particular circumstances may require a review of police methods' (1981: para. 4.75–4.76). Had such a review been undertaken, he believed, 'a street "saturation" operation would not have been launched when it was' (1981: para. 4.77). The implications of Scarman's analysis for the use of stop and search were made clear in a Home Office report published shortly afterwards (Willis, 1983: 23):

> Without a secure base of community support ('consent') the use of powers of this kind, however extensive or circumscribed, rapidly becomes hazardous and ineffective. To maintain their effectiveness, therefore, their exercise needs constantly to be re-assessed not merely in relation to their contribution to arrests, but also in the light of their effect on individuals and on the temper of the community as a whole. In other words, the satisfactory and fruitful exercise of powers in this area depends crucially in the long-term on police action being perceived by individuals and groups as acceptably fair and rational.

A large body of empirical evidence has been developed subsequently that supports this conclusion. It has been well established in both Britain and the US that contact with the police has a negative net effect on public trust and confidence: poor or unsatisfactory contact does considerable damage to people's perceptions of the police, while good or satisfactory contact has a much smaller positive effect (Skogan, 2006; Bradford et al., 2009; Tyler, 2011; Singer, 2013; see also Chapter 6). Police-initiated contacts, including stop and search, it appears, have the potential to be especially damaging to people's perceptions of police fairness and legitimacy (Bradford et al., 2009; Jackson et al., 2012b; Myhill and Bradford, 2012). When people feel they are treated fairly and with respect they are more supportive of the police and more respectful of the law, but when they feel they have been treated unfairly or disrespectfully they are less supportive and less respectful (Sunshine and Tyler, 2003;

Tyler and Fagan, 2008; Hough et al., 2010). Thirty years after the Brixton 'riots', the damaging effects of stop and search were, once again, implicated in the outbreak of serious public disorder that started in London and spread to 66 areas across England (Riots, Communities and Victims Panel, 2011).

As well as the damage to community relations and police legitimacy, stop and search carries considerable opportunity costs. A million or so stop-searches per year, to say nothing of the much larger number of stops that do not lead to searches, represents a significant investment of resources that could be used to do other, potentially more effective, things. While there is strong evidence to support 'hot spot' policing, the effectiveness of this approach varies depending on the type of activity undertaken. There is some evidence that police patrols can have a moderate deterrent effect on crime (Sherman and Weisburd, 1995) and that increased police presence alone leads to reductions in crime and disorder (Koper, 1995), but other, more focused, interventions have been found to be more effective. Drawing on the results of a randomised controlled trial in Massachusetts, US, Braga and Bond (2008) examined the causal pathways of key crime-prevention mechanisms associated with hot spot policing, paying particular attention to the role of increased misdemeanour arrests, situational prevention strategies and social service actions. They concluded that the strongest crime-prevention gains were generated by situational prevention strategies that sought to modify conditions that are conducive to crime and disorder using a range of interventions that were specifically designed to address the problem in an area. Such interventions included cleaning and securing vacant lots, demolishing abandoned buildings, improving street lighting, adding video surveillance and performing code inspections of disorderly venues. A subsequent review of 19 studies covering 25 hot spot policing interventions came to a similar conclusion, noting that problem-oriented policing interventions, including situational crime-prevention measures, had more impact than 'increased policing interventions' (Braga et al., 2012: 32; see also Taylor et al., 2011).

> While arresting offenders remains a central strategy of the police and a necessary component of the police response to crime hot spots, it seems likely that altering place characteristics and dynamics will produce larger and longer-term crime prevention benefits...Implementing situational prevention strategies that reduce police reliance on aggressive enforcement strategies may also yield positive benefits for police-community relations.

The value of 'problem-solving' approaches that often involve police working in partnership with local communities and other agencies has also been highlighted specifically in relation to drug law enforcement. Mazerolle et al. (2007) point to a hierarchy of effectiveness, with unfocused police patrols at the bottom, followed by targeted place-based approaches. While unfocused approaches do not appear to reduce drug markets or associated harms, targeted place-based approaches have demonstrable benefits that tend not to be sustained once policing resources are withdrawn. At the top of the hierarchy, Mazerolle et al. identify a combination of problem-solving and geographically targeted approaches that create sustained partnerships and can help to achieve long-term reductions in drug markets and associated crime.

The enduring appeal of stop and search

Given the relative costs and benefits involved, why do the police continue to invest so heavily in stop and search? Part of the answer lies in the observation that it has a purpose other than the avowed one of crime reduction. According to Brogden (1981), stop and search serves a more diffuse social control function and provides the police with a means of maintaining control of the streets rather than detecting crime. While such powers were originally designed to enable police to contain and, where necessary, apprehend 'rogues', 'vagabonds' and other 'unruly' persons, something of this original purpose remains despite the introduction of tighter procedural safeguards. The police are frequently called on to deal with various 'troublesome' populations, including protestors, homeless people, beggars, the mentally ill and groups of young people 'hanging around'. Stop and search often provides the preferred method by which the police deal with such groups and arguably has more to do with monitoring, controlling and disciplining 'suspicious' people than detecting crime or criminals (Choongh, 1997; Sanders and Young, 2007; May, 2010). It is precisely this kind of tenuous and discriminatory approach that is likely to undermine trust and confidence, alienating impacted communities.

Proactively engaging in stop and search also enables officers to demonstrate they are doing 'real police work' (Reiner, 2010; Sanders et al., 2010). The pressure for 'results' provides a 'basic motivating force within police culture' and has been formalised over the last 20 years or so by a growing emphasis on performance management (Reiner, 2010: 121; see also Cockcroft and Beattie, 2009). Attempts to assess performance on the basis of statistical indicators has created a 'numbers game', distorting police performance by creating perverse incentive structures and encouraging officers to concentrate on measurable activities (Loftus, 2009; Eterno and Silverman, 2012). Stop and search provides one such activity that is emphasised through a range of formal and informal means, including performance development reviews, performance meeting minutes, individual and team 'league tables', applications for promotions, and targets for patrol officers set during briefings (Ainsworth, 2011; The Metropolitan Police Federation, 2014). The impact of this regime was described by one officer quoted in a recent scoping study looking at the policing of young adults (Graham and Karn, 2013: 21; see also Eastwood et al., 2013):

> I have to say, certainly when I was in the response team, we were under pressure to get a certain amount of searches each month. So it's much easier, when you've got a group of kids engaging in a bit of antisocial behaviour, albeit very low level, there's a smell of cannabis, you think great, here's my chance. You can justify it very easily and it's an easy win for a young police officer.

According to another officer quoted in a report by the Metropolitan Police Federation drawing attention to the 'burgeoning and deleterious use of targets as a management tool' (Metropolitan Police Federation, 2014: 1, 12),

> We are set individual targets of four arrests per month and 10 stop and searches... There should be at least one positive stop and search per month (i.e. leading to arrest), and there is also the 'suggestion' that should you be called to an incident, perhaps stop and search them first or whilst investigating the incident (obviously that is a serious breach of procedure and law) in order to get a search figure.

Conclusion

The effectiveness of stop and search is largely assumed. Familiar claims about the value of this tactic as a tool in the fight against crime are not supported by the available evidence and fail to consider the associated costs. Stop and search yields meagre returns in the form of measurable outcomes, such as arrests, and systematic evaluation indicates that its role in reducing crime is a marginal one at best. The costs, by contrast, are significant and well documented. Stop and search, particularly when done badly, damages police/community relations, reduces public trust and confidence, discourages cooperation and, ultimately, undermines the legitimacy of the police. Current levels of stop and search activity also absorb considerable resources that could be better used on other activities. The negative consequences of stop and search weigh particularly heavily on black communities, imposing a double burden that is neatly encapsulated in the claim that 'the experience of black people over the last 30 years has been that we have been over policed and to a large extent under protected' (David Muir, cited in Macpherson, 1999: para. 45.7). For politicians and police officers to maintain that stop and search is effective against the weight of the evidence offers a false sense of security and does a disservice to the communities they serve because it leaves them exposed to this double burden. There is a growing body of evidence that there are things the police can do that have a measurable impact on crime, but stop and search does not appear to be one of them, or at least not one of the most effective. It is time that the use of this tactic was subject to the rigours of an evidence-based approach that is alert to potential costs as well as possible benefits.

6
Unintended Consequences
Ben Bradford

What effect does stop and search have on those who experience it? For officers, these encounters may seem fleeting, constitute little more than a moment's inconvenience for all involved and, of course, are part of the normal working day. Yet, those stopped often have a rather different experience, finding it unsettling and sometimes profoundly disturbing. In this chapter, though, I want to move beyond consideration of what people *think* or *feel* about being stopped and searched to examine the material effect such experiences may have on them, their friends and families, and the communities in which they live. While people's emotional and cognitive reactions are, of course, important in their own right, stop and search may also have significant long-term implications that should refocus the way we think about this element of police practice. By locating itself in wider criminological debates, this chapter also constitutes an attempt to move beyond ethnic disproportionality as the sole locus of concern towards a more rounded picture of the (unintended) consequences of stop and search.

Using procedural justice theory (Tyler and Huo, 2002; Tyler, 2006a) as the primary lens through which to view stop and search, the discussion below aims to flesh out an argument most succinctly put by Bowling and Phillips (2007: 959–60):

> There is no compelling 'business case' for the present level of stop and search ... it has a deeply damaging effect on society; it impacts negatively on the law abiding population and is cause of a loss of public support for and de-legitimation of the police. It increases the frequency of adversarial encounters – some of which have the potential to trigger public disorder – and contributes to accelerating the flow of young black people disproportionately into the criminal justice system.

To anticipate the key points, as currently practised in England and Wales, stop and search appears likely to undermine legitimacy and cooperation between police and public (and thus the effectiveness of policing in the long run); suck people unnecessarily into the criminal justice system; and perhaps cause, rather than prevent, offending. Furthermore, and relatedly, stop and search may be an important aspect of wider processes of social exclusion that damage people's social identities and connection to wider society while, at the same time, promoting affiliation with problematic group identities and/or creating alienation and anomie.

The chapter proceeds in five distinct but interconnected parts. First, it addresses the fundamental issue of the fairness of this type of policing, as experienced from the perspective of ordinary citizens; second, it considers the role police stop activity[1] can have in driving a wedge between individuals, communities and the police, thus damaging trust, legitimacy and the potential for cooperation between police and public; third, it explores the links between the experience of stop and search and wider forms of social exclusion; and, fourth, the focus switches to the potential role of police stops in criminal justice net-widening and in pulling young people into the criminal justice system. The chapter closes with some thoughts about lessons to be drawn in relation to how police – and, indeed, society more widely – might think differently about the effectiveness of stop and search as a policing tool.

Data from a survey of young men from black and minority ethnic (BME) groups are used to illustrate the discussion at various points. This survey was administered in the summer of 2010 on behalf of the London Metropolitan Police Service (MPS) as an add-on to its London-wide Public Attitudes Survey (see Bradford et al., 2009; Jackson et al., 2013; Bradford, 2014).[2] A total of 1,017 young men aged 16–30, living in four London boroughs, were interviewed, with questions probing their attitudes towards police, crime and disorder, their sense of identity, their social bonds to family and community, and a range of other issues. Some 19 per cent of the sample reported having been stopped by police in the past year, while still more reported other forms of personal and vicarious contact with officers (such as seeing police interact with others), making the survey an ideal source for analysing the effects of stop and search on relations between police and public.

A couple of initial provisos are required. The fact of ethnic disproportionality in the exercise of police stop and search powers is taken here as a given (Equality and Human Rights Commission, 2010), and the reasons for this disproportionality are not discussed. This assumption is significant, given that it implies the likely effects of stop and search described below will not be evenly spread across the population but will be concentrated among those groups who experience a disproportionate volume of stops and/or searches. Equally, no consideration is given to the different stop and search powers used and their number: it is, in any case, highly unlikely that members of the public distinguish between them (Macpherson, 1999; Bowling and Phillips, 2007). Finally, the focus is limited primarily to England and Wales, although relevant work from other jurisdictions is also drawn upon.

The issue of basic fairness

Police stop and search practice is currently, and perennially, a topic of significant debate in the UK, and this debate concerns particular issues of fundamental fairness. The level of public concern about stop and search over the last 30 years means that this aspect of police practice is widely known; furthermore, the prevalence of stops of one kind or another is high enough to view this type of police contact as one of which a significant proportion of the population have direct, personal experience (the Crime Survey of England and Wales, formerly the British Crime Survey, regularly finds that around 10 per cent of people report being stopped on foot or in a vehicle each year), and one of which an even larger proportion have vicarious experiences via friends, family or colleagues. Most recent research (e.g. Delsol and Shiner, 2006; Bowling and Phillips, 2007; May et al., 2010; Miller, 2010) concludes that not only are such experiences unevenly distributed across different population groups; there is, furthermore, a component of the ethnic disproportionality in the experience of police stop (and stop and search) activity that cannot be justified. That is, whether one considers arguments such as the population 'available' to be stopped (MVA and Miller, 2000; Waddington et al., 2004), differential offending rates (Bowling and Phillips, 2002) or differences in the 'hit rates' of stops in terms of arrests, there is an essential element of disproportionality that cannot be explained away.

We should not underestimate the extent to which public experiences of police stops constitute in and of themselves an 'impact' of the police power to stop, question and search citizens, particularly in cases where the exercise of this power is experienced as *unfair*. This is an issue that goes right to the heart of the relationship between the police, as a core state agency, and the people it polices. Stop and search, and analogous practices, have historically been and are currently a key element of police practice; this is one of the more important ways in which police *do* policing. Stop and search does generate arrests and seizures of contraband, although its effectiveness remains a matter of debate (see Chapter 5), and few people challenge the idea that the police require the ability to intervene in the business of citizens and to ask them to account for their behaviour in some way and/or search them. However, in democratic, plural societies people have a right to be free from unnecessary or abusive state intervention, to be treated equally, to expect decent treatment at the hands of state agents (Margalit, 1996) and to expect that the state will represent them and defend their interests. Indeed, as will be shown below, the police themselves have an interest in demonstrating to the public that this is the case. The criminal justice system should not simply aim to ensure or reproduce order and security, but should also be centrally concerned with treating people fairly and decently, and with seeking to align itself with the normative expectations of those it governs.

Whatever the effectiveness of stop and search, instrumental matters cannot, therefore, be considered in isolation from questions of fairness, a point to which I return at the end of this chapter.

Assessments of the fairness of stop and search among those who experience it (either directly or vicariously) should thus be central to any evaluation of the practice. Research on the psychology of justice has produced a detailed specification of the place of fairness in people's relationships with the police. This work has underlined that issues of justice and fairness are at the centre of our understandings of the way the criminal justice system *should* work; equally, fairness is the primary lens through which we judge our actual encounters with system agents such as the police (Tyler and Huo, 2002; Tyler, 2006a; Tyler and Fagan, 2008). Work in the UK has started to pick up, apply and expand Tyler's procedural justice model (Tendayi et al., 2006; Bradford et al., 2009; Hough et al., 2010; Jackson et al., 2012a, 2012b; Tankebe, 2013; Bradford, 2014), while related studies have also focused on the importance of openness and transparency in trust-building between police and community more widely (e.g., Spalek, 2010). The procedural justice model appears to be highly relevant in the British context, where, as in the US, research consistently finds, that in their dealings with the police, people care most about the fairness with which they are treated, and fair treatment is linked to trust, legitimacy, cooperation and compliance with the law.

Based on a social-psychological understanding of the role of group membership in people's lives, procedural justice theories stress that treatment at the hands of important group representatives such as the police carries status-relevant messages concerning an individual's inclusion and status within the group(s) the police represent. In essence, we care about procedural justice because we want to feel included in and valued by overarching social groups. In the context of policing, procedural justice theories, therefore, chime with more sociologically oriented research that has underlined the association of the police with images, and ideologies, of nation, community and the dominant social order (Waddington, 1999; Reiner, 2000; Loader and Mulcahy, 2003; Jackson and Bradford, 2009).

Much work on procedural justice tends to stress that people value process fairness over both instrumental concerns and assessments of distributive fairness (e.g. Tyler and Huo, 2002). It is important to recognise that this is an empirical rather than a normative claim. To note that it seems to be the case that, on average, people place a greater emphasis on process rather than instrumental or distributive outcomes is not to claim that this is either inevitable or necessarily desirable. In the present context, the distinction between procedural and distributive fairness seems key. Procedural fairness in the context of policing is characterised by neutrality, transparency and evidence-based decision-making on the part of officers; voice on the part of individuals during their encounters with the police; and treatment that is mutually respectful, open, dignified and conducive to the development of trust. By contrast, distributive fairness is characterised by an equal distribution of the goods and impositions of police activity. When people believe they are singled out for disproportionate 'special treatment' by officers, for example, they are unlikely to believe police to be distributively fair.

It is an interesting finding from research on public perceptions of policing that people can and do distinguish between procedural and distributive fairness, and tend to prioritise the former. When it comes to police stops in general, and stop and search in particular, however, the situation may be somewhat more complex, since experiencing police activity of this type seems likely to influence assessments of police procedural and distributive fairness in a complex and interactive manner. In terms of officer behaviour during the encounter, people will make judgements about the quality of the interaction: on the extent to which they are treated with dignity and respect, allowed a voice, and so on. Yet, they will also make a judgement concerning the reason the encounter happened in the first place, and, in particular, they may ask themselves whether they were stopped not because of what they were doing but because of who they are. Their answer to this question may be both informed by and reflect back on their assessments of procedural fairness. If they decide that they were, indeed, stopped because of who they are – that is, if they believe the police were acting in a distributively unfair way by singling them out for different treatment in comparison with others – this seems almost certain to undermine their sense that the police are neutral, make decisions based on evidence, and have their best interests at heart (Tyler and Wakslak, 2004; McAra and McVie, 2005; Sharp and Atherton, 2007). Moreover, if people feel that the way police officers treat them is premised on their race, gender, age or some other personal characteristic, this will raise questions about whether they are accorded rights pertaining to membership of the superordinate group the police represent (Tyler and Blader, 2003: 359). If, on the other hand, police do treat people in a procedurally fair way, for example by explaining properly and openly the reasons for the stop, this can serve to alleviate suspicions of distributive unfairness by forging links of motive-based trust between officer and citizen (Tyler and Wakslak, 2004).

In this context, procedural justice and distributive justice are, therefore, significantly intertwined. Perceptions or experiences of (in)justice of one type may predict or inform judgements about the (in)justice of police activity in relation to the other. Yet this is not inevitable, and people who experience procedurally fair stop encounters may still come away with a sense of injustice based on distributive criteria, most notably, perhaps, if they have experienced a large number of such encounters in the past. Furthermore, while distributive injustices may often be premised on procedural injustices (such as prejudiced or dishonest decision-making), it also seems plausible to suggest that fair processes during individual-level encounters will not automatically prevent distributively unfair outcomes: for example, inequalities in the distribution of police activity may have causes prior to or separate from the behaviour of street-level officers, such as high-level decisions concerning resource allocation.

Experiences of unfairness, whether procedural, distributive or both, during stop and search encounters risks undermining people's trust in the police and the wider criminal justice system. Furthermore – and particularly so due to the extent to which procedural and distributive concerns are, in this instance, so closely interconnected – if people experience stop and search as disproportionate this risks undermining their sense that police respect and represent them, and, by extension, the legitimacy they invest in both the police and the system they represent (Tyler, 2006b). The associations between negative contact with the police, particularly encounters experienced as procedurally unfair by those involved, and lower levels of trust and legitimacy are explored in more detail below.

Stop and search, trust and legitimacy

The negative correlation between the experience of disproportionate police attention and lower levels of trust and confidence among ethnic minority and other youths in the UK is perhaps the best researched topic among those considered in this chapter. Such research stretches back to the first 'Policing for London' report (Smith, 1983) and continues right up to the present day (e.g. Sharp and Atherton, 2007; Jackson et al., 2012b). These and similar studies are a subset of a wider body of work looking at the relationship between contact with officers, public trust, and the legitimacy of the police, and there are two elements to this wider body of work that are particularly relevant when considering the effect of stop and search on individuals and communities.

First, it is one of the core findings of almost all research in this area that the net impact of contact with the police on public confidence is negative, and that levels of trust, legitimacy and support for the police appear to be lower among those who have had recent personal contact with officers than among those who have not (FitzGerald et al., 2002; Bradford et al., 2009; Walker et al., 2009). This effect appears to be largely due to an asymmetry in the effect of contact on confidence (Skogan, 2006). Poor or unsatisfactory contacts have a large negative impact on people's opinions; good or satisfactory contacts have a much smaller positive impact. While the extent of this asymmetry may have been overplayed (Tyler and Fagan, 2008), current UK research suggests that it is considerably stronger in relation to police-initiated contacts than in relation to those initiated by members of the public (Bradford et al., 2009; Myhill and Bradford, 2012). That is, there seems to be something about police-initiated contacts such as street or traffic stops that makes them particularly likely to damage the relationship between police and public. Police-initiated contacts seem to have a major impact on perceptions of police fairness, assessments of the extent to which police understand and act on community issues (Bradford et al., 2009), and, partly through these factors, on the legitimacy of the police (Jackson et al., 2012b).

The second factor highlighted by existing work is the multiplicative effect of repeat stops and other forms of police-initiated contacts. People who are stopped by the police often, particularly those from BME groups and other minority groups, are considerably more likely to experience multiple forms of police-initiated and other contacts with officers (Bowling and Phillips, 2007; Sharp and Atherton, 2007), and this seems likely only to accentuate the negative association between contact and trust. One poor experience at the hands of police officers may be discounted or gradually forgotten; a series of such contacts, whether experienced personally or vicariously, can seriously damage individuals' relationships with the police.

Cooperation between police and public

The fact that contact with officers seems to have a net negative impact on public trust in the police is, again, a significant issue in and of itself. The now defunct 'PSA23' target that gave police forces in England and Wales one overarching performance management task – to improve public confidence – was very possibly misguided in its design and application (FitzGerald, 2010b; Myhill et al., 2011). But it did at least acknowledge the idea that public validation of the police service is a core element of its democratic accountability. If a certain section of society, by dint of excessive rates of contact with officers, has less trust in the police and grants it less legitimacy, this should be of some concern, quite aside from any concrete consequences that might follow.

Yet, recent UK studies have also started to apply ideas from procedural justice theory to probe more deeply into the potential effects of personal contact with officers on public cooperation with the police and compliance with the law. Tyler's model links the experience of fair treatment at the hands of police officers, through the intervening mechanisms of trust and legitimacy, to public cooperation with the police and compliance with the law (Tyler and Fagan, 2008; Tyler, 2011; Jackson et al., 2012a, 2012b). Unfair treatment, by contrast, undermines cooperation and promotes cynicism about the law (Hough et al., 2010). Police stop and search activity, if it is experienced negatively by those involved and felt to be procedurally unfair, is therefore likely to damage the potential for cooperation between police and public, something which has implications for both individuals and communities.

Despite the growth of private policing in recent years, for most people in the UK the public police are still the monopoly provider of security, offering the sole possibility of legally sanctioned redress in the face of criminal victimisation. Individuals who feel unwilling or unable to engage with the police and access the sorts of help officers may be able to provide are significantly disadvantaged compared with those who *do* feel able to turn to the police at times of need. Furthermore, the communities in which they live will suffer collectively, as law and disorder-related problems are less likely to be addressed and, even when police action is forthcoming, its effectiveness will be diminished if officers are unable to rely on the assistance of local people, whether as victims, witnesses or sources of information (Kirk and Matsueda, 2011). Willingness to cooperate with the police can thus be seen as an element of the social capital carried by individuals and communities, where social capital is defined in its broadest sense as inhering in social relations that have (potentially) productive benefits.

Data from the MPS survey seem to confirm that stop and search activity damages public cooperation. In this survey, as in the wider Public Attitudes Survey (Bradford et al., 2009) and the Crime Survey of England and Wales (Walker et al., 2009), the net effect of police stops on opinions of the police is negative. While many of the encounters reported by respondents were felt to be positive, trust in the fairness of the police was on average lower among those who had been stopped than among those who had not (see Jackson et al., 2012b). Figure 6.1 lays out the implications of this in terms of individual's willingness to cooperate with the police (measured in the survey by questions such as 'if the situation arose, how likely would you be to call the police to report a crime you witnessed?'). The figure summarises the results of a structural equation model[3] replicating a core aspect of procedural justice theory –

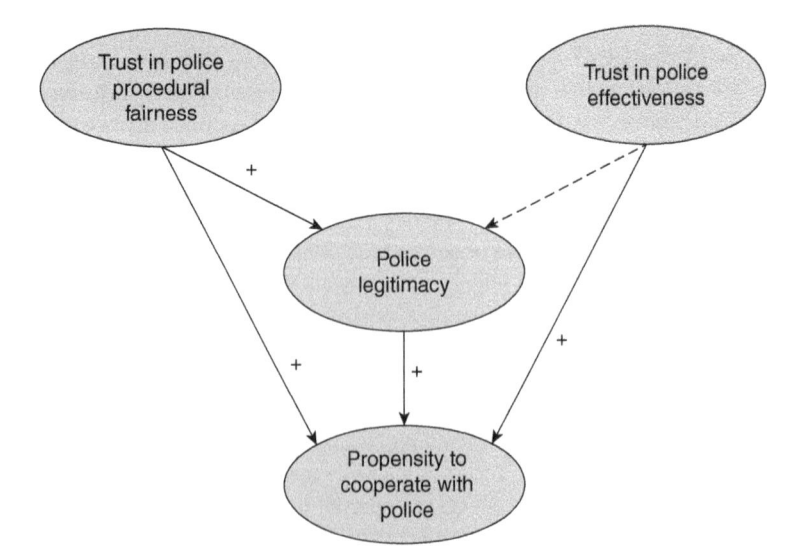

Figure 6.1 Unfairness damages legitimacy and cooperation
+ Indicates positive statistical effect; – Indicates negative statistical effect.
Note: Summary of results from a structural equation model predicting self-reported propensity to cooperate with the police.

that police legitimacy rests heavily on the public's sense that officers act in a fair way, and that both procedural fairness and legitimacy are linked to propensities to cooperate. Both relationships hold strongly in this data – as they do in the PAS and other UK surveys (Bradford and Jackson, 2010; Hough et al., 2010; Jackson et al., 2012a, 2012b). People who tended to trust in the procedural fairness of the police also tended to regard police as legitimate and report a greater willingness to cooperate with them. As found in many other studies, officer behaviour that damages trust in the fairness of the police does indeed seem to undermine the potential for cooperation between police and public.

Self-help violence

According to Tyler's model, procedural fairness encourages people to feel that the police have the right intentions towards them and that they are 'on the same side'. It is this sense of motive-based trust and group belonging that generates legitimacy and promotes cooperation and compliance with the law. Trust, shared group membership and legitimacy may also encourage individuals to cede to the police the right to define proper behaviour (Kelman and Hamilton, 1989; Jackson et al., 2012a). In situations where the potential or actual use of force is needed to reach a desired outcome – for example, to apprehend someone who has committed an assault – a legitimate police force is able to convince citizens that it should be entrusted to apply such force and that they (citizens) should not take it upon themselves to act. An illegitimate police force, by contrast, is unable to do so, and, in effect, encourages people to take the law into their own hands.

Individuals who, whether because of the experience of procedural injustice or for some other reason, do not hold the police to be legitimate may thus be more likely to engage in 'self-help' violence (Black, 1998). Given the nature of the law and the criminal justice system in a country such as the UK, those who do so are likely to find themselves in confrontation with the police. Individuals who try to solve such problems themselves may also be more likely to suffer physical injury, financial loss and other negative outcomes. In short, those who feel they can or must use violence to protect themselves, their property or their honour are likely, on average, to be significantly disadvantaged when compared with those who feel they can and should leave things to the police.

The House of Commons Home Affairs Select Committee (2007: 52) described just how such a process may come about. The Committee relays comments made to it by witnesses from police, community and faith groups, who concluded that 'a lack of trust in the police was leading young people to turn to informal "street justice", in which friends, relatives or the victims themselves took action to seek redress'. The London survey data again appear to support this argument. Respondents were asked a series of questions about how 'right' they thought it was for people to use violence to solve problems they might encounter, such as being attacked in the street or being involved in a neighbour dispute. One interpretation of the answers given to these questions is that they collectively reveal an individual's underlying orientation towards the use of violence, with more positive answers revealing a greater acceptance of the desirability of using violence as a response to dangers or problems.

Results from a structural equation model predicting this latent propensity are summarised in Figure 6.2. Orientations towards the possible use of violence were strongly associated with perceptions of police fairness and legitimacy: on average, respondents who felt the police were procedurally just, and who granted them legitimacy, were considerably less likely to say that using violence to solve problems is the right thing to do, and this association persisted even once other possibly

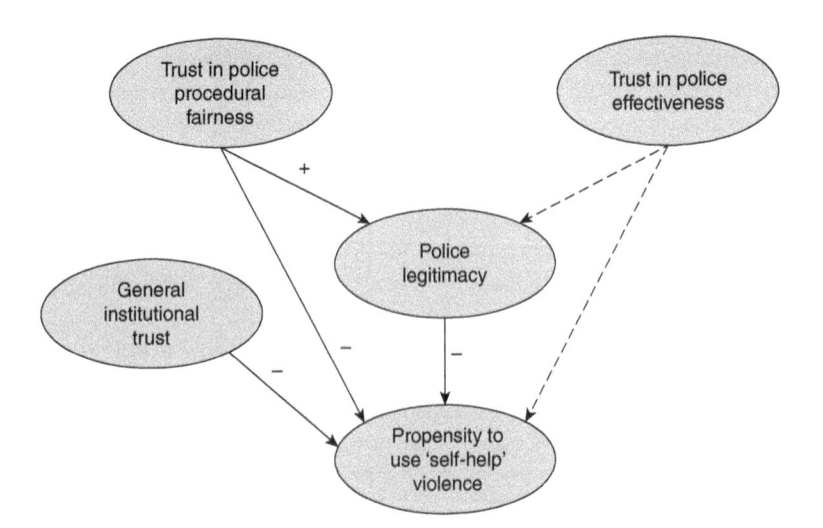

Figure 6.2 Trust in police fairness is linked to readiness to use self-help violence
+ Indicates positive statistical effect; − Indicates negative statistical effect.
Note: Summary of results from a structural equation model predicting self-reported propensity to use 'self-help' violence.

pertinent factors, such as general institutional trust, were taken into account (see Jackson et al. (2013) for more in-depth analysis of this issue). Conversely, people who trusted less in the procedural fairness of the police, and who granted them less legitimacy, were more likely to feel that the use of violence to solve problems was justified.

Wider issues of social exclusion

Current evidence, therefore, strongly suggests that experiences of police unfairness damage trust, legitimacy and the potential for cooperation, while simultaneously promoting a sense that the use of personal violence can be justified. Recall that the effect of police-initiated contact on trust is highly asymmetrical; positive encounters have little positive effect, while negative encounters have a large negative effect. Police stop activity, especially when concentrated on particular people and groups, is therefore highly likely to affect the relationship between the police and those who experience it. The net result, at both community and individual levels, is to distance people targeted for stops from a key element of the assistance the state, in the form of the police, can offer its citizens.

Furthermore, recall that the causal mechanism at the heart of the procedural justice model is shared group membership. Through the way they treat those they encounter, police officers communicate powerful messages to them about their inclusion and status within the social group(s) the police represent, whether these are conceptualised as the nation or state (Reiner, 2000; Loader and Mulcahy, 2003), the respectable community (Waddington, 1999), or some other similar social group. Experiencing unfairness may be linked not only to distrust in the police organisation, but also to a wider sense – or subjective experience – of exclusion.

Contact with the police is therefore likely to be associated with actual and symbolic exclusionary processes. Social exclusion has been defined as a 'lack or denial of resources, rights, goods and services, and the inability to participate in ... normal relationships and activities.... It affects both the quality of life of individuals and the equity and cohesion of society as a whole' (Levitas et al., 2007: 25). People who are socially excluded are more likely to be subject to police interventions for a whole host of reasons, which extend well beyond considerations of how police officers exercise their power (see, for example, McAra and McVie, 2005). But the argument here is that police activity may *promote* social exclusion, in some circumstances at least (McAra and McVie, 2012).

Symbolically, when unfairness communicates that people are not valued and held in respect, officers' actions can push people out from the social groups that the police represent. More concretely, police contact can drag individuals into the criminal justice system and away from more socially productive roles.

The London survey provides evidence of the potential for 'symbolic' exclusion based on responses to a series of questions concerning identities, affiliations and belonging. To take just one example, a paired set of questions asked how strongly respondents felt they 'belonged' to London and Great Britain. Answers to these two questions were highly correlated, and loaded onto one underlying factor that might represent their sense of belonging to the wider society. Most respondents did feel they belonged (nearly 80 per cent, for example, felt 'very' or 'fairly' strongly that they belonged to Great Britain) but, as Figure 6.3 illustrates, those who felt the police to be less fair were less likely to feel they belonged to the wider society (see Bradford (2014) for more detailed analysis). This association was robust to the inclusion of several

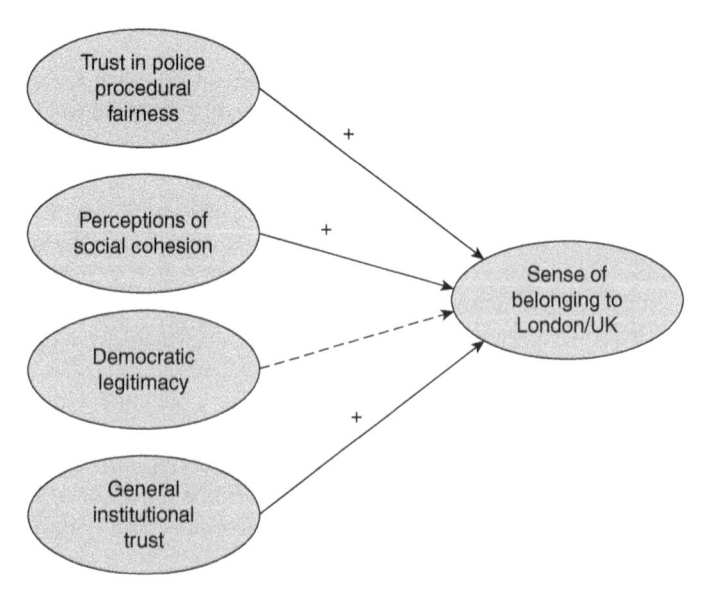

Figure 6.3 Trust in police fairness is linked to people's sense of belonging to the UK
+ Indicates positive statistical effect; − Indicates negative statistical effect.
Note: Summary of results from a structural equation model predicting sense of belonging to London/the UK.

potentially confounding variables, such as general institutional trust (the extent to which institutions in general are considered trustworthy), democratic legitimacy (the extent to which people feel aligned with democratic values) and perceptions of social cohesion (the extent to which people feel their local community is stable and that others living there are trustworthy).

Many of these issues may coalesce around recent experiences of policing among British Muslims and people with South Asian or Middle Eastern heritage thought by others to be Muslim. Several authors have noted that many current methods in counter-terrorism policing – including stop and search – undermine trust, turn communities inward and away from the majority society and the state, and ultimately may create a vicious spiral as aggressive police tactics (and political rhetoric) engender radicalisation, which in turn triggers yet more repressive responses (Spalek and Lambert, 2008; Spalek et al., 2009; Vertigans, 2010; see Chapter 7).

Beyond this specific context, criminal justice practices that serve to exclude people from valued social categories may encourage a wider turn towards alternate identities that are not, for example, defined by a positive relationship with the police and society more widely. Indeed, unfair policing may actively *place* people in such categories, and labelling theory (Becker, 1963; Ericson, 1975) provides an important reference point: people may begin to take on and internalise a sense of self that is problematic for themselves and those around them when they feel police and other criminal justice agents are assigning them to such an identity (see below). Alternatively, exclusion from identities oriented towards the nation, state and/or respectable community may be linked to a sense of anomie, disconnection or drift (Matza, 1964) that has similar implications for future behaviour.

Criminal justice net-widening and the criminogenic effects of stop and search

For evidence of the possible link between police stop activity and more literal forms of exclusion, we can turn to a body of literature concerned with the implications arising from police contact in terms of individuals' entry into the wider criminal justice system. Contact with the criminal justice system among young people, such as that initiated by a street stop, is thought by police and government alike to reduce the risk of their (re)offending. For the minority who are stopped and found to have committed an offence, the sanctions that arise are intended to have a deterrent effect on future behaviour, while any intervention programmes they may enter aim to address the 'root causes' of their offending. Presumably, on this account, the majority who are not guilty of any offence will also be deterred from potential future offences by the active demonstration of police power and efficacy. However, McAra and McVie (2007, 2012) note that a growing body of international research suggests that 'system contact', such as involvement with the youth justice system and, in particular, experience of more severe forms of sanctioning, is more likely to result in enhanced offending than in diminished offending. 'Taken to its extremes, this research would suggest (in a manner akin to labeling theory) that contact with the youth justice system is inherently criminogenic' (2007: 318).

Evidence to this effect has accrued over a relatively long period of time. Farrington (1977) found that self-reported delinquency was higher among a group of boys from London first convicted at age 14–18 than among a matched group of unconvicted boys (matching was via similarity on a self-reported delinquency scale at age 14). Farrington et al. (1978) found a similar effect for those who had their first convictions aged between 18 and 21, again compared with a group not convicted between those ages. Similar results have been reported elsewhere (e.g. Tracey and Kempf-Leonard, 1996; Huizinga et al., 2003).

In their own study, McAra and McVie (2007) use data from the Edinburgh Study of Youth Transitions and Crime to examine this issue. The Edinburgh study is a longitudinal study of a cohort of young people in Edinburgh aged 11 or 12 in 1998. It then returned to them annually for the next six years (and at less frequent intervals subsequently). Two findings are of particular relevance here. First, in a model predicting a charge between sweeps three and four (aged around 14–15), which controlled for socio-demographic and behavioural correlates such as socio-economic status and self-reported offending, the strongest predictor by far of reporting a police charge at sweep four was having been charged by police at earlier sweeps. This pattern was also evident at other stages of the Scottish youth justice system. Second, a detailed analysis considering desistance from offending concluded that contact with the criminal justice system was associated with a diminished likelihood that young people would cease committing crime: 'significant desistance from offending is apparent among young people who have either no or minimal system contact, whereas those who are drawn furthest into the system with the aim of receiving intervention to address their behavioural problems are inhibited in this regard' (2007: 334).

Stop and search is one of the gateways into the criminal justice system, and may be implicated in processes such as those described above to the extent that it draws people (differentially) into the system. Yet, even stops/stop and searches that do not result in an arrest or other sanction have been linked to later offending. A recent paper using multi-wave longitudinal data from a 'gang resilience' project in the US (Wiley and Esbensen, 2013) reported that merely experiencing a police stop at Wave two was associated with greater self-reported offending at Wave three. Again drawing on labelling theory, the authors also found that experiencing a police stop was associated with lower anticipated guilt in relation to, and greater neutralisation of the effects of, potential acts of crime. That is, being stopped by police seemed to alter young people's perceptions of crime in a more permissive direction.

If the findings from these studies apply in England and Wales – and there is no reason to suggest they would not – the implication would be a kind of ratcheting effect, as increased contact predicts increased offending and further contact. One important point is that these studies take into account the idea that young people with more permissive orientations towards crime, and who commit more delinquent acts, are more likely to be stopped or charged. In McAra and McVie's (2007) study, for example, the estimated effect of previous charges on the odds of a charge at sweep four was conditional on self-reported offending. It was not simply that those who reported an earlier charge were offending more at the later date – there was something about earlier criminal justice system attention *in and of itself* that predicted a greater chance of a later charge.

In Edinburgh, much of this ratcheting effect appears to take effect by agencies identifying the 'usual suspects' (McAra and McVie, 2005), often on class and geographical bases, who become the principal focus of official attention and who are constantly recycled through the system. Add to this the likely effects of institutional racism (and personal bias), and it is not hard to envisage that many of those from BME populations regularly targeted by stop and search activity will find themselves classed as the usual suspects and pulled into the processes described above.

Work by May et al. (2010) in England and Wales suggests exactly this. Looking at police and criminal justice practice across four police Basic Command Units and 12 Youth Offending Teams, they found that 'proactive policing', of the type characterised by high levels of stop and search, was unevenly spread both geographically and in terms of the types of crime targeted. They concluded that in the areas studied 'a considerably higher proportion of arrests of Asian, black and mixed race teenagers originate from proactive work than arrests for other groups' (2010: 34). They also found that, once arrested, mixed-race defendants were more likely to be charged than their white counterparts, while black and mixed-race defendants were more likely to be remanded in custody (2010: vi). May et al. thus concur with the Home Affairs Select Committee, which noted, in 2007, that young black people are nearly twice as likely as their white counterparts to enter the criminal justice system as a result of being stopped and searched (Home Affairs Select Committee, 2007: 45).

As well as having a net negative effect on the relationship between the police and the policed, then, stop and search may undermine citizens' sense of belonging to the social groups the police represent. It might also trigger more concrete processes of social exclusion, as those who are stopped run higher risks of being drawn into the criminal justice system, with negative implications in terms of deviancy amplification, deepening entry into the system, and consequent reduction in life chances. This is fully in line with the predictions of the procedural justice model, which posits that unfair experiences at the hands of criminal justice agents, such as the police, will damage people's assessments of their legitimacy (and, indeed, the legitimacy of the law) and undermine their sense of belonging to the social groups the police, in particular, represent, making them more likely to break the law (Tyler, 2006). In their recent study, for example, Jackson et al. (2012b) found that 'unsatisfactory' contact with the police was associated with a higher probability of self-reported offending behaviour, with most of this statistical effect flowing through procedural justice judgements.

Reconsidering 'effective' stop and search

The research outlined above contains four core messages. First, ordinary people as well as academics and human rights lawyers care deeply about the fairness of the police and the wider criminal justice system. Encouraging a sense that the criminal justice system is unfair may in itself be a negative impact of current stop and search practice. Second, when it comes to interactions between police and public, notions of fairness play out most importantly at the level of process. People place less emphasis on outcome or distributive fairness, although in relation to stop and search questions of procedural and distributive fairness are closely intertwined. Third, due to the asymmetry effect described above, excessive use of stop and search undermines people's sense of the procedural fairness of police and undermines legitimacy and cooperation. Fourth, excessive or disproportionate police-initiated contact is linked with social exclusion. Symbolically, when it is experienced as unfair, officer behaviour can communicate to people that they are not valued or respected within, and serve to push them away from, the important social groups the police represent. Materially, it may drag people into the criminal justice system and damage their future potential to participate fully in society.

Taken together, these messages have significant implications for the willingness – indeed, ability – of individuals and communities to cooperate with the police and for the ways in which people seek to manage the 'law and order' problems that confront them. Attempting to solve such problems without the assistance of the police may carry a significant social and economic penalty that could itself predict further confrontational contact with the police, creating a downward spiral of lost trust, alienation and confrontation.

Contrast the evidence outlined above, and described in depth in many other studies, with the uncertainty concerning the effectiveness of stop and search. Recall that this is one of the core methods of British policing: the formal powers are used over one million times a year, and there are many more stops that do not make it into formal records. There is, however, essentially no evidence relating to the effectiveness of stop and search in comparison with other policing methods, and, furthermore, very little evidence concerning the marginal effectiveness of stop and search in apprehending or deterring offenders or reducing crime. It is unclear how much, if at all, increasing general levels of stop and search would improve outcomes in terms of offenders caught or deterred (see Miller et al., 2000).

There is some research suggesting that highly targeted 'applications' of stop and search activity can produce positive results, particularly when they are part of problem-oriented or 'pulling levers' policing strategies prioritising the highest-crime areas (Ratcliffe et al., 2011). Yet there is also much to suggest that stop and search is not only often instrumentally ineffective but also actively counter-productive. Research into the use of police stops in relation to drug use and dealing, for example, has suggested that many users are not deterred from offending by the threat of being stopped and searched, but merely move their activity elsewhere or make a greater effort to conceal it (Ream et al., 2010). Delsol discusses these issues in more depth in Chapter 5 of this volume. In sum, it seems that, while stop and search can provide useful results in some places at some times, we simply do not know whether it is more or less effective than other modes of policing, or whether it generates desired outcomes, such as increased arrest rates, detection rates or deterrence.

While we know very little about the effectiveness of stop and search in instrumental terms, though, we know quite a lot about the damage it may do to trust, legitimacy, cooperation and compliance.[4] Furthermore, the effectiveness and fairness of stop and search, often treated as separate aspects of the practice, are in reality likely to be closely intertwined. To be effective in dealing with crime, the police need the support and cooperation of the people and communities they serve, and all available evidence suggests that, *as currently practised*, stop and search damages this, certainly at the individual level and possibly also at the community level. In as much as it undermines the legitimacy of the police in the eyes of those who experience it, moreover, far from deterring crime, stop and search may actually encourage offending (Tyler, 2006; Jackson et al., 2012a; see also Sherman, 1993); and there are other reasons to suggest that stop and search may be actively criminogenic, promoting, instead of inhibiting, the likelihood of future offending. Any immediate or short-term 'returns' from stop and search, in the form of crimes prevented or deterred, or arrests, may be offset, in the long run, by its unintended negative consequences.

A further potential effect of stop and search, at least at some times and in some places, may thus be to make policing more difficult and less effective, and generate higher, not lower, levels of crime. On a more optimistic note, it follows that a more parsimonious use of the power, targeted to the times and places where it may be most useful and more stringently governed in terms of ensuring procedural and distributive fairness, might minimise the damage done to trust, legitimacy and cooperation, making policing easier and more effective.

Conclusion

There is much we still do not know about the impact of stop and search on individuals and communities. Perhaps partly because of this, current debates and research in the UK seem stuck in a groove of argument and counter-argument about the existence of, and reasons for, ethnic disproportionality. It seems to me that this debate has yet to produce a resolution precisely because the *effects* of stop and search have received relatively little attention. There are significant gaps in existing research, particularly in relation to the identification and quantification of the concrete outcomes of current practice. This gap is often filled by 'abstract' arguments concerning the inherent unfairness of the current situation, which are as compelling to those on one side of the discussion as they are unconvincing to many on the other.

One way out of this impasse may be to move towards a more integrated approach that considers questions of fairness alongside, and as part of, questions of effectiveness. At the present time, the weight of evidence favours the hypothesis that because stop and search damages trust and legitimacy, and sucks people unnecessarily into the criminal justice system, it generates at least as many dis-benefits as benefits in relation to police effectiveness and efficiency. This hypothesis remains subject to further testing, and may need to be revised. But, if correct, it suggests that in the long run making stop and search fairer (both procedurally and distributively) may make it more effective, precisely because greater fairness would minimise many of the potential negative effects outlined above.

Notwithstanding the possibility of such a positive-sum relationship, it may equally be the case that, unlike other areas of policing (Bradford et al., 2013), effectiveness and fairness are separate and even competing aspects of this aspect of police practice, and that a zero sum relationship pertains between them (Bowling, 2008). That is, in terms of stop and search specifically, more effective policing may well mean less fair policing, and vice versa. If this is so, proponents of the status quo (and advocates of change) should ask themselves not whether stop and search can undermine police effectiveness, but how much unfairness they are prepared to tolerate for incremental increases in effectiveness, howsoever both are defined. How many people drawn unnecessarily and disproportionally into the criminal justice system is too many? Is it right that police practice can serve to (pro)actively exclude people from identities and social groups they value? How much damage to the public's readiness to cooperate with the police is too much? Answers to these and related questions may, in and of themselves, promote a new way of thinking about stop and search.

Notes

1. Stop and search conducted under the Police and Criminal Evidence Act (PACE) 1984 and other legislation comprises only a proportion of the overall number of 'police stops' that occur each year. Significantly more people are stopped than are stopped and searched, one obvious example of the wider category being 'stop and account' encounters. In this chapter, I am interested not simply in stop and search as legally defined but in the wider category of police–public interactions initiated by officers in an enforcement context. I therefore use the term 'police stop' (or just 'stop') to refer to any encounter in which police interdict citizens and ask them to account for themselves in some way; such encounters may or may not go on to become 'stop and searches', and they may or may not have a legal basis; the key point is, perhaps, that they are experienced as a stop by the individual concerned. Stop and search, by contrast, refers directly to encounters conducted under the relevant legislation. In practice this may often be a rather fine distinction,

and the ideas described here will apply equally to 'stops' and 'stop and searches'.
2. The author would like to thank the Metropolitan Police Service for permission to analyse the 2010 BME Survey. This paper constitutes part of a wider collaboration between the author and the MPS Strategy, Analysis and Research Unit. Research produced by this collaboration has enabled structured discussions within the MPS concerning approaches to improving Londoners' experiences of policing, and is part of a wider programme of research on confidence and satisfaction in London policing.
3. Structural equation modelling (SEM) is a statistical technique that allows simultaneous estimation of (a) latent or unobserved variables and (b) the relationships between them. SEMs have two components. The first is the 'measurement model', wherein observed indicators (here, survey questions) are used to measure unobserved latent constructs (such as trust in police procedural fairness). The second component is the structural model, wherein relationships between latent constructs are estimated via standard regression techniques. Two advantages of this technique are that latent variable techniques allow better measurement of key constructs, and that SEMs allow estimation of direct and indirect statistical effects in a transparent fashion.
4. It should be noted that the negative implications of much research in this area are somewhat tempered by findings which suggest, first, that procedural fairness during stop encounters might mitigate their negative implications (Mazerolle et al., 2012), and, second, that there appears to be support among the public for the use of the power in a general or abstract sense, albeit with many reservations about the way it is used in practice (FitzGerald, 1999; FitzGerald et al., 2002; Quinton and Olagundoye, 2004).

7
Counter-Terrorism Policing
Tara Lai Quinlan and Zin Derfoufi

The policing landscape has been dramatically reshaped by the emergence of 'the new terrorism' (Zedner, 2009; see also Innes, 2008; Field, 2009). Exemplified by a series of al Qaeda-inspired attacks, including the 2001 bombings of New York and Washington (9/11), the new terrorism is said to be unprecedented in terms of its global scale as well as the catastrophic nature of its aims and methods. While much terrorism activity is covered by standard criminal law, special procedures may be justified 'when there is an operational need for them, when their use is confined to cases of need and when it is proportionate to their impact on individual liberties' (Anderson, 2011: 5–6). Official responses to the new terrorism threat have been characterised by vastly expanded state power, enhanced anti-terrorism legislation, increased security measures, expanding counter-terrorism budgets and the strategic deployment of police resources towards counter-terrorism. As part of this trend, the UK has seen a 'vast increase' in 'counter-terrorism resources over the past five to 10 years' (Anderson, 2011: 5). While government officials repeatedly argue that some individual human rights and civil liberties may have to be sacrificed to promote collective security (Cole, 2003a), elements of the counter-terrorism strategy have proved controversial even among those who accept that special measures are required. Some of the sharpest criticisms have been reserved for the use of stop and search.

This chapter begins by providing a historical account of the development of modern terrorism laws, before going on to explore how stop and search powers have been deployed in the 'new terrorism era'. In many ways, it will be argued, stop and search for the purposes of counter-terrorism echoes the use of stop and search more generally: what was supposed to be an 'exceptional' power to combat the threat of terrorism has been normalised and used for routine policing matters;

black and minority ethnic groups have been disproportionately subject to the use of these powers; and the associated costs appear to outweigh the benefits. Rather than enhancing our collective safety, the misuse of terrorism-related stop and search powers has, it is argued, been counter-productive, harming targeted communities and jeopardising their willingness to cooperate with law enforcement agencies. In a further parallel with more general developments, a recent legal challenge has been followed by efforts to rein in some of the excesses associated with the use of stop and search for counter-terrorism purposes (see Chapter 3).

The development of exceptional terrorism powers

Although we may have entered a 'new terrorism' era, there are, nonetheless, significant continuities (Field, 2009). Various counter-terrorism measures, including stop and search powers, were established across the UK well before the emergence of al Qaeda-inspired terrorism, as successive governments sought to address the conflict over Northern Ireland. The 'Troubles' lasted from the late 1960s to the late 1990s, and involved considerable violence as Republican groups sought to bring an end to British rule. Government efforts to counter the Republican terrorist threat hinged on an expanded set of police powers that did not exist under standard criminal law (Bonner, 2007). This separate set of laws was broader and more extensive than that dealing with regular criminal offences, and laid the foundations for a dual legal system, which was unprecedented in British history, and was justified by the government on the basis that it would help to restore public order (Hillyard, 1993; Bonner, 2007). A separate system was deemed necessary because standard criminal law was considered hamstrung by procedural rules, including legal mechanisms of accountability and transparency that hampered the effective management of the terrorism threat (Bonner, 2007). Newly created counter-terrorism powers were unencumbered by such safeguards, allowing police to operate with broad authority and without significant public scrutiny of their practices. As a result, terrorism suspects were dealt with more severely than regular criminal suspects, and faced greater restrictions on their civil liberties, including internment without trial as well as restrictions on residence and movement (Hillyard, 1993; Bonner, 2007).

The Prevention of Terrorism Act 1974 provided the primary basis for countering the terrorism threat from Northern Ireland. This legislation was enacted weeks after two bombings in Birmingham city centre which killed 21 people and injured 162 others (Bonner, 2007). At the time, the then home secretary Roy Jenkins argued that the Act was needed to address 'a different order of casualties from anything we previously had known' (quoted by Bonner, 2007: 98). The legislation granted police the power to stop and search anyone they suspected of being a supporter or member of the Irish Republican Army (IRA); to conduct warrantless arrests where there were reasonable grounds to suspect that a relevant offence had been committed, such as belonging to, or providing financial support to, the IRA or wearing clothing or carrying an article showing support for the group; to arrest without reasonable grounds anyone who was believed to be engaged in acts related to the 'commission, preparation or instigation' of terrorism; and to detain them without charge for 48 hours (HM Government, 1974: II 3.3). According to Hillyard (1993), the Act was used by the British state to treat Irish people as a 'suspect community'. Those drawn into the criminal justice system under this legislation, he argued, were considered suspect not because they were thought to be guilty of an illegal act, but because they were Irish: 'In attempting to prevent the spread of political violence to Britain, anyone living in Ireland as well as anyone with an Irish background living in England could 'be seen as falling within a category of people who may legitimately be stopped' (1993: 33). In this sense, the Irish community as a whole was viewed as suspect. More than 7,000 individuals were detained under the Prevention of Terrorism Act between 1974 and 1991, 86 per cent of whom were released without charge or arrest, and the Act was implicated in a series of miscarriages of justice involving Irish suspects, including the Birmingham Six, the Guildford Four and the Maguire Seven, all of whom were eventually exonerated after spending lengthy periods in prison.

The Prevention of Terrorism Act was accompanied by a system of independent review that formed part of the renewal process for what was, theoretically, a temporary set of provisions (Anderson, 2014). Lord Shackleton was commissioned to undertake the first independent review and paid particular attention to the effectiveness of the legislation and its impact on the liberties of the subject. Further occasional reviews were undertaken in 1983 and 1984 before the review process was put on an annual footing. The independent reviewer is unable to investigate individual cases, but has unrestricted access to classified documents, ministerial correspondence and national security personnel, meaning that any 'criticism has the potential to be devastating' (Anderson, 2014: para. 2). Although both the independent reviewer (see Rowe, 1994) and the Royal Commission on Criminal Justice (1993) noted serious concerns about the Prevention of Terrorism Act, including its role in several miscarriages of justice, it was repeatedly renewed until it was replaced by the Terrorism Act 2000.

The Terrorism Act 2000

The Terrorism Act 2000 built on the temporary provisions designed to address the terrorism threat from Northern Ireland and provides 'an apparently complete anti-terrorist code' (Anderson, 2013: para. 1.7). By the mid-1990s the Troubles appeared to be heading towards a peaceful resolution, and Michael Howard, then home secretary, appointed Lord Lloyd of Berwick to investigate whether permanent anti-terrorism legislation was required (Gearty, 1999). Lord Lloyd concluded that such legislation was necessary to provide a general deterrent and recommended that the emergency stop and search powers provided by the Prevention of Terrorism Act be incorporated into permanent anti-terrorism legislation (Roach, 2011). The government accepted most of Lord Lloyd's recommendations, which formed the basis of the Terrorism Act 2000 (Bonner, 2007; Walker, 2008), and expanded these powers not only to address lingering Northern Irish terrorist threats but also to deal with a range of other domestic and international threats (Bonner, 2007). The new legislation adopted most of the central features of the Prevention of Terrorism Act, including modified criminal prosecution rules for terrorism suspects; enhanced stop, search and detention powers; travel restrictions at ports and airports; and the proscription of a number of terrorist organisations. By expanding and making permanent the provisions of previous temporary legislation, the Terrorism Act reinforced the general approach whereby terrorism offences are governed by a separate regulatory framework from other crimes. It also made broad, discretionary, proactive forms of policing that had, until then, been considered 'exceptional' a regular feature of British society.

The Terrorism Act 2000 contains three stop and search powers. Section 43 provides a conventional power that officers may use to stop and search anyone they 'reasonably suspect' of being a terrorist to determine whether they have anything in their possession which may constitute evidence that they are a terrorist (HM Government, 2000). The Act also included an 'exceptional' power that went beyond anything then present in Northern Ireland (Dickson, 2009). Section 44 allowed officers to stop and search a person or vehicle in an authorised area 'for articles of a kind which could be used in connection with terrorism' regardless of 'whether or not' they have 'grounds for suspecting the presence of articles of that kind' (HM Government, 2000: 45.1). Senior officers could authorise the use of this exceptional power in a specified area if they considered it 'expedient for the prevention of acts of terrorism' (2000: 44.3). Authorisations had to be confirmed by the secretary of state within 48 hours and could be renewed. Section 44 was authorised for the whole of London immediately after the Act came into force and remained in place for most of the decade, but was little used outside the capital (Dickson, 2009; Sanders et al., 2010).

Section 44 was effectively dismantled in 2011 after the European Court of Human Rights (2010) ruled that it contravened the right to privacy. The case was bought by Pennie Quinton and Kevin Gillan, a photographer and a protestor, respectively, who had been stopped and searched at an arms fair in East London in September 2003. Although the UK's domestic High Court held that the stop and search powers were provided for by law and were not disproportionate, a decision upheld by the Appeal Court and the House of Lords, the European Court (2010: 87) took a different view:

> In conclusion, the Court considers that the powers of authorisation and confirmation as well as those of stop and search under sections 44 and 45 of the 2000 Act are neither sufficiently circumscribed nor subject to adequate legal safeguards against abuse.

As a result of this ruling, Section 44 was repealed in March 2011, when it was replaced by Section 47A, which provides a more tightly circumscribed stop and search power. Section 47A still represents 'a significant divergence from the usual requirement to have reasonable suspicion', but the test for authorising its use requires that the person giving it '*must reasonably suspect that an act of terrorism will take place and considers that the powers are necessary to prevent such an act*' (Home Office, 2011c: 3.1.1, original emphasis). These conditions have proved so hard to satisfy that, to date, Section 47A has never been authorised in England, Scotland or Wales, and has only been authorised once in Northern Ireland (Anderson, 2013).

The Terrorism Act 2000 makes special provision for stop and search at ports, replacing similar powers that were available under the Prevention of Terrorism Act 1974 (Anderson, 2013). Schedule 7 provides a 'formidable' set of powers that are 'among the strongest of all police powers', requiring neither reasonable suspicion nor prior authorisation for use (Anderson, 2012: para. 9.3). These powers enable 'examining officers', who may be police, immigration or customs officers, to stop and question anybody to determine whether they appear to be, or to have been, concerned in the commission, preparation or instigation of acts of terrorism. Persons, luggage and vehicles may be searched for the same purpose. Examining officers were initially able to detain individuals for up to nine hours, subsequently reduced to six hours, in order to conduct thorough searches of the person and their property, to subject them to more in-depth questioning, to collect biometric information and to retain data on electronic equipment such as mobile phones and laptops (Home Office, 2014, 2014d). Reasonable force may be used to effect searches, and failure to comply with a duty under the Schedule, including answering questions, is a criminal offence punishable by a fine or up to three months' imprisonment. The 'right' to consult a solicitor is only made available once a person has been detained, although the High Court recently ruled that refusing access to legal advice prior to detention is unlawful and gave permission for a legal challenge to proceed to judicial review (High Court of Justice, 2013; *The Guardian*, 2014b).

Policing the crisis

The Terrorism Act 2000 had been in place for little more than a year when the attacks on New York and Washington reverberated around the world. Further al Qaeda-inspired attacks followed in Bali (2002), Madrid (2004) and London (2005) (7/7). The then New Labour government, like many other governments around the world, responded by accumulating more terrorism-specific powers to combat 'the most acute and prolonged threat from international terrorism that the UK has ever faced' (Anderson, 2014: para. 13), while also demonstrating solidarity with the US-led 'war on terror' (Bonner, 2007; Zedner, 2009; Roach, 2011). Officials argued that existing terrorism and criminal justice mechanisms were not sufficient to stop or investigate 9/11-style attacks, and that broader counter-terrorism measures were required (Zedner, 2007). They also insisted that the evolving global terror threat required greater deviation from standard criminal law, resulting in new legislation, procedures and tools that operated outside established procedural safeguards (Lowe, 2005; Zedner, 2009). Such developments proved controversial, as legal scholars observed that the hasty implementation of expansive counter-terrorism measures reflected the tendency of governments to overact in times of fear and crisis, resulting in severe curtailment of human rights and civil liberties (Cole and Dempsey, 2006; Walker, 2008) with potentially disastrous consequences for perceptions of state legitimacy (Innes and Thiel, 2008).

One of the first new pieces of legislation to be introduced was the Anti-terrorism, Crime and Security Act 2001, which came into force just three months after 9/11, and was described by one commentator as 'the most draconian legislation Parliament has passed in peacetime in over a century' (Tomkins, 2002: 205; see also Bonner, 2007; Roach, 2011). As well as enhancing existing investigative powers for terrorist financing, the Act provided measures to improve information-sharing and cooperation between international agencies; increased security at ports, borders and potential target sites like nuclear plants; and, most controversially, enhanced immigration rules to permit the indefinite detention of foreign national terrorism suspects who for practical or legal reasons could not be removed from the country (Bonner, 2007). Two years later, in 2003, the government launched a four-pronged Countering International Terrorism (CONTEST) strategy that assembled all aspects of the country's counter-terrorism arsenal and associated agencies under a single unified framework and focused their efforts on four strands: to *prevent* violent extremism, to *pursue* terrorists, to *protect* vulnerable areas, and to *prepare* to better withstand future attacks (Roach, 2011; see also Anderson, 2011). The expansion of the country's counter-terrorism capacity continued after 2005, when the 7/7 bombings and failed attacks of 21/7 'made it plain' that UK targets 'were threatened at least as much by home-grown terrorists as by those from abroad' (Anderson, 2011: para. 2.26). Less than a month after the 7/7 bombings killed 56 people, including the four bombers, and left more than 700 injured, the then prime minister Tony Blair announced that 'the rules of the game have changed' (quoted by Anderson, 2011: para. 1.8). The attacks on London challenged the general perception that the threat of al Qaeda-inspired terrorism emanated from foreign agents rather than domestic sources, sparking fears that existing policing measures were insufficient to stop the phenomenon of home-grown cells (Bonner, 2007). Such concerns gave rise to further expansion of existing powers through the introduction of more legislation, including the Terrorism Act 2006, which created a series of new offences, including encouragement of terrorism and dissemination of terrorist publications.

A new suspect community?

The expansion of the UK's counter-terrorism capacity to combat the threat of al Qaeda-inspired terrorism in the aftermath of 9/11 and 7/7 raised particular concerns about the role of ethnic or racial profiling and its impact on Muslim communities. Definitions of racial profiling vary along a continuum, ranging from the use of 'race' as the sole reason for the intervention through to its use alongside other factors (Ramirez et al., 2003; Delsol, 2009a). While there is no internationally agreed definition, Goodey (2006: 207) notes that 'ethnic profiling' is 'generally interpreted to mean the police practice of stopping someone for questioning or searching on the basis of their ethnic or "racial" appearance and not because of their behaviour or because they match an individual suspect description'. Ramirez et al. (2003: 1204) define racial or religious profiling as a circumstance where 'a law enforcement officer relies upon race, ethnicity, national origin, or religion as one of several factors in determining whom to stop, search, or question', while Delsol (2009a: 263) suggests:

> Racial profiling refers to the use by the police of generalizations based on race, ethnicity, religion or national origin, rather than individual behaviour, specific suspect descriptions or accumulated intelligence, as the basis for suspicion in directing discretionary law enforcement actions such as stops, identity checks, questioning or searches among other tactics.

Having generally been associated with the targeting of minorities in the US, particularly African Americans and Hispanics, for drug offences and traffic stops, racial profiling has become a controversial feature of the 'war on terror' (Goodey, 2006; Delsol, 2009a). After 9/11, counter-terrorism activities extended racial profiling to include Muslims and those perceived to be of Arab or Middle Eastern descent, subjecting them to a range of adversarial encounters, including car stops, aggressive enforcement of immigration laws, intrusive security screening at airports and removal from planes. Such encounters have served to reshape the experience of some British Asian communities, prompting claims that Muslims are being treated as a new 'suspect community' (Pantazis and Pemberton, 2009, 2011; McGovern, 2010). Traditional representations of British Asians and, by association, Muslims as hard-working, respectful, law-abiding citizens who were more likely to be victims than perpetrators of crime began to fragment from the late 1980s against a backdrop of protests over the publication of Salman Rushdie's novel *The Satanic Verses*, clashes over the first Gulf War, and a series of ethnically charged civil disturbances in Oldham, Bradford and Leeds during the summer of 2001 (Alexander, 2000; Parmar, 2007; Webster, 2007; Bowling et al., 2008). Such incidents fuelled concerns about an 'Asian crime "time bomb"' (Alexander, 2000: 7) and contributed to a perceptible shift in media portrayals of British Asians, particularly young Bangladeshi and Pakistani males, as angry, violent and pre-disposed towards crime and anti-social behaviour (Webster, 1997; Alexander, 2000; Lee, 2007; Parmar, 2007; Choudhury and Fenwick, 2011). The events of 9/11 and 7/7 cemented the position of Asian, and particularly Muslim, young men as the folk devils of the new terrorism era (Bowling et al., 2008; Mythen et al., 2009; Khalid, 2011; Pantazis and Pemberton, 2011).

While noting some important differences between the experiences of Irish people during the Troubles and British Muslims today, McGovern (2010) maintains there is much to be gained from comparing them (see also Pantazis and Pemberton, 2009, 2011; Hickman et al., 2011). 'The first and most obvious reason' for comparison, he notes, is because 'communities that find themselves at the sharp end of anti-terror legislation and policies tend to find much in common in what they experience and are made to feel' (McGovern, 2010: 9). Many of the measures adopted by the state to combat the conflict in Northern Ireland provided a template for more recent counter-terrorism measures, producing some notable continuities 'in the nature and scope of counter-insurgency policy and law' (2010: 9). One of the most striking elements of continuity is evident in the way emergency laws have been normalised. While Northern Ireland always had 'emergency legislation', counter-insurgency legislation has become a permanent feature of UK law since 9/11. As was the case in Northern Ireland, moreover, much of what is being done to combat terrorism in Muslim communities appears to be counter-productive: in both settings 'extraordinary measures' have undermined confidence in the rule of law and damaged state–community relations, leading to poorer intelligence and an increased potential for the very 'radicalisation' that such interventions were designed to combat.

Use of the powers

Stop and search under Section 44 of the Terrorism Act 2000 proved to be a particularly controversial feature of the government's attempts to combat the new terrorism. The number of stop-searches carried out under this provision increased sharply during the decade or so after 9/11 (see Figure 7.1), attracting considerable criticism. Increases in the use of Section 44 did not seem proportionate to the apparent scale of the terrorism threat, and formed part of a more general increase in use of stop and search, particularly that involving 'exceptional' powers (see Chapter 3). Lord Carlile, who served as the independent reviewer from 2001 to 2011, was highly critical of the use of Section 44, noting: 'If there is a single issue that can be identified as giving rise to most assertions of excessive and disproportionate police action, it is the

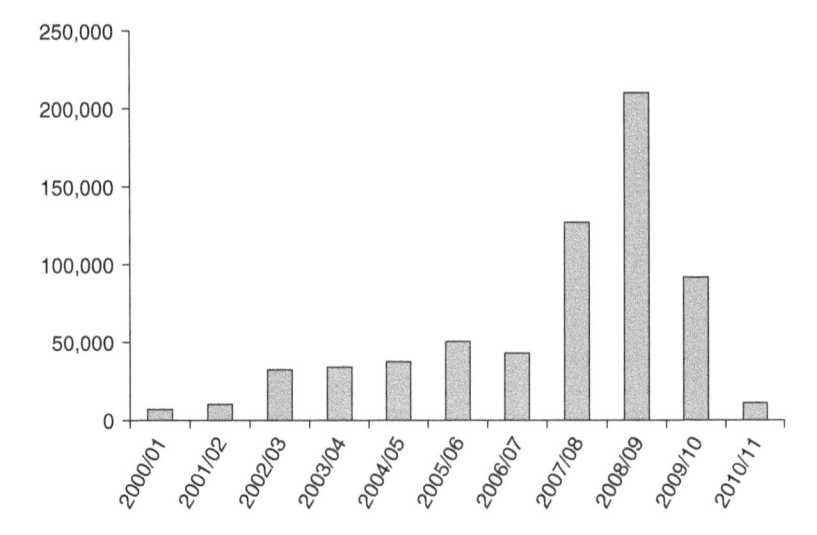

Figure 7.1 Stop-searches under Section 44 of the Terrorism Act 2000 in England and Wales
Note: Figures for 2000/2001 relate to stop-searches under Section 13 of the Prevention of Terrorism (Temporary Provisions) Act 1989, which was repealed under the Terrorism Act 2000.
Source: Home Office (2011c, 2014b).

use of Section 44' (Carlile, 2009: para. 42). While Section 43 searches were considered 'relatively straightforward' because of the requirement for 'reasonable suspicion', Section 44 searches were judged problematic for several reasons (2009: para. 143). First and foremost, Lord Carlile repeatedly asserted that Section 44 searches were being over-used and deployed for purposes other than those for which they were intended, noting (2009: para. 147):

> The alarming numbers of usages of the power (between 8,000 and 10,000 stops per month as we entered 2009) represent bad news, and I hope for better in a year's time. The figures, and a little analysis of them, show that *Section 44* is being used as an instrument to aid non-terrorism policing on some occasions, and this is unacceptable.

While making it clear that he had no criticisms of the careful use of Section 44 'to deal with operationally difficult places at times of stress, when there is a heightened likelihood of terrorists gaining access to a significant location', Lord Carlile was troubled by the inconsistent application of the power: 'I find it hard to understand why *Section 44* authorisations are perceived to be needed in some force areas, and in relation to some sites, but not others with strikingly similar risk profiles' (2009: para. 146). The vast majority of Section 44 searches were conducted in London, and this concentration proved stubbornly resistant to criticism, prompting Lord Carlile (2009: para. 147) to note:

> I now feel a sense of frustration that the Metropolitan Police still does not limit their *Section 44* authorisations to some boroughs only, or parts of boroughs, rather than to the entire force area. I cannot see a justification for the whole of the Greater London area being covered permanently, and the intention of the section was not to place London under permanent special search powers.

A similar sense of frustration was apparent over 'self-evidently unmerited searches' (Carlile, 2010: para. 177) and the role of racial profiling. While insisting that 'the criteria for *Section 44* stops should be objectively based, irrespective of racial considerations', Lord Carlile (2010: para. 177) maintained that 'ethnic imbalances' do not necessarily provide evidence of poor practice: 'if an objective basis happens to produce an ethnic imbalance, that may have to be regarded as a proportional consequence of operational policing', and yet:

> Examples of poor or unnecessary use of *Section 44* abound. I have evidence of cases where the person stopped is so obviously far from any known terrorism profile that, realistically, there is not the slightest possibility of him/her being a terrorist, and no other feature to justify the stop. *Section 44* stops and searches in the past year have included a senior retired Cabinet Minister and a 64 year old Q.C., both so obviously not possible terrorists as to make the procedure laughable, were it not for the intrusion into their civil liberties. In another case the subject was a lawyer of whom the only possible factor giving rise to the stop is that he is British Asian: in no way other than on a crude racial basis could an intelligent decision have been made to stop him. Chief officers must bear in mind that a *Section 44* stop, without suspicion, is an invasion of the stopped person's freedom of movement.

The progressively greater use of Section 44 during the decade after 9/11 weighed heavily on minority ethnic communities. Sharp increases were evident across all ethnic groups, including whites, but were particularly

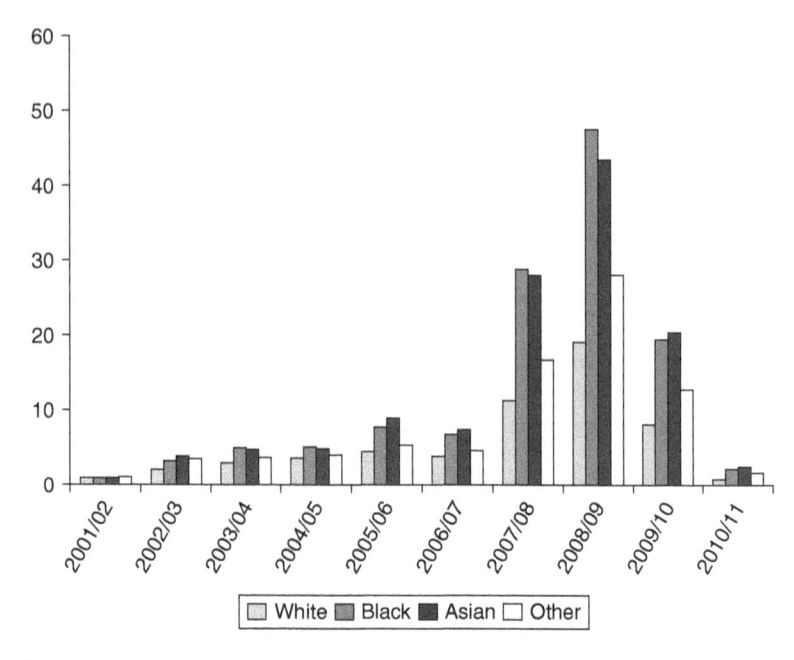

Figure 7.2 Trends in stop-searches under Section 44 of the Terrorism Act 2000 in England and Wales by ethnic appearance (numbers indexed to 2001/2002)

Note: The number of searches for each ethnic group per year is shown as a multiple of the number in 2001/2012. A value of two indicates that the number of searches within a specific ethnic group was double the number in 2001/2012 and a value of 20 indicates that it had increased by 20-fold. In 2001/2002 there were 6,629 searches of white people, 529 searches of black people, 744 of Asian people, 358 of people who were classified as being ethnically 'other' and 260 searches of people whose ethnicity was not known.

Source: Home Office (2004a, 2006); Ministry of Justice (2008, 2010, 2011).

marked in relation to Asian and black groups (see Figure 7.2). Searches of white people increased by almost 20-fold between 2001/2002 and 2008/2009, though this increase may have been inflated by police attempts to manipulate the figures, as Lord Carlile pointed to 'ample anecdotal evidence' that some people were being stopped 'in order to produce a racial balance' (2009: para. 140; see also 2010: para. 177). Even if police records are taken at face value, it is clear that increases in the number of Section 44 searches targeting white people were overshadowed by increases in the number targeting black and Asian people. The proportion of searches that were carried out on black or Asian people doubled over the course of the decade, from 15 per cent in 2001/2002 to 30 per cent in 2008/2009 and 2009/2010 (Home Office, 2004a; Ministry of Justice, 2010, 2011).[1] When Section 44 searches peaked in 2008/2009, the number of searches per 1,000 population varied from 2.6 for whites to 7.8 for Asians and 10.3 for blacks.[2] In other words, Asian people were stopped and searched under Section 44 at 3.0 times the rate of white people (up from 2.2 in 2001/2002) and black people were stopped and searched under this power at 3.9 times the rate of white people (up from 2.6 in 2001/2002).

Since 2007/2008 the Ministry of Justice has published stop and search data classified according to the self-defined ethnic identity of the person searched as well by their ethnic appearance as judged by the officer conducting the search. This data facilitates a more detailed assessment of variations in the experience of stop and search under Section 44 (see Table 7.1). The data is consistent with the suggestion that there is a general 'Asian' effect: Bangladeshis, Indians, Pakistanis and those who were classified as Asian 'other' all experienced heightened rates of Section 44 stop and search compared with the white British group. It is notable that Indians, who are a multi-faith group, were stopped and searched at a higher rate than Pakistanis, who are overwhelmingly Muslim, though both groups were stopped and searched at a lower rate than Bangladeshis, who are also overwhelmingly Muslim. These variations may reflect different patterns of residence, as Bangladeshis and, to a lesser extent, Indians are concentrated in London, whereas the vast majority of Pakistanis live outside the capital (see Heath and Martin, 2013). The relatively high rate of Section 44 stop and search experienced by Indians may also reflect the similar appearance of Sikh religious garments and those of South Asian Muslims, resulting in the former being mistaken for the latter (see Parmar, 2007). Black Caribbeans and black Africans also experienced heightened rates of stop and search under Section 44 – rates that were consistently higher than those experienced by Indians and Pakistanis – even though they are overwhelmingly Christian in their religious affiliation or secular (see Heath and Martin, 2013). While this may, once again, reflect patterns of residence (the majority of people in all the black groups live in London), it supports the notion that 'exceptional' counter-terrorism powers have been extended beyond their original purpose and absorbed into general crime control strategies that disproportionately target black communities (Hallsworth, 2006).

As with stop and search more generally, 'other' ethnic groups are subject to particularly high rates of intervention under Section 44. Such groups may include relatively recent migrant communities, and may be susceptible to police attention due to their youthful age structure

Table 7.1 Section 44 stop-searches by self-identified ethnicity in England and Wales (2008/2009 and 2009/2010)

	2008/2009		2009/2010	
	Rate per 1,000	Disproportionality Ratios	Rate per 1,000	Disproportionality Ratios
White				
British	1.6	1.0	0.7	1.0
Irish	4.1	2.6	1.8	2.6
Other	16.5	10.2	7.5	11.0
Black				
African	10.3	6.3	4.6	6.7
Caribbean	11.4	7.0	4.6	6.8
Other	18.3	11.3	6.9	10.1
Asian				
Bangladeshi	11.7	7.2	5.3	7.7
Indian	6.9	4.3	3.4	4.9
Pakistani	5.1	3.1	2.5	3.7
Other	12.0	7.4	5.8	8.5
Mixed				
African	3.2	2.0	1.2	1.8
Asian	2.4	1.5	1.0	1.4
Caribbean	2.2	1.4	0.9	1.3
Other	7.6	4.7	3.3	4.8
Chinese	8.0	4.9	3.2	4.6
Other	9.9	6.1	4.4	6.4

Notes: 1) Disproportionality ratios are calculated by dividing the rate per 1,000 for a minority group by the rate per 1,000 for the white British group. There are some slight anomalies due to rounding errors.
2) Stop and search rates were calculated using figures published by the Ministry of Justice (2011) and population estimates based on the 2011 Census (Office for National Statistics, 2012).

and distinct patterns of residence, as they tend to include a proportionately large number of people living in London (see Chapter 3 for discussion).

Schedule 7 may not have attracted the same level of public interest as Section 44 (Anderson, 2012), but it has placed considerable strain on Muslim communities, 'silently eroding' their 'trust and confidence in policing' (Choudhury and Fenwick, 2011: 28). Both independent reviewers since 9/11 have criticised the way Schedule 7 has been used. Lord Carlile (2010: para. 192) maintained that Schedule 7 remains 'a very important' aspect of the Terrorism Act 2000, but repeatedly suggested that 'the number of random or intuitive stops could be reduced considerably' without risk to national security. To this end he proposed that Schedule 7 powers should no longer be available to all ports officers, but should be confined to those who satisfactorily complete behavioural analysis training. Anderson (2013: para. 10.35) similarly noted that, while 'nobody disputes that the ability to stop and examine passengers at ports is an essential tool in the fight against terrorism', whether 'the power is proportionate in its current form' is a 'legitimate subject for both public debate and judicial scrutiny'. In his first annual report on the operation of anti-terrorism legislation, Anderson acknowledged that questions could be asked about whether elements of the power 'are necessary and subject to sufficient safeguards' (2011: 7). He also acknowledged concerns about the discriminatory application of Schedule 7, but noted: 'reliable figures are lacking, and I have not seen evidence that the ethnic breakdown of those examined is disproportionate to the terrorist threat (or even, though this is less relevant, to the ethnic composition of the travelling public)' (2011: 7).

Ethnic monitoring data covering the use of Schedule 7 has only been publicly available since May 2011, when it was first released in response to a freedom of information request (Anderson, 2012). Since then such data has been routinely assessed by the independent reviewer. In his 2013 report, Anderson presented data on Schedule 7 stops for the previous four years, noting that the number of people examined had fallen from 87,218 during 2009/2010 to 61,145 during 2012/2013. These numbers, he noted, should be set against the large number of people travelling through UK airports, seaports and international rail terminals, estimating that the figure for 2010/2011 represented fewer than 0.5 per cent of travellers. Of those who were examined each year, 3–4 per cent were held for more than one hour, while approximately 1 per cent were detained and had their biometric data taken (generally finger prints). In terms of ethnicity, Anderson concluded that the distribution 'changed very little over the period', noting: 'The central point remains that self-defined members of minority ethnic communities continue to constitute a majority of those examined under Schedule 7, and a very large majority of those detained and fingerprinted' (2013: para. 10.12 ; see also Table 7.2).

Although ethnicity data is not available for all port travellers, Anderson (2013: para. 10.14) claims 'it is overwhelmingly likely' that travellers from some minority ethnic groups – particularly those of Asian and 'other' (including North African) origin – are subject to

Table 7.2 Schedule 7 examinations by self-identified ethnicity in the UK (percentages)

	Examined Less than One Hour	Examined More than One Hour	Detained	Biometrics
2010/2011				
White	46	14	8	7
Black	8	15	21	21
Asian	26	45	45	46
Other	16	20	21	20
Mixed or not stated	4	6	5	6
2011/2012				
White	46	12	8	6
Black	8	14	23	23
Asian	25	36	35	35
Other	16	24	23	24
Mixed or not stated	5	14	11	12
2012/2013				
White	42	14	9	9
Black	8	14	22	24
Asian	22	33	31	30
Other	17	25	22	22
Mixed or not stated	11	15	16	15

Source: Anderson (2013).

examinations and detentions at a disproportionately high rate. In and of itself, however, he insists that this likely pattern provides 'no basis for criticism of the police', noting that if 'the power is being properly exercised' we 'would expect it to correlate not to the ethnic breakdown of the travelling population, but rather to the ethnic breakdown of the *terrorist* population' (2013: para. 10.15; original emphasis). In the absence of a 'definitive ethnic breakdown' of the terrorist threat, Anderson compares Schedule 7 detentions with stop-searches carried out by the Metropolitan Police Service under Section 43 of the Terrorism Act 2000 between 2009 and 2012 and charges for terrorist offences in Great Britain between 2005 and 2011: of those stopped and searched under Section 43, 10 per cent were black and 30 per cent were Asian, while 21 per cent of those charged with terrorist offences were black and 44 per cent Asian. These figures 'lend no support to the idea that persons of Asian appearance are more likely to be stopped under Schedule 7 than they are to be stopped under a suspicion-based power, arrested on suspicion of committing a terrorist offence or charged with terrorism' (2013: para. 10.16), prompting Anderson to conclude: 'As in previous years, I have seen no evidence, either at ports or from the statistics, that Schedule 7 powers are exercised in a racially discriminatory manner' (2013: para 10.17).

Comparisons with other criminal justice statistics should be treated with caution, not least because, as Anderson (2013: para. 10.16) notes, they provide 'only the roughest of indicators'. We might add that various criminal justice outcomes are subject to discrimination (Bowling and Phillips, 2002) and may not, therefore, provide a valid baseline for comparison. In addition, such comparisons arguably involve a degree of tautology, because who gets charged is partly a function of who is suspected and subject to police attention. It is, in other words, unsurprising that minority groups constitute a sizeable proportion of those charged for terrorist activities, given that they are subject to heightened rates of counter-terrorism policing. The question remains whether this disproportionate focus on minorities is reasonable and fair.

Impact and effectiveness

Preventative measures like Section 44 and Schedule 7 depend on the ability to identify potential terrorists in the absence of 'reasonable suspicion'. This kind of predictive law enforcement often relies on profiling individuals and identifying those at 'risk' of offending on the basis of group characteristics (Harcourt, 2007). Such an approach was seemingly endorsed by Ian Johnston, then chief constable of the British Transport Police, in the wake of the 7/7 attacks on London, when he argued (cited in Dodd, 2005):

> Intelligence-led stop and searches have got to be the way. We should not waste time searching old white ladies. It is going to be disproportionate. It is going to be young men, not exclusively, but it may be disproportionate when it comes to ethnic groups.

A similar underlying logic was outlined by Hazel Blears, then Home Office minister for community safety, crime reduction, policing and counter-terrorism, when she told the Home Affairs Select Committee on Terrorism and Community Relations (Home Affairs Select Committee, 2005: 167):

> Dealing with the terrorist threat and the fact that at the moment the threat is most likely to come from those people associated with an

extreme form of Islam, or falsely hiding behind Islam, if you like, in terms of justifying their activities, inevitably means that some of our counter-terrorist powers will be disproportionately experienced by people in the Muslim community. That is the reality of the situation, we should acknowledge that reality and then try to have as open, as honest and as transparent a debate with the community as we can. There is no getting away from the fact that if you are trying to counter the threat, because the threat at the moment is in a particular place, then your activity is going to be targeted in that way.

According to critics, profiling is ineffective and 'encourages sloppy policing and wasteful expenditure of resources' because the 'proxies of ethnicity and political or religious association are so inexact and overboard that the vast majority of those questioned or detained are certain to be wholly innocent' (Cole, 2003b: 302; see also Ramirez et al., 2003; Delsol, 2009a). Attempts by law enforcement officers to predict what are statistically rare forms of behaviour on the basis of general characteristics run the risk of false positives and false negatives, where innocent people are wrongly suspected and would-be offenders are wrongly deemed to be innocent (Harcourt, 2007). The problem of false positives is graphically illustrated by the low 'hit rate' associated with Section 44 and Schedule 7. Fewer than 0.5 per cent of the many thousands of Section 44 searches carried out each year yielded an arrest for terrorist offences, and these searches were more likely to result in

Table 7.3 Stop-searches and resultant arrests under sections 44 and 47A of the Terrorism Act 2000 in England and Wales

	Searches	Arrests	Terrorism Arrests	Terrorism Arrests (%)
2000/2001	6,400	45	1	0.02
2001/2002	10,200	189	20	0.20
2002/2003	32,087	380	19	0.06
2003/2004	33,798	491	19	0.06
2004/2005	37,013	468	64	0.17
2005/2006	50,047	563	105	0.21
2006/2007	42,834	495	28	0.07
2007/2008	126,706	1,234	19	0.02
2008/2009	210,013	1,249	10	< 0.01
2009/2010	91,567	438	2	< 0.01
2010/2011	10,994	78	0	0.00

Source: Home Office (2011c, 2014b).

an arrest for other offences (see Table 7.3). Outside Northern Ireland, no Section 44 search has ever led to a conviction for terrorism offences, prompting Lord Carlile (2009: para. 148; see also 2010: para. 185) to conclude: 'I am sure that safely it could be used far less. There is little or no evidence that the use of *Section 44* has the potential to prevent an act of terrorism as compared with other statutory powers of stop and search.'

Similar problems have been identified with Schedule 7. According to Anderson (2013: para. 10.18), Schedule 7 examinations produced 31 terrorism-related arrests at ports during 2010/2011 and 24 such arrests during 2011/2012.

> This means that only 0.04% and 0.03% respectively of those examined under Schedule 7 were arrested: a minuscule proportion when compared with the arrest rates after exercise of stop and search powers, including under TA 2000 section 43. These striking figures underline the point that terrorists make up an infinitesimal proportion of the travelling public. It is important for police to recognise that in the absence of clear incriminating intelligence, the overwhelming likelihood is that any person stopped will not be a terrorist, regardless of their ethnicity.

Most of the Schedule 7 stops that resulted in terrorism-related arrests were said to have been made on the basis of intelligence rather than intuition or 'copper's nose'. Having made the necessary inquiries, Anderson (2013: para. 10.56) was unable to identify 'any case of a Schedule 7 examination leading directly to arrest followed by conviction in which the initial stop was not prompted by intelligence of some kind'. Noting that UK terrorists are 'of all colours', including a substantial proportion who are white, Anderson (2012: para. 9.26) reminded those involved with the application of Schedule 7 that 'perceived ethnic background or religion should not be used, alone or in combination with each other, as the sole reason for selecting a person for examination'. The focus on minority ethnic groups, he argued, provides 'no basis for criticism of the police', but does 'underline the need for vigilance, particularly when some minority communities are understandably sensitive about the application of Schedule 7' and when 'apparently innocuous decisions (for example, to check the plane from Pakistan rather than the plane from Canada) may reflect unconscious racial bias' (2012: para. 9.26).

The diversity of the terrorism threat also highlights the potential for false negatives. There are various examples, often involving Muslim converts, of individuals engaging in al Qaeda-inspired terrorist attacks who do not conform to narrow appearance-based profiles. These include Richard Reid, the mixed-'race' 'Shoe Bomber', who attempted to detonate a bomb hidden in his shoes on a transatlantic flight during 2002; Jamaican-born 7/7 bomber Germaine Lindsay and his British wife, Samantha Lewthwaite, dubbed the 'White Widow', who is suspected of being a member of the al-Shabaab terror group; Umar Farouk Abdulmutallab, the Nigerian 'Underwear Bomber', who attempted to detonate explosives on a transatlantic flight from Amsterdam to Detroit during 2009 after his father had alerted the authorities to his potentially radicalising conduct; and Michael Adebolajo and Michael Adebowale, both British-born Muslim converts of Nigerian heritage, who killed Fusilier Lee Rigby in May 2013. Appearance-based profiles may also be actively subverted by the recruitment of 'clean skins' (persons not known to the police) who do not fit the profile of a terrorist suspect (Anderson, 2013).

Assessing the benefits of preventative measures like Section 44 and Schedule 7 is obviously difficult, but the associated arrest rates are low even by the modest standards of suspicion-based powers. As such, it is unclear what these 'exceptional' measures add that could not be achieved through other means, including more carefully circumscribed stop and search powers. It is likely that 'exceptional' powers carry higher costs than suspicion-based powers because they are applied less selectively and are subject to fewer procedural safeguards (See Chapters 2, 6 and 8). The damage that counter-terrorism policing has done to community relations has been well documented, with the former independent reviewer stressing: *'terrorism related powers should be used only for terrorism-related purposes*; otherwise their credibility is severely damaged. The damage to community relations if they are used incorrectly can be considerable' (Carlile, 2010: para. 176, original emphasis). Levels of trust and confidence in the police are lower now among Asian and Muslim communities than they were before 9/11, and the disproportionate use of stop and search has been identified as a particular grievance, creating a sense that these communities are being unfairly targeted, generating feelings of intimidation, powerlessness and anger (Kundnani, 2009; Mythen et al., 2009: 744; Choudhury and Fenwick, 2011; Hickman et al., 2011; Parmar, 2011; Awan, 2012). Section 44 is said to have been 'catalytic in generating social and political disenfranchisement' (Parmar, 2011: 377), while similarly detrimental effects have been described in relation to Schedule 7. Being questioned and possibly detained at ports has become a routine feature of the travel experience for some Muslims (Choudhury and Fenwick, 2011), prompting decisions to travel from distant ports in an attempt to reduce the risk of being stopped (Anderson, 2013). The intrusive nature of the searches and questioning about religious practices is said to have compromised carefully balanced and mutually reinforcing British Muslim identities by giving greater prominence to Islamic characteristics at the expense of national pride (Choudhury and Fenwick, 2011; Hopkins, 2011; Blackwood et al., 2012a, 2012b).

The relationship between procedural justice, trust and confidence, and cooperation with police (see Chapter 6) has particular implications for stop and search in the context of counter-terrorism. Where communities feel they are unfairly targeted, the police are less likely to be viewed as a legitimate authority (Weitzer and Tuch, 2002; Tyler and Wakslak, 2004). Reduced trust and confidence among Asian and Muslim communities has been associated with less willingness to engage with police, even on safety issues including hate crime, while reluctance to pass on potential intelligence has been attributed to fear of an excessive police response and a perceived lack of police interest in non-terrorism-related matters (Spalek et al., 2009; Choudhury and Fenwick, 2011; Huq et al., 2011). Suspicion and concerns about exploitation have also shaped community responses to police attempts to develop voluntary law enforcement–community partnerships, particularly where such initiatives are geared towards obtaining short-term community intelligence on terrorism (Spalek, 2010; Choudhury and Fenwick, 2011). Attempts to create partnerships have been more positively received and secured greater cooperation where they have involved longer-term trust-building efforts and addressed a variety of community concerns beyond terrorism (Spalek, 2010).

Striking a balance?

After almost a decade of expanding counter-terrorism resources, the UK entered a period of 'cautious liberalisation' (Anderson, 2013: para. 1.7). This process was ushered in by the European Court's decision on Section 44 and accelerated by a change of government and a growing sense of security after 'several years without a fatal terrorist attack in Great Britain' (2013: para. 1.8). Some changes, including the repeal of Section 44 and introduction of enhanced safeguards on biometric data, have been welcomed by the independent reviewer as being of 'considerable practical significance' (2013: para. 1.9). The loss of Section 44 'appears on balance to have been a positive development', removing 'an important source of resentment amongst Muslims' without any apparent 'countervailing disadvantage' (2013: para. 9.17). Other welcome developments include the more modest use of Section 43, at least in London; the introduction of stricter time-limits on examination and detention under Schedule 7; and the restraint shown in relation to Section 47A, which has never been activated except for a single use in Northern Ireland (2013: para. 9.19):

> Overall, the development of stop and search since 2010 has been positive. It demonstrates that in some fields at least, terrorism-specific powers can be significantly scaled back without noticeable damage to public safety. Indeed the argument can be made that the removal of a widely-used and much-resented power has reduced community tension and assisted policing by consent.

While commending the government for the action it was taking, the independent reviewer retained reservations about the patchiness of some of its efforts, including the limited nature of the consultation and proposed reform of Schedule 7. It was particularly 'regrettable' that the consultation did not consider whether it is necessary to have such a power without the requirement for reasonable suspicion. Some of what has been put in place, moreover, has been accompanied by contingency plans that have been designed to be used if 'the threat picture worsened' (Anderson, 2013: para. 9.19). Several factors, including the murder of Private Lee Rigby and ongoing violence in Northern Ireland, have prompted the stricter application of existing laws and renewed interest in developing further measures. Given these competing influences, we find ourselves 'at a crossroads, from which the future direction of travel is not clear... History suggests, however, that a strong influence on the future direction of antiterrorism law will be the incidence (or otherwise) of terrorist violence in the years ahead' (2013: para. 1.10–1.11).

Conclusion

Stop and search in the context of counter-terrorism offers a cautionary tale, encapsulating many of the worst features of this kind of intervention. A threat-based rhetoric has been used to justify a disproportionate police response, circumventing conventional procedural safeguards and further alienating already marginalised communities. Mirroring earlier experiences in Northern Ireland, 'exceptional' powers have been routinised and absorbed into general crime control strategies. As a result, examples of misuse 'abound' involving individuals far removed from any known terrorism profile. Particular concerns have been registered about the way Asian, and particularly Muslim, groups have been cast as the new 'suspect community', while counter-terrorism measures have also contributed to the continued over-policing of black people. The costs associated with such tactics have been well documented, and include loss of trust and confidence in the police, alienating the very communities whose cooperation is most needed to combat the threat of terrorism. Tangible benefits are harder to identify, and the irony is that, where civil liberties and security are pitted against each other, both may ultimately be compromised. After nearly a decade of expanding counter-terrorism resources, we have arguably entered a new phase involving attempts to find a better 'balance' between liberty and security. Such efforts have produced a tentative, precarious settlement, but one that may be upset at any time. It remains to be seen whether the real lessons of the 'new terrorism era' have been learned.

Notes

1. These figures exclude cases where the ethnicity of the person searched was not known.
2. Stop and search numbers were taken from Home Office (2004a) and the Ministry of Justice (2010, 2011). Disproportionality ratios for 2001/2002 were calculated using population estimates based on the 2001 Census (see Home Office, 2004), while those for 2008/2009 and 2009/2010 were calculated using population estimates from the 2011 Census (ONS, 2012). Disproportionality ratios for Section 44 searches in 2009/2010 were very similar to those for 2008/2009: 3.7 for black/white and 3.2 for Asian/white.

8
Regulation and Reform
Michael Shiner

The general democratic principle that police can intervene in the lives of citizens only under limited and carefully controlled circumstances (Marx, 2001) has significant implications for stop and search. As a coercive power, stop and search impinges on what the late Bernie Grant, former member of parliament for Haringey, described as the 'fundamental right' to 'walk the streets', raising important questions of liberty, fairness and equality (see NACRO, 1997: 3). Concerns about procedural justice focus on the quality of such encounters and the way negative experiences serve to undermine people's trust and confidence in the police, potentially fuelling a more general sense of alienation (see Chapter 6). Distributive justice, on the other hand, concentrates on who it is that is stopped and searched, raising particular concerns about the disproportionate focus on black and minority ethnic groups and the potential for discrimination. Although stop and search operates at the shallow end of the criminal justice system, it has important knock-on effects, helping to define who gets caught in the net, driving ethnic disparities at later stages of the process (May et al., 2010; Eastwood et al., 2013). Potential inequalities and injustices in the use of stop and search, therefore, are important not just in and of themselves, but because of the way they reverberate throughout the system.

Regulating police conduct is notoriously difficult, due partly to inherent features of the police role. Policing requires considerable discretion, not least because full enforcement of every law is impractical, and the degree of discretion afforded to officers increases further down the organisational hierarchy (Reiner, 2010; Cockcroft, 2013). Much of what front-line officers do, moreover, including stop and search, occurs away from the police station, out of sight of supervisors and managers. Different jurisdictions have responded to the challenges of regulating police stops differently, and the following analysis draws a distinction between 'consensus' and 'conflict' approaches. The consensus approach that has prevailed in England and Wales has sought to embed stop and search in an extensive body of regulations, but has floundered in the face of substantial barriers to reform, including police resistance. Ultimately, it is argued, such efforts have failed to get to grips with an unavoidable central paradox, whereby the police cannot be relied upon to ensure robust regulation themselves, yet are likely to resist and subvert external efforts to this end. In an attempt to chart a way out of the current impasse, a synthesis of consensus and conflict approaches is proposed, drawing on Braithwaite's (2002) model of responsive regulation.

Modes of regulation

The regulation of police conduct draws on two principal mechanisms: forward-looking policy interventions that seek to ensure officers comply with certain standards of behaviour; and remedial procedures, including litigation, that seek to provide some kind of redress when things go wrong. To the extent that either of these mechanisms is prioritised, quite different approaches may result. In the US, the emphasis is on court decisions rather than statutory legislation or 'managerial professionalism', creating a much more adversarial system than in England and Wales (Epp, 2009; Harris, 2013). After the collapse of the Civil Rights Movement, a flurry of 'law-inspired professional reforms' came together from the late 1970s to create 'a common policy framework' of 'legalized accountability', which aims to 'bring bureaucratic practice in line with emerging legal norms' (Epp, 2009: 2–3). A key source of legal accountability was virtually eliminated by a Supreme Court decision in 2001 that the Civil Rights Act 1964 does not provide a 'private right of action' to ordinary citizens or civil rights groups (Alexander, 2010), but other options remain. A recent class action lawsuit against the New York City Police Department proceeded on the basis that its use of stop and frisk was unconstitutional. In a landmark judgement, the Federal Court agreed that the Police Department's tactics amounted to a policy of 'indirect racial profiling' and called for a federal monitor to oversee a programme of reform (Goldstein, 2013). In light of this case, the Civil Rights Committee of the New York City Bar Association urged the City Council to pass a local law granting 'a private right of action' that is 'virtually identical' to the one that was previously available under the Civil Rights Act (New York City Bar Association, 2013). Stop and frisk practices may also be challenged under Section 14141 of the Violent Crime Control and Law Enforcement Act 1994, which prohibits 'the pattern or practice' of law enforcement that deprives people of their legal or constitutional rights (Chanin, 2014). Where evidence of misconduct is found, the Department of Justice is empowered to pursue prospective policy changes in order to enhance compliance with the law. Since the Act came into force, more than 20 state and local police departments have been found to be in violation of Section 14141, the vast majority of which have decided to settle rather than litigate, triggering a range of interventions, including policy change, enhanced officer training and the development of early warning systems. Such interventions remain exceptional, however, and have been criticised for being overly legalistic and for focusing on substantive compliance rather than sustainable reform (Chanin, 2014).

The regulation of policing in England and Wales leans heavily towards a consensus approach based on 'broad, programmatic policy reforms to the virtual exclusion of responsiveness to individual complaints' (Epp, 2009: 143). Rather than relying on judicial checks as in the US, the British government has favoured high-level official inquiries, national legislative reform and managerial control. Stop and search is subject to a legal code of practice, breaches of which constitute a disciplinary offence and are admissible as evidence in criminal or civil proceedings (Reiner, 2010; see Chapter 2), though compliance is largely treated as an internal police matter. Some remedial procedures have been put in place that potentially enable members of the public to pursue grievances against individual officers, including civil action and an independent complaints system that may lead to disciplinary action or criminal charges, but none of them operate very effectively (Reiner, 2010). There are, moreover, in-built features that militate against the use of these procedures. Following a wave of successful lawsuits against the police from the late 1980s, the Court of Appeal put a cap on exemplary damages, which drastically reduced the size of individual awards and stemmed the flow of cases (Epp, 2009). Financial barriers are also evident in the way remedial procedures are starved of necessary resources, with legal aid being cut for civil actions and not covering police complaints (Sanders et al., 2010).

Even when remedial procedures are pursued, they operate within some fairly tight constraints. Police officers are given 'unusually broad discretion in gathering evidence' and are rarely convicted (Epp, 2009: 143). This is partly because much that 'would be criminal if done by "normal" people is not criminal when done by the police' and it 'seems that many police actions take place in a legal wilderness' (Sanders et al.,

2010: 675, 717). Given this lack of legal provision, many fundamental 'rights' are not catered for, which means there are 'no effective remedies' (Sanders et al., 2010: 717). Evidencing misconduct can also be difficult because stop and search is often conducted in the absence of independent witnesses, with the result that few complaints are upheld (Independent Police Complaints Commission, 2012).

The road to regulation

The formal regulation of stop and search across England and Wales is a relatively recent development that has emerged as part of a broader cycle of crisis and reform that has engulfed the police (Reiner, 2010). Until the mid-1980s, officers had at their disposal a variety of ad hoc legal powers to stop and search suspects based on a mixture of local and national legislation (Rowe, 2004). In most instances police officers could use these powers when they had the slightest suspicion that a person had committed an offence and without any objective indicators, such as witness descriptions or crime reports. Subsequent attempts to regulate police stop and search have often arisen in response to particular crises that demonstrate malpractice, prompting various commissions and inquiries. Among the most influential inquiries were those led by Lord Scarman into the 1981 Brixton 'riots' and Sir William Macpherson into matters arising from the death of Stephen Lawrence. Although precipitated by very different events, both inquiries were centrally concerned with the policing of black communities and both were publicly heralded as 'watersheds' in Britain's relationship with 'race' (Neal, 2003: 56).

The beginning of always

The impetus behind the introduction of formal regulations governing the use of police powers was provided by the wrongful conviction of three teenage boys on charges arising from the murder of Maxwell Confait in 1972 (Reiner, 2010). Evidence that the boys had falsely confessed to the charges, having been maltreated while in police custody, prompted the creation of the Royal Commission on Criminal Procedure in 1977. The Commission's core concern was to balance the rights of the suspect with the requirement to tackle crime, which was reflected in its call for a uniform stop and search power that would be exercised within strict safeguards. This recommendation was eventually enshrined in the Police and Criminal Evidence Act (PACE) 1984, but only after one of the most serious outbreaks of public disorder in recent British history.

A few months after the publication of the Royal Commission report, concerns about the potential misuse of police powers were crystallised by a wave of urban unrest. Although disturbances occurred in numerous locations, it was the Brixton 'riots' that captured the public imagination and seemed to epitomise the pervading sense of crisis. Lord Scarman was appointed to head a public inquiry into the causes of the disturbances and to make recommendations with the aim of preventing further disorder. His report triggered 'a multifaceted reorientation of police thinking, which dominated police reform debates' for the rest of the decade (Reiner, 2010: 245). Insisting that the maintenance of public tranquillity should be prioritised over law enforcement, Scarman (1981) made several pointed criticisms of the way Brixton had been policed in the lead up to the disorder. The deprivations, frustrations and racial tensions of inner city life, he argued, had been aggravated by 'unimaginative and inflexible' police tactics, which lacked local support and impacted disproportionately on minority ethnic communities, alienating many innocent people who were caught up in them (1981: para. 4.50). The mass use of stop and search, in the form of Operation 'Swamp 81', was identified as the immediate trigger of the 'riots' and was judged to have been a serious mistake. Pointing to a general failure of formal liaison with local communities, Scarman reasserted the role of 'consent', which he considered essential to securing legitimacy for policing in a democratic society.

Racial tensions featured prominently in Scarman's assessment of the 'riots', which he characterised as 'essentially an outburst of anger and resentment by young black people against the police' (1981: para. 8.12). While noting 'the ill-considered, immature and racially prejudiced actions of some officers' (1981: para. 4.63), Scarman rejected the notion that British society was institutionally racist in the sense of discriminating 'knowingly, as a matter of policy' (1981: para. 2.2) and concluded that the 'direction and policies' of the police 'are not racist' (1981: para. 4.62). Although much criticised by left-wing commentators, this conclusion was, perhaps, largely presentational. Scarman's analysis of the 'disastrous impact' of stop and search demonstrated his awareness of the problem of institutional racism in the broader sense of the unintended consequence of organisational policies and he 'soft-peddle[d] the terms in which he couched his criticisms of the police' in part because he wanted to avoid 'a closing of the ranks against change' (Reiner, 2010: 163, 246). To prevent further disorder, Scarman's recommendations included greater police recruitment from minority ethnic communities; increased consultation through the introduction of statutory liaison committees; the creation of an independent review of complaints against the police; and the tightening of regulations against racially prejudiced behaviour by officers. While endorsing stop and search as being essential to confront street crime, Scarman called for safeguards to ensure that it was exercised with reasonable grounds for suspicion.

The Police and Criminal Evidence Act 1984

Reflecting the concerns of the Royal Commission and the Scarman Report, the Police and Criminal Evidence Act (PACE) sought to introduce the principles of balanced powers and safeguards, while guarding against the possibility of discrimination. As well as granting a new national stop and search power, the Act introduced a series of safeguards governing the use of such powers that are specified in a code of practice. PACE Code A outlines the principles governing the use of stop and search, emphasising that the powers must be used fairly, responsibly, with respect and without unlawful discrimination. Officers are reminded of their duty, under the Equality Act 2010, 'to have due regard to the need to eliminate unlawful discrimination, harassment and victimisation, to advance equality of opportunity between people who share a relevant protected characteristic and people who do not share it, and to take steps to foster good relations between those persons' (Home Office, 2013a: para. 1.1). The requirement that there are 'reasonable grounds' for suspicion attempts to guard against discrimination by ensuring officers have an 'objective basis' for suspecting somebody before they proceed with a stop and search (see Chapter 2). In addition to distributive concerns about discrimination, PACE reflects procedural concerns, placing a series of duties on officers regarding the application and monitoring of stop-search powers. Before proceeding, front-line officers must take 'reasonable steps' to inform the subject of the search of the officers' name and station; the legal power that is being exercised; the purpose of the search; and the grounds for it. Officers also have a general duty to make a record of the search, which conveys much of this information, and provide it to the person being searched. Supervising officers and senior officers are required to monitor the use of stop and search, taking action where necessary to ensure compliance with the regulations.

PACE has been billed as 'the single most significant landmark in the modern development of police powers' (Reiner, 2010: 212). By providing a statutory codification and rationalisation of police powers, alongside safeguards governing their use, PACE serves an important symbolic and practical function. While critics insisted the police would exceed their new extended powers, just as they had previously, the evidence is mixed. There are some areas, such as the handling of suspects, where much of what PACE calls for has become routine practice. Assimilation 'of the PACE rules into police culture and working practices has been uneven and incomplete', however, with much of it being 'ritualistic and presentational' and affecting 'little of substance' (Reiner, 2010: 215). Various problems have been identified with the regulations governing stop and search. Reasonable suspicion has been described as a 'slippery concept', which invites multiple interpretations and is often not met in practice; forms are not always completed, though rates of recording have improved over time; and supervision occurs only rarely (Sander et al., 2010: 74; See also Quinton et al., 2000; HMIC, 2013).

The Stephen Lawrence Inquiry

Despite the limitations of PACE, it took another crisis before concerns about the misuse of police powers translated into something more tangible. Four years after the then unsolved racist murder of black teenager Stephen Lawrence,[1] the newly elected Labour government established a public inquiry to examine matters arising from his death. The Inquiry, led by Sir William Macpherson (1999: para. 46.1), famously concluded that the flawed investigation into the case had been marred 'by a combination of professional incompetence, institutional racism and a failure of leadership by senior officers'. Institutional racism was said to exist 'both in the Metropolitan Police Service and in other Police Services and other institutions countrywide' (1999: para. 6.39). The Inquiry made 70 detailed recommendations covering a wide range of police activities, prompting the 'most extensive programme of reform in the history of the relationship between the police and ethnic minority communities' (Bowling and Phillips, 2003: 546).

Although stop and search was not the focus of the Inquiry, it came to feature prominently in its deliberations. The Inquiry held a series of public meetings and was struck by 'inescapable evidence' of a lack of trust between the police and minority ethnic communities, who 'clearly felt themselves to be discriminated against by the police and others' (Macpherson, 1999: para. 45.6). If there was one area of complaint that was universal, it was said to be the use of stop and search, while ethnic disparities in stop and search were identified as one of four areas where institutional racism was primarily apparent. While noting that other factors might be used in an attempt to explain these disparities, including demographic mix, school exclusions, unemployment and recording procedures, the Inquiry insisted: 'there remains, in our judgment, a clear core conclusion of racist stereotyping' (1999: para. 6.45).

The Macpherson Report is often compared favourably with the Scarman Report because it 'grasped the nettle of institutional racism' (Reiner, 2010: 251; see also Bowling and Phillips, 2003). But, on the specifics of stop and search, Macpherson followed Scarman's lead, endorsing the need for such a power and posing the issue as one of disproportionality rather than as one of an inherently problematic tactic (Lea, 2000). The issue for Macpherson, as for Scarman, was to regulate stop and search in a way that prevents racist stereotyping by officers. What this meant in practice was a call to tighten up the procedures introduced by PACE, with Recommendation 61 proposing that the recording requirement should be extended to cover all stops, including non-statutory stops, and all stop-searches made under any legislative provision, not just PACE (Macpherson, 1999: para. 47.61). Following this recommendation, PACE was revised so as to abolish 'voluntary' or 'consensual' stop-searches. Officers were also required to record stops that fell short of a search, but where they asked members of the public to account for themselves (that is to say, their actions, behaviour, presence or possession of anything) (see Chapter 2).

The impact of the Lawrence Inquiry has been mixed. Research commissioned by the Home Office reported positive changes in several areas, including police responses to hate crime, the management of murder investigations and the general elimination of racist language from the police service (Foster et al., 2005). But such improvements were not evident in all areas, and it was noted that forces had tended to focus on those changes that were most obviously identifiable and achievable. The greatest continuing difficulty was said to exist in relation to understanding and designing responses to the problem of 'institutional racism'. Despite 'the intentions of police forces and their staff', it was said that 'certain groups still receive an inappropriate or inadequate service because of their culture or ethnic origin' (Foster et al., 2005: ix). Similarly mixed findings were reported by two reports marking the 10-year anniversary of the Lawrence Inquiry, both of which identified enduring problems with disproportionately high rates of stop and search among black and minority ethnic groups (Bennetto, 2009; Rollock, 2009).

A more adversarial approach?

According to Sanders et al. (2010: 75), 'the enormous growth' in stop-searches since the introduction of PACE indicates that existing regulations have been 'largely ineffective' in restraining police conduct. This conclusion is reinforced by the stubbornly disproportionate focus on black and minority ethnic groups and steadily declining arrest rates (Miller, 2010; Sanders et al., 2010). The limitations of PACE became evident quite quickly, prompting calls for more litigious and judicial checks: 'By the mid-1990s many observers characterized the centralized reforms of British policing of the 1980s as a failure: managerial reform had no bite' (Epp, 2009: 145). Litigation against the police started to increase sharply shortly after the introduction of PACE, attracting considerable media attention and bringing 'into full public view the long-held complaints by minority communities of discriminatory and abusive police action' (Epp, 2009: 163). By routinely exposing the police to public embarrassment, these lawsuits hit them 'where it matters – in adverse publicity' and helped to 'redefine the problem from a conception of individual officer responsibility (the "bad apple" syndrome) to institutional responsibility' (Epp, 2009: 164). When the Court of Appeal put a cap on payments in 1997, the size of awards against the police plummeted and media attention faded.

Since the Lawrence reforms were implemented, stop and search powers have been rebalanced in ways that have effectively seen crime control values eclipse concerns about accountability and due process (Reiner, 2010; see also Sanders et al., 2010). As stop and search activity reached an all-time high, with massive increases in the use of exceptional powers circumventing the need for 'reasonable suspicion' (see Chapter 3), recording requirements were watered down as part of a concerted campaign against 'unnecessary' bureaucracy (see Shiner, 2010). Revisions to PACE, which took effect from early March 2011, removed the national requirement to record stop and account, with the vast majority of forces choosing to abolish this practice, and reduced the amount of recorded information required for stop-searches from 12 to 7 fields (The Police Foundation, 2012). Among the fields that have been dropped are the name and address of the person being searched and the outcome, which makes it more difficult to monitor repeat searches, measure effectiveness and hold officers to account (StopWatch, 2011).

The rebalancing of police powers away from concerns about accountability and due process had a polarising effect, giving rise to more adversarial responses. A successful legal challenge against Section 44 of the Terrorism Act 2000 was followed by a similar, though as yet unsuccessful, challenge to Section 60 of the Criminal Justice and Public Order Act 1994 (see Chapter 3). Both cases subjected police activities to adverse media attention (see, for example, Johnson, 2005; Dodd, 2011). The threat of enforcement action under equalities legislation has also been used by the Equalities and Human Rights Commission (EHRC, 2013) to intervene in a handful of forces where stop and search was deemed to be particularly problematic, leading to legal compliance action against two forces. While the use of exceptional powers plummeted following (impending) legal action, the EHRC intervention was accompanied by striking overall reductions in the number of suspicion-based searches, as well as some limited reductions in the disproportionate focus on black and minority groups, without any discernible impact on crime (EHRC, 2013; See Chapter 3).

Barriers to reform

The apparent failure to establish effective regulations governing the use of stop and search is, perhaps, unsurprising given the inherent difficulties involved and given what we know about police reform. In addition to substantial structural constraints, the prospects for effective regulation have been hindered by political barriers and internal police resistance.

Structural inequality

According to Reiner (2010), police reform strategies invariably lack a sociological analysis, which means they systematically fail to confront the nature of policing. Because police officers are routinely confronted by disorder, crime and other inherently contentious situations, he notes, it is only in the most exceptional circumstances that they will be regarded as anything other than a regrettable necessity. It has also been argued that there are aspects of the day-to-day work of the police organisation which generate and sustain an occupational culture supportive of racism (Lea, 2000). The use of stop and search as a means of policing 'dangerous populations' means predominantly white officers routinely coming face-to-face with members of black communities in confrontational situations, while rarely doing so outside law enforcement situations, making them particularly susceptible to stereotyping. As 'a form of generalised policing of whole communities and groups', therefore, stop and search is 'a major factor in generating police racism' (Lea: 2000: 231). The failure to address these structural dimensions has been identified as a substantial barrier to successful reform (Reiner, 2010: 251):

> With the 20:20 vision of thirty years' more experience of police discrimination in relation to race, it is clear that the Scarman Report

failed to end racial discrimination in policing. This was not because of its own failings, however, but because of the lack of political commitment to achieve the transformation of black people's social and economic circumstances, as well as the reforms of police organization and policy that it called for. In the continuing absence of a fundamental attack on economic and social disadvantage experienced by black and other ethnic minority people the widespread anger and sorrow produced by the Lawrence tragedy is likely to prove equally unsuccessful in achieving a real breakthrough in the vexed relationship between black people and the police and criminal justice system.

Although clearly important, structural constraints do not preclude the possibility of improving police/community relations. There is a large and growing body of literature on procedural justice showing that police conduct matters, in the sense that it can have a small positive impact on public trust and confidence and a much larger negative impact (see Chapter 6). At the very least, then, damage to police–community relations might be minimised by promoting procedurally just modes of intervention. As Reiner (1985) noted, moreover, the post-riots experience in the US suggests that police–public relations can be improved even in the face of worsening socio-economic deprivation and injustice if policing is predominantly based on a 'peace-keeping' philosophy (see Sherman, 1983). Improving relations between the police and black communities during this period were due largely to the influence of 'system' factors, particularly the rise of black political power in the form of massive increases in the number of black elected officials.

Lord Scarman's recommendations incorporated many of the features that contributed to the changes in the US and, 'in the absence of the possibility of black political control', were 'the nearest it might be possible to get in terms of a clear signal to police forces of the need for reform' (Reiner, 1985: 201). Scarman's emphasis on the need for improved community liaison and independent oversight is embodied in the PACE requirement that, in 'order to promote public confidence in the use of the powers', arrangements must be made for stop-search records 'to be scrutinised by representatives of the community, and to explain the use of the powers at a local level' (Home Office, 2013a: para. 5.4). The nature of these arrangements has, however, failed to confront the basic structural dimensions of police–community relations. For Lea (2000), the key regulatory problem is the lack of power within black and minority ethnic communities, which requires far-reaching structural changes in operational policing and the constitutional relationship of police forces with minority communities. If there were a developed system of police accountability in which elected representatives had the power to determine the general strategies and priorities of policing, he argued, black and minority ethnic groups could contribute to the setting of police goals and be taken seriously as a constituency. The introduction of elected police and crime commissioners in 2012 notwithstanding, established systems of accountability have fallen a long way short of such arrangements, not least because the potential for local influence has waned with the long-term trend towards greater centralisation (Jones, 2003; Reiner 2010). The form of accountability that police are expected to provide to external bodies, moreover, is 'explanatory and co-operative' rather than 'subordinate and obedient' (Marshall 1978: 61–3), which means that chief constables are required to give account for their decisions but are under no legal requirement to take account of any critical response (Reiner, 2010). Finally, local consultative committees are generally run by the police and lack independence. While noting there have been some successes, Lea (2000: 225) argues that most groups are largely 'talking shops' and have had little impact on relations between police and minority communities:

> What had been ignored was the issue of power. Police were willing to listen to those who agreed with them and would act as their supporters. But otherwise there was little incentive to listen to the demands or grievance of those not perceived to be politically powerful at either a local or a national level.

Subsequent research has confirmed that the 'damage limitation' approach to community consultation remains widespread, ensuring there is little meaningful independent scrutiny of police stops (Delsol and Shiner, 2006; Shiner, 2006). According to this approach, oversight of front-line officers is treated as an internal police matter, so that, outside the complaints procedure, there is little room for external agents to call individual officers to account for specific incidents. Where external scrutiny is carried out, moreover, it is typically based on corporate modes of accountability involving statistical information and passive forms of community engagement geared towards demonstrating there is not a problem.

Organisational resistance

The British police are famously 'reform resistant' and have been uniquely able to 'undermine, frustrate, withstand, invert and deny' externally imposed change agendas (Savage, 2003: 171). Nowhere has this been more evident than in response to the Scarman Report and the Lawrence Inquiry. Scarman's proposals met stiff resistance and outright hostility from the police organisation and were undermined by a police-orchestrated 'counter attack' that fostered 'the racist stereotype of the black, male, mugger' (Sim, 1982: 74). Shortly after the publication of the Scarman Report, the Metropolitan Police Service released annual crime statistics analysing street robbery by the ethnicity of the offender, 'highlighting the stereotype of the black mugger' in 'an unprecedented use of official statistics in a manner that had clear political implications' (Reiner, 1985: 90). Scarman's call for greater emphasis on community policing was also usurped by an ongoing process of militarisation, and his proposals to this end 'became a secondary appendage to the technological imperatives of the force' as police powers were extended and riot equipment made available on an unprecedented scale (Sim, 1982: 57; see also Institute of Race Relations, 1987).

The Lawrence Inquiry received a similarly hostile reception from police. Widespread anger was evident among officers, who felt the Inquiry had been unfair and that the failings it identified were rooted in incompetence rather than racism (Rowe, 2004; Foster et al., 2005). The 'accusation' of 'institutional racism' was widely viewed as an affront to the integrity and professionalism of the service (McLaughlin, 2007; Shiner, 2010). This reaction contrasted sharply with the prevailing response among people from black and minority ethnic groups, who widely welcomed the Inquiry's findings and saw them as a vindication of longstanding complaints about mistreatment at the hands of the police (Reiner, 2010). Viewed from a police perspective, the finding of institutional racism may have been counter-productive. As the single most powerful message officers received from the Inquiry, the label of 'institutional racism' was widely taken to signify a widespread problem of individual racism, giving rise to considerable anger and acting as a possible barrier to reform: 'Despite the avowed intention of the Lawrence Inquiry...the extraordinary resonance of the word *racism within* the term *institutional racism* was sufficient to deflect considerable police service attention away from the complex problem of indirect corporate discrimination' (Foster et al., 2005: 97). While certain media coverage, together with the reaction of some key stakeholders, encouraged this (mis)reading, the Inquiry's own definition was also implicated. In particular, the claim that institutional racism can be seen or detected in 'processes, attitudes and behaviour which amount to discrimination through unwitting prejudice, ignorance, thoughtlessness and racist stereotyping' (Macpherson, 1999: para. 6.34) was said to be more suggestive of individual than institutional racism, creating the potential for confusion (Foster et al., 2005; Souhami, 2007).

Although areas of conceptual confusion may have facilitated such a (mis)reading, the Lawrence Inquiry went to some lengths to distance itself from claims that individual police officers are necessarily racist. The Inquiry expressed the hope and belief that 'the average police officer' and 'average member of the public' will accept that 'we do not suggest that all police officers are racist' and 'will both understand and accept the distinction we draw between overt individual racism and the pernicious and persistent institutional racism which we have described' (Macpherson, 1999: para. 6.46). It also noted that, while 'It is in the implementation of policies and in the words and actions of officers acting together that racism may become apparent', 'we say with emphasis that such an accusation does not mean or imply that every police officer is guilty of racism. No such sweeping suggestion can be or should be made' (1999: 6.24). These passages alone give the reader permission to see the report as focusing on something other than individual racism and invite an alternative reading. But such an invitation was not widely accepted within the police service.

Anger over the 'accusation' of 'institutional racism' does not fully explain why the police failed to get to grips with some of the more challenging aspects of the Lawrence Inquiry. After all, the Scarman Report was given a similarly hostile reception and was effectively 'mugged' by the police (Reiner, 1985: 90) despite its insistence that the fundamental problem was not one of institutional racism. Organisational change often gives rise to defensive responses that have been likened to the resistance psychotherapists encounter when working with individual clients (Bovey and Hede, 2001). From this perspective, police responses to the Lawrence Inquiry are, perhaps, best viewed as a form of psychological defence. What was widely viewed as an 'attack' on the integrity of the service produced a palpable sense of loss, disorientation and trauma, triggering a series of well-known psychological defence mechanisms and analogous conscious processes (Shiner, 2010). In this manner, officers routinely explained the disproportionate focus of stop and search on black and minority ethnic groups in ways that did not implicate police behaviour. Obviously contradictory claims that had little regard for issues of evidence or consistency worked in tandem with carefully constructed criticisms of the Lawrence Inquiry, with the common aim of protecting the reputation of the police service. In practice, these psychological defences translated into various forms of resistance, so that the recording of stop and account was sold to officers, not as a way of improving monitoring and accountability, but as an additional source of intelligence, effectively rebranding the whole exercise and diverting attention away from the broader reform agenda.

The politics of denial

In the case of both the Scarman Report and the Lawrence Inquiry, police hostility formed part of a broader backlash against reform. Police attempts to discredit Scarman by playing on fears about the spectre of black criminality were readily taken up by Conservative politicians and news media, sparking a full-blown debate about 'law and order' (Sim, 1982). An acquiescent home secretary helped ensure Scarman was outmanoeuvred and that any challenge he posed to police authority was quickly neutralised. The hostile police response to the Lawrence Inquiry also formed part of a broader campaign orchestrated by Conservative politicians and news media against what was very much a New Labour initiative (McLaughlin, 2007). Among others, William Hague, then Conservative leader, complained about the way the Inquiry report 'has been used to brand every officer and every branch of the force as racist', claiming it had 'contributed directly to a collapse of police morale and recruitment, and has led to a crisis on our streets' (Travis, 2000). After returning to power as part of a coalition government, the Conservative Party oversaw the diminution of PACE recording requirements, while supporting police efforts to deflect attention away from the disproportionately high rates at which black and minority ethnic groups are stopped and searched. Responsibility for stop and search practice transferred to the National Police Improvement Agency in 2007, and its principal piece of work in this area was described by Nick Herbert, then minister for policing and criminal justice, in the following terms (Herbert, 2010: 298WH):

> the 'Next Steps' process developed by the National Policing Improvement Agency... helps the police to understand the way in which they use stop and search and how the population of an area and the apparent levels of disproportionality might in some circumstances not present a true picture. The early feedback on 'Next Steps' is positive, and we hope to be able to expand it to other areas shortly.

A decade or so after the Lawrence Inquiry, this was a clear rejection of the associated reform agenda, sanctioning the kind of obfuscation that had been so roundly dismissed. Macpherson was clear: 'Nobody in the minority ethnic communities believes that the complex arguments which are sometimes used to explain the figures as to stop and search are valid' (1999: para. 45.8). Attempting 'to justify the disparities through the identification of other factors, whilst not being seen vigorously to address the discrimination which is evident', he insisted, 'simply exacerbates the climate of distrust' (1999: para. 45.10).

The coalition government's position on stop and search shifted significantly after the August 2011 riots. In its immediate response, the government stuck to the familiar 'law and order' line, with the home secretary, Theresa May, attributing the riots to 'sheer criminality' and insisting on 'robust policing' (Camber, 2011). As aggressive police tactics were repeatedly implicated in the causal mix leading to the riots, however (see Ball and Taylor, 2011; Riots, Communities and Victims Panel, 2012), the home secretary commissioned Her Majesty's Inspectorate of Constabulary (HMIC) to carry out a review of stop and search. A month or so later, the commissioner of the Metropolitan Police Service, Sir Bernard Hogan-Howe, announced a plan to dramatically cut the amount of stop and search, while increasing the arrest rate, in an attempt to improve relations with black and minority ethnic communities (Davenport, 2012).

The HMIC (2013: 6) review of stop and search uncovered 'alarming' and 'disturbing' evidence of non-compliance with the PACE Code of Practice. Approximately a quarter of forms examined did not include sufficient grounds to justify the lawful use of the power and almost half of forces 'did nothing to understand the impact of stop and search encounters upon communities, with only a very small number proactively seeking the views of the people and communities most affected' (2013: 6). Use of stop and search was also said to be 'rarely based upon evidence of what works best to cut crime' and officers were given little training on how to use these powers effectively (2013: 48). In terms of broader developments, the review pointed to 'noticeable slippage' in the level of attention given to stop and search by senior officers since the publication of the Lawrence Inquiry report, while reductions in the recording requirements were said to have diminished the capability of forces 'to understand the impact of the use of stop and search powers on crime levels and community confidence' (2013: 8). Anticipating the publication of the HMIC report, the home secretary announced there would be a public consultation on stop and search, citing particular concerns about the disproportionate focus on black people and the low arrest rate, which led her to 'question whether stop and search is always used appropriately' (Travis, 2013b).

The home secretary's response to the public consultation was delayed by several months as her determination to do something about stop and search was apparently held up by 'regressive attitudes' at senior levels of the Conservative Party (BBC, 2014a). When it came, however, her statement to the House of Commons was unrecognisable from the 'law and order' rhetoric she had favoured just a few years earlier. When 'innocent people are stopped and searched for no good reason', she declared, it is not only 'hugely damaging to the relationship between the police and the public', but is also 'an unacceptable affront to justice' (May, 2014: column 831). In particular, the misuse of stop and search was said to be 'unfair, especially to young black men' (May, 2014: column 833). As politicians on both sides of the House vied over which was the real party of reform, the 'misuse of stop and search' was described by one Conservative back-bencher as 'probably the worst form of legal racial abuse in our country' (Fuller, 2014: column 843). Another Conservative member of parliament asserted that the figures on stop and search were 'a stain on British policing', before asking: 'Do not the figures indicate that, sadly, in a large number of cases it is nothing but the colour of the skin of the person being stopped that has caused the stop-and-search to happen?' (Ellis, 2014: column 841). The home secretary concurred, before agreeing with her colleague that the situation was 'disgraceful' (Ellis, 2014: column 841; May, 2014: column 841).

As part of her statement, the home secretary announced several new initiatives to guard against the misuse of stop and search. These initiatives included revisions to PACE to clarify what constitutes reasonable suspicion and to emphasise that officers who do not use their powers properly will be subject to formal performance or disciplinary proceedings; training for officers with a focus on 'unconscious bias'; and an invitation to all police forces to sign up to a 'best use of stop and search' scheme. The home secretary also announced that the College of Policing had been commissioned to review the national training on stop and search, with a view to developing robust professional standards, and to introduce an assessment of officers' fitness to use stop and search powers. These initiatives were designed 'to send the clearest possible message: if officers do not pass this assessment, if they do not understand the law, or if they do not show they know how to use stop-and-search powers appropriately, they will not be allowed to use them' (May, 2014: column 832). The 'Best Use of Stop and Search Scheme' was launched in August 2014, with all 43 territorial police forces in England and Wales having signed up to it (Home Office, 2014a; Rush, 2014). Under the Scheme, forces will record a broader range of stop and search outcomes (arrests, cautions, penalty notices for disorder and so on) to show the link between the object of the search and its outcome; provide opportunities for members of the local community to accompany police officers on patrol; and introduce a local community complaint policy. The Scheme also makes revisions to the 'exceptional' stop and search power under Section 60 of the Criminal Justice and Public Order Act 1994, which include raising the level of authorisation to a senior officer (above the rank of chief superintendent), who must reasonably believe that an incident involving serious violence will, rather than may, take place and limiting its duration to 15 hours, down from 24 hours. (For more on Section 60, see chapters 2 and 3.)

Although these are significant developments, they do not live up to the tough talk on stop and search. The reforms announced by the home secretary 'do not match the scale of the problem that she herself has described' and fall short of what she called for previously (Cooper, 2014: column 834). The voluntary nature of the 'Best Use of Stop-and-Search' scheme has been singled out for particular criticism (Cooper, 2014: column 834) and has raised questions about what will happen if it does not work (Vaz, 2014: column 836). If the 'voluntary code' fails and the number of stop-searches does not come down, if stop and search does not become more targeted, and if the ratio of arrests to stops does not 'improve considerably', the home secretary promised that the government will return with primary legislation to make these things happen (May, 2014: column 833). She refused to be drawn on the timescale (2014: column 837), however, and it was extremely unlikely that any such legislation could have been introduced before the general election in May 2015. Rather than dealing directly with the need for reform, then, the government fudged the issue and played for time.

Why, though, has the home secretary gone as far she has in tackling the misuse of stop and search? While the 2011 riots put stop and search firmly under the spot-light, her willingness to publicly criticise police tactics may be due, in part, to emerging tensions in the longstanding alliance between the Conservative Party and the police. Certainly May's critical comments came on the back of several high-profile clashes over funding cuts, which saw her being roundly booed at a Police Federation conference (Peachey, 2012), and the resignation of the Conservative Party chief whip, Andrew Mitchell, amid claims he abused police officers outside the Houses of Parliament – claims Mitchell described as a 'sustained attempt' to 'toxify the Conservative Party' and 'destroy' his career (Churcher, 2012). To date, three officers have been dismissed for gross misconduct over the Mitchell affair, one for lying about witnessing the incident and two for leaking information to the press (Laville, 2014). The officer who lied about witnessing the incident has also been imprisoned and two other officers are awaiting disciplinary hearings for passing information to the press. For his part, Mitchell claimed the incident had shaken his faith in the police, noting that African Caribbean staff at his wife's surgery had told her 'countless stories of what happened to their families just because of the colour of their skin' (Hurst, 2014). He has also started to campaign against stop and search powers that do not require reasonable suspicion, asserting: 'As an elected politician I am ashamed of having not fully understood the truth of this before. It's time we took responsibility and made stop and search without suspicion a thing of the past' (quoted by Hurst, 2014).

There are other signs that the political landscape may be shifting in ways that help to mitigate opposition to police reform. The appointment of directly elected police and crime commissioners has created lobbying opportunities for campaign groups to shape local policing agendas by raising matters such as the use of stop and search (Gill, 2012; Derfoufi, 2013). Although majoritarian forms of government tend to militate against the interests of minority groups (Reiner, 2010), demographic changes mean that black and minority ethnic voters hold the balance of power in a quarter of parliamentary constituencies across England and Wales, including almost two-fifths of seats in London (Holloway, 2013). Because of this, perhaps, some Conservative politicians in constituencies with sizeable black and minority ethnic populations are becoming more vocal about the need to do something about stop and search (Barwell, 2013; but see O'Flynn, 2013).

Promoting organisational change

There are various things that can be done to regulate police stop and search. Following the Lawrence Inquiry, several forces developed internal performance management procedures that had 'scope to enhance the legitimacy of searches' (Bland et al., 2000b: viii), but they are rarely used (HMIC, 2013). A number of forces have drawn on technological developments, including electronic mapping systems that cross-reference stop-search activity with local crime patterns (Open Society Justice Initiative, 2011), the use of body-worn video cameras that appear to improve the conduct of officers as well as those they stop, and detection devices, such as metal detectors, that enable screening without a full search (HMIC, 2013). The Metropolitan Police Service has also committed to halving the number of unsuccessful stop-searches for drugs as part of its attempt to improve police–community relations (HMIC, 2013). Minor drug searches might be further discouraged by discounting cannabis possession from 'sanctioned detections', removing the perverse and unintended incentive structure that rewards officers for targeting such offences (Eastwood et al., 2013; see also Chapter 3).

These are little more than piecemeal developments, however, and, after more than a quarter of a century of PACE, it seems clear that existing regulations have been largely ineffective in restraining police use of stop and search. While various factors are implicated in this apparent failure, police resistance has been crucial, giving rise to an unavoidable central paradox that reform efforts have failed to confront – the police cannot be relied upon to ensure robust regulation themselves, yet are likely to resist and subvert external efforts to this end. Part of the problem is that PACE lacks an effective enforcement mechanism, prompting calls for a more adversarial approach, but litigation only ever deals with a minority of cases and is costly, uncertain and slow. Based on the US experience, it has also been noted that court cases do not make for good prospective regulation or productive policy-making (Harris, 2013). Punitive sanctions tend to be divisive and often promote defiance rather than compliance, with the result that behavioural change becomes less, not more, likely (Braithwaite, 2002). Previous experience suggests that reform efforts should anticipate resistance and build in responses to it (Shiner, 2010). This may mean finding ways of working with, or around, psychological defences, as well as rewarding good practice. A regulatory system can incentivise compliance by employing carrots as well as sticks, rewarding the kinds of behaviour it wants to encourage, while imposing sanctions for the kinds of behaviour it is seeking to eradicate. Including rewards, as well as punishments, provides a useful counterweight to the idea that regulation represents an attack on the police (Delsol and Shiner, 2006; Shiner, 2010).

Organisational change will almost inevitably activate psychological defence mechanisms among those affected because it is an anxiety-inducing process (Bovey and Hede, 2001). The way change is packaged and marketed can heighten or soothe anxieties, making compliance more or less likely. By tying its recommendations to the finding of institutional racism, the Lawrence Inquiry amplified the inherent reform resistance of the police organisation, ensuring a predictably defensive reaction that distanced the new recording requirement from its intended purpose. The key lesson, perhaps, is that the 'softly, softly approach' is likely to be more effective than name-calling or 'charging...head-first' (Reiner, 1985: 212). As a general proposition, we might suppose that reform is most likely to succeed when it coincides with an organisation's priorities and appeals to its self-interest. While the finding of institutional racism inflamed police opinion, the general principles underlying the recording of stop and account were much more widely endorsed (Shiner, 2006). There was, for example, widespread support among police personnel for increased accountability, and those involved in implementing the new recording requirement felt it would have a positive impact by providing people who were stopped with credible reasons for the stop, increasing accountability and promoting fairness.

Such responses suggest that compliance might be improved by framing the regulation of police stops more explicitly in terms of the underlying principles of fairness, legitimacy and procedural justice. According to the procedural justice model, fair treatment at the hands of police officers promotes trust and legitimacy, encouraging public cooperation and compliance, while unfair treatment undermines cooperation and promotes cynicism about the law (see Chapter 6). By ensuring that police powers are used parsimoniously and efficiently, in ways that are procedurally and distributively fair, it follows that effective regulation might minimise the damage done to trust, legitimacy and cooperation, making policing easier and more effective. Appeals to fairness, legitimacy and procedural justice are more likely to motivate compliance than denunciations of racism because they coincide with police priorities and self-interest, while having the added advantage of emphasising to officers the wider purpose of regulation and its motivating principles (Delsol and Shiner, 2006).

While procedural justice is forward looking in the sense that it seeks to ensure certain standards of conduct, a rounded regulatory system also requires remedial procedures that provide some kind of redress when things go wrong. Braithwaite's (2002) model of responsive regulation has much to offer in this regard. Originally developed as a way of dealing with corporate wrongdoing, responsive regulation rests on the basic idea that regulatory authorities should be responsive to the conduct of those they seek to regulate in deciding whether a more or less interventionist response is required. In particular, regulators should take account of how effectively citizens or corporations are regulating themselves before deciding whether to escalate intervention. The potential for escalation is built into the structure of responsive regulation by integrating a range of different types of response to wrongdoing, starting with persuasion before moving onto deterrence and punishment as proves necessary. Consistent punishment and consistent persuasion are, according to Braithwaite (2002: 29), both 'foolish strategies' because

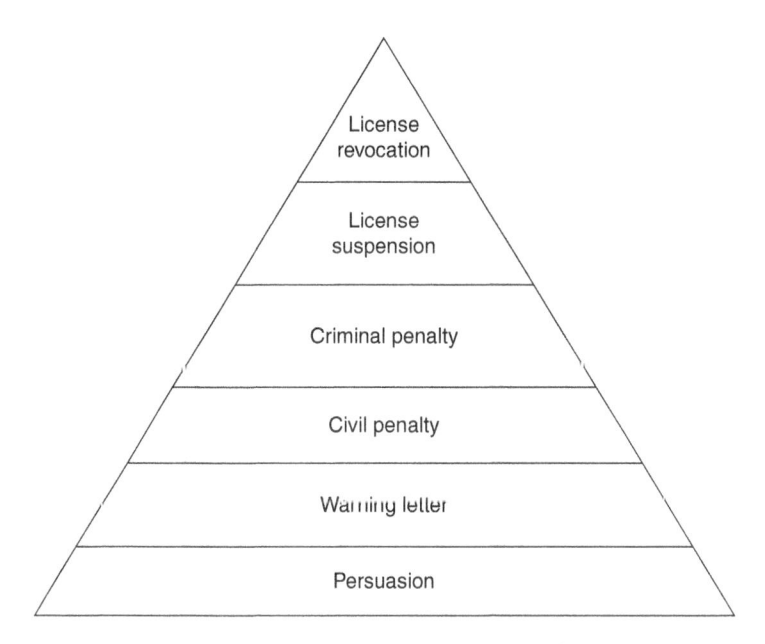

```
         /\
        /  \
       /License\
      /revocation\
     /------------\
    /   License    \
   /   suspension   \
  /------------------\
 /   Criminal penalty  \
/----------------------\
/      Civil penalty     \
/------------------------\
/       Warning letter     \
/--------------------------\
/         Persuasion         \
/----------------------------\
```

Figure 8.1 An example of a (corporate) regulatory pyramid
Source: Braithwaite (2002: 31) (by permission of Oxford University Press); see also Ayres and Braithwaite (1992).

neither works all the time and each works some of the time. The puzzle is deciding when to persuade and when to punish.

The regulatory pyramid is the most distinctive aspect of responsive regulation and seeks to resolve this puzzle (see Figure 8.1). At the base of the pyramid is a restorative dialogue-based approach, where the emphasis is on persuasion and motivating rule-breakers to make amends to those they have harmed. As well as being more ethical, the presumption of persuasion, rather than punishment, is said to be more effective, as there 'seem to be good empirical grounds for optimism that restorative justice can "work" in restoring victims, offenders, and communities' (Braithwaite, 2002: 69; see also Sherman and Strang, 2007). The assumption is that we should always start at the base of the pyramid and only escalate to more demanding or punitive approaches when dialogue fails. Once compliance is forthcoming, the process of escalation is put into reverse as we move back down the pyramid. The particular strength of the regulatory pyramid is two-fold. On the one hand, restorative justice is said to work best with the threat of punishment in the background, incentivising compliance earlier rather than later – something

Braithwaite refers to as 'the active deterrence of escalation' (2002: 42) or 'trust in the shadow of the axe' (2002: 36). Engaging in persuasion before moving on to more demanding and potentially punitive sanctions also means that coercion is likely to be seen as more legitimate and procedurally fair if it has to be used, increasing the prospect of compliance.

By integrating persuasion, deterrence and punishment, responsive regulation combines the strengths of consensus and conflict approaches, each compensating for the weaknesses of the other. One of the particular strengths of restorative justice is that it confronts rule-breakers with the harms they have caused in ways that are difficult to neutralise because commonly used defences, such as denial, are difficult to sustain in light of direct testimony from the victim (Braithwaite, 2002). As well as neutralising commonly used defences, restorative processes seek to promote the internalisation of restorative values among participants, thereby providing a mechanism for cultural change.

As a means of regulating stop and search, responsive regulation would begin by seeking to persuade officers of the case for exercising their powers fairly and lawfully. At the base of the pyramid this might involve training in procedural justice, incorporating the voices of impacted communities, before moving up to restorative dialogue with people officers have wrongly stopped and searched. 'Restorative policing' has been billed as 'the next logical step' in 'community policing and police reform', which offers 'new tools and new principles' for building social capital and efficacy (Bazemore and Griffiths, 2003: 344). Some forces have incorporated restorative principles into their complaints procedures in the belief that they might provide a constructive solution to conflict between police and the public as well as between police officers and their colleagues or employers (Hoyle and Young, 2003). If persuasion and dialogue fail to ensure compliance, further misconduct would trigger ever more punitive responses that might include disciplinary action, fines, suspension of stop and search powers and, ultimately, dismissal or prosecution.

Conclusion

The Riots, Communities and Victims Panel (2011: 11–12) was 'disturbed' by evidence of a 'breakdown in trust between some communities and police', recommending that 'Stop and Search needs immediate attention to ensure that community support and confidence is not undermined.' Thirty years after the Scarman Report, the Panel reflected: 'it is a sad fact that in some respects, the underlying challenges are strikingly similar' (2011: 5). Having documented the many failings of the existing regulatory system, the HMIC (2013), like the Lawrence Inquiry before it, went on to recommend more of the same – monitoring, training, supervision and community consultation in an attempt to ensure compliance with the PACE Code of Practice and equalities legislation. Despite talking tough, the home secretary has followed this lead. As history seems to be repeating itself, we are in danger of doing the same thing over and over again, hoping for a different outcome – a commonly cited definition of insanity. The fundamental problem with PACE is that it lacks an effective enforcement mechanism, without which it is little more than a paper tiger. This leaves us with a dilemma, because any attempt to move towards a more adversarial, US-style approach is likely to be seen as a hostile one and to be resisted by the police organisation. It is, perhaps, time to talk more softly and carry a bigger stick (Ayres and Braithwaite, 1992).

Note

1. Two of the original five suspects were eventually convicted of Lawrence's murder in January 2012, nearly 20 years after the incident.

9
Towards a Transnational and Comparative Approach

Ben Bowling and Estelle Marks

The power to stop people in public places, to question them and to search their person and belongings is common to policing worldwide. Drawing on the small, but growing, academic literature on 'stop and search' in a range of different geographical and institutional settings, this chapter examines the use of this power in theory and in practice. It explores the range of purposes for which stop and search is deployed, including the often vaguely defined general goals of security, crime prevention and counter-terrorism. Here it is contended that stop and search is the widest and least circumscribed coercive power of government. Although it is often socially invisible, stop and search is among the first and most frequent contacts between police and public and has far-reaching consequences. The chapter reflects on the problems of ensuring that police power is constrained by mechanisms of transparency, accountability and respect for human rights, and notes that this is particularly important as police power globalises. We argue that the way forward is to develop an agenda for transnational and comparative research to provide the basis for mechanisms to ensure that increasingly globally connected police power can be held to account.

Defining the power to 'stop and search'

The command 'Stop, police!' asserts authority in any language. Issued in the street, at a roadblock or at a border, the official instruction to stop initiates a coercive and intrusive process that is available to law enforcement agencies around the world (Weber and Bowling, 2012). Markus Dubber (2005: xi) argues that 'among the powers of government none is greater than the power to police and none less circumscribed'. We agree, and contend that, among the powers of the police, the capacity to stop and search is perhaps the widest and least circumscribed of all. In most, if not all, jurisdictions, police officers have almost unfettered power to stop people in public places, question them and search personal items of clothing, bags or motor vehicles.

It is important to understand that when an agent of the state instructs a person to stop as they walk in the street, drive their car or pass through an airport, they are – in effect – using state-sanctioned coercive power to detain them. The person who is stopped is prevented from moving unless and until the officer allows them to do so. In all jurisdictions where evidence exists, a police instruction to stop is non-negotiable and is backed up by coercive power and punishment for non-compliance. In Hungary, failure to identify oneself to the police may result in custody or a fine (Tóth and Kádár, 2012). In India, those who refuse to stop can be fined or imprisoned for up to six months (Belur, 2012). In England, a person who fails to stop, or to stop a vehicle, when required to do so by a constable in the exercise of his powers under the Criminal Justice and Public Order Act 1994 commits a criminal offence punishable by a fine and/or one month's imprisonment. Under Schedule 7 of the Terrorism Act 2000, anyone passing through a UK border who refuses to submit to a search or to answer questions commits an offence punishable by a fine or three months in prison.

Although detaining a person on the street for the purposes of questioning them, establishing identification or a search may not be the 'paradigm case' of detention (e.g. placing a person in a prison cell), we agree with the European Court of Human Rights' (2010) opinion that it is a coercive act consistent with the notion of a detention. The detention may be for a very short period of time, for the purpose of checking identification or simply to ask some brief questions. It could lead to a longer period of detention for more in-depth questioning or for the purpose of a search, and may eventually lead to arrest. The power has a rather different quality when officers demand that civilians stop and account for themselves – to justify their presence in a place, to give their personal details, such as name and address, or to officially identify themselves. In this case they are intruding into the private life of the individual.

A physical search of a person's clothing, belongings or vehicle is considerably more of an interference with a person's privacy and liberty than a request to stop and identify or explain oneself. A search may be more or less physically intrusive; it may involve being scanned with a metal detector or entail a pat down or 'frisk' of outer clothing. It may involve more extensive searches of outer clothing and belongings, when a person may be asked to remove jackets, hats, shoes and socks to allow them to be searched. In some instances, a person may be subject to a 'strip search'. Bags and luggage may be searched, as may the passenger and storage areas of vehicles. Searches can be extremely thorough and detailed or, in other circumstances, simply cursory. When people are searched in public places, the interference with their private person and belongings inevitably causes inconvenience and has the potential to cause unease, embarrassment, humiliation and anger. This is true even when the police officer explains the reason for the stop and conducts it courteously and professionally. Greater problems arise when it is carried out disrespectfully and on flimsy grounds.

The range of 'police-like' agencies that use stop and search powers

The power to stop and search is most frequently exercised by and associated with 'blue uniformed' police officers on the beat. As such, most research is focused on this area, and in Britain, the US, Canada, Australia and, to a lesser extent, continental Europe there is growing academic literature on stop and search by uniformed constables (Weber and Bowling, 2012). In other parts of the world, researchers have documented how traffic police use the power at roadblocks to stop and search vehicles at random (Belur, 2012) or, in the case of South Africa, 'super-roadblocks' of all vehicles passing on a particular route (Marks, 2012).

However, our theoretical and methodological lens should pan out to take into account the wide range of police-like agencies, from customs and border officials to military agencies and private security guards (Bowling, 2010; Loftus, 2013). Special paramilitary forces and military forces undertaking policing roles (e.g. in public order functions) make extensive use of stop and search powers. In some jurisdictions these agents are the primary users of stop and search. For example, a 2004 survey of stops in Brazil found that 90 per cent were conducted by military forces rather than civilian police (Ramos and Musumeci, 2004).

Since the 18th century the navy, marine police and customs officers have had the power to hail, stop, board and search vessels – known as 'visitation' – in their role patrolling the world's seas and oceans for pirates, smugglers and slavers (Bowling, 2010). Stop and search powers are available to border agencies and are frequently aimed at 'suspect passengers' at airports, ports and railway stations. Immigration and customs officials at borders around the world have a wide discretion to detain and question individuals, to search their belongings and to grant or deny entry.

Private security firms use the power to search in both public and private settings. In the UK, Canada and the US, private security agencies play major roles in the delivery of public services, particularly in the penal system: here the power to search prisoners and visitors is frequently used by private actors. The power to search people's belongings is frequently used by private security guards at the entrance to both public and private buildings; whether a quick glance into a handbag on entry into a nightclub or a full bag search and ion scan on entry into sensitive public buildings such as New York's Statue of Liberty or the CN Tower in Toronto, these searches are non-negotiable if entrance is to be permitted.

Very little research has been conducted in relation to non-police use of stop and search, but the limited information available relating to border control shows a need to examine and understand the use of this power in the wide variety of settings in which civilians encounter it. The evidence of discrimination by both police and border control officials raises questions of disproportionality in all areas in which it is used. We return to this issue later in the chapter.

Contract theory and police power

The power to stop and search impacts upon, and interferes with, the 'human rights' or 'civil rights' of the individual, most fundamentally their rights to liberty and privacy. It also interferes with their inherent moral rights to unrestricted travel and to be free of state coercion unless the interference can be explicitly justified in terms of both its means and its ends. Although this point is self-evident to lawyers and social scientists, some police officers – especially constables assigned to street duties – find this baffling. The idea of stop and search as a 'routine' practice seems to be so ingrained in police cultural expectations that they find it difficult to conceive the power as a coercive one and resent the idea that they should be required to justify its use in general or in specific instances. Sometimes, in their defence of the power, police officers assert that if a person has nothing to hide, then they have nothing to fear from a relatively brief detention to ask a few questions or a quick search of their clothes or vehicle.

The key point is that, in a democratic society, state powers to physically coerce and intrude on the private lives of civilians cannot simply exist without circumscription. The state must provide a justification for the existence of these powers in general and for their use in each and every individual case. The principles of Lockean contract theory tell us that, in return for the protection of our safety and security, we give over some power to the state to interfere with our lives. However, the same principle demands that any exercise of this power should be justified with specific reference to the end of protecting our safety and security. As Kleinig (1996: 13) argues, there is 'a moral onus on those who limit the freedom of others to provide a justification of that limitation'.

The principles of contract theory provide the background for all discussions of policing and state interference with human rights. When applied to the individual stop and search context, they require that an officer have grounds for each and every stop. These grounds must be objectively justifiable, explicable and acceptable to the person stopped, and the officer using them (and their supervisors) should be held accountable. This principle is a fundamental aspect of the rule of law (Bingham, 2011) and is enshrined in human rights legislation (Bowling and Weber, 2013). In the common law world, the principle that state interference with personal and property rights must be justified by law manifests itself clearly in case law as early as the 1600s.[1]

More recently, this principle is reflected in various articles of the European Convention on Human Rights, which restricts state interference with rights to instances where it is legal, necessary, proportionate and accountable (Bowling and Weber, 2013). Particularly relevant to police powers of stop and search are articles 5, 8 and 14, which protect individual rights to liberty and privacy and prohibit discrimination on grounds such as sex, race, colour, language, religion, political or other opinion, national or social origin, association with a national minority, property, birth or other status. A close look at police practice demonstrates that the reality of modern policing frequently falls short of these requirements.

The police power to stop and search is so 'taken for granted' that in some contexts little or no justification is ever articulated, or it is defended in only the broadest terms. Such power is said to be necessary for 'routine' street policing with the goals of, *inter alia*, 'officer safety', 'public order', 'public protection', 'public safety', 'crime control' and the detection and prevention of crime. It is deployed to prevent offences ranging from anti-social behaviour and drunk driving to serious gang violence and terrorism. Advocates claim that it is essential to detect stolen goods, drugs and weapons and illegal immigrants.

It is also clear that, whatever the official justification, police frequently use the powers for other purposes. For example, they have been used to break up and disperse groups, to police public protests (going so far as to discourage people from attending demonstrations), to gather intelligence or simply to exert power for the purpose of social discipline (Choongh, 1997). Although these practices are not legally sanctioned or justifiable in a democratic society, they are commonplace in many countries.

To clear a path through the disparate claims, it is helpful to look carefully at the investigative and deterrent justifications that underpin the modern power to stop and search.

The investigative justification

The primary justification for stop and search powers advanced by police officers and government officials is its purpose in facilitating the investigation, detection and prevention of crime. In England and Wales, Section 1 of the Police and Criminal Evidence Act 1984 permits officers to stop and search individuals to allay or confirm their 'reasonable suspicion' that a person has committed or is about to commit a criminal offence, and the officer may search for stolen or prohibited items based on a reasonable suspicion that such items will be found. These powers allow officers to stop, question and investigate individuals without exercising their more coercive power of arrest. In principle, this seems sensible; it provides officers with an intermediate power that allows them to investigate allegations or suspicions rather than being left with a choice to arrest or do nothing, a situation that many police officers and wrongly suspected individuals would rather avoid. The ability to take immediate action to confirm or disprove an allegation of personal theft, for example, without the need to arrest the person suspected of the offence is practical.

If the existence of the power is justified on the basis of its investigative value, then in individual cases the power must be circumscribed to ensure it is used for this purpose and to protect against arbitrary interference with rights. In the UK, the requirement of reasonable suspicion provides this protection. In New York, the Fourth Amendment requires stops to be based on 'probable cause' that a crime has been or will be committed. 'Terry stops', which require a lower threshold of 'reasonable suspicion', are justified on the basis of officer safety and allow officers to 'frisk' individuals to search for weapons, though the decision in *People v De Bour* (1976) forbids inquiries 'based on mere whim, caprice or idle curiosity'. It has, however, been demonstrated that under 3 per cent of Terry stops result in the recovery of weapons (Geller and Fagan, 2010).

A close look at New York's UF-250 forms, where these stops are recorded, reveals that in almost half of stops suspicion is attributed to 'furtive movements', a vague assertion which is difficult to contest and leaves a significant margin for officer discretion to justify a stop (Center on Race, Crime and Justice, 2010). In Japan, stop and account is regulated by Article 2(1) of the Police Official Duties Execution Act 1948, which requires 'sufficient ground to suspect that a person has committed or is likely to commit a crime judging reasonably from surrounding circumstances': this 'sufficient ground' should be based on objective factual criteria. In Spain, searches must be based on a 'motive' that is not specifically defined, although the constitutional court has ruled that stops must be within the framework of prevention and investigation of criminal activity, even if there is no indication that the person has committed a crime (Delsol, 2009b). The Spanish Supreme Court has further ruled that stops may be carried out based on 'simple suspicion' that must not be 'illogical, irrational or arbitrary' (cited by Delsol, 2009b: 81). This leaves an uncomfortably wide margin for officer discretion in deciding whom to stop and for what purpose.

In Moscow, Article 1(2) of the Police Patrol Statute establishes a duty 'to prevent and suppress crimes and administrative offenses'. Here again, stops must be based on reasonable suspicion (Adjami, 2006). Article 107 defines this reasonable suspicion very broadly and requires officers to 'pay particular attention to persons that are suspiciously watchful and anxious, that are unseasonably dressed, or dressed in clothes that do not fit their body type and height, and also to those who have bandages and injuries' (cited by Adjami, 2006: 42), highlighting a legislative focus on the poor and vulnerable within society, who are most likely to fit into these categories.

In some jurisdictions the requirements are even less stringent: in Hungary, 'mere suspicion' – which presumably does not have to be 'reasonable' – is sufficient justification for a stop and search (Tóth and Kádár, 2012). In our view, no person should be stopped and subjected to a search unless the officer has well-founded suspicion or a genuine reason to believe that an offence has been or is going to be committed, or that the individual is in possession of prohibited items, such as drugs, stolen goods or an illegal weapon. What is debatable is what the content of that reasonable suspicion, motive or probable cause should be, on what objective criterion such suspicion might be based, and how accurate or reliable the suspicion must be in order to describe it as reasonable.

Paul Quinton (2011) suggests that, in practice, police officers believe that almost anything can form the basis of reasonable suspicion.

Research on this topic over many years bears this out (Bowling and Phillips, 2007). It suggests that very broad behavioural cues such as 'running, hurrying or loitering' are often given by police officers as grounds for suspicion. Even personal characteristics such as age, style of dress, criminal history or physical appearance are cited as grounds. Many questions are raised about the formation of reasonable suspicion and how it can be justified; officers frequently refer to hunches or intuition and other highly subjective criteria that would fail to satisfy a neutral observer (Bowling and Weber, 2012). The question of reasonableness remains a vexed question in many jurisdictions, including Bulgaria and Spain (Delsol, 2009b).

From an investigative perspective, very few stop and searches yield fruit. In the UK, fewer than one in ten stops based on reasonable suspicion result in the discovery of prohibited items or the arrest of the suspect (Bowling and Phillips, 2007). This means that, from the point of view of effective investigative practice, nine out of ten searches are a waste of police time and resources. Furthermore over 100,000 'suspicionless' searches carried out under the Terrorism Act 2000 resulted in the identification of no terror suspects whatsoever, with the most frequent 'successful' result being a warning for the possession of cannabis (Parmar, 2011). In Brazil, around 5 per cent of stops result in action of any kind (Ramos and Musumeci, 2004), and in Paris, 78 per cent of stops recorded resulted in no further action by police (Goris et al., 2009).

The deterrent justification

Advocates of stop and search powers argue that, even if they make only a small contribution to the investigation and detection of crime, they can still be justified on the grounds of crime prevention through deterrence. This could be 'individual deterrence', where those people who are arrested and brought to justice as a result of stop and search will be deterred from committing future crimes, or where those people who experience stop and search – irrespective of the result in terms of discovering contraband – 'think twice' before carrying prohibited items in the future. Furthermore, advocates argue that extensive use of stop and search may have a 'general deterrent' effect, in the sense that the entire population will be more cautious with what they carry if they imagine that they might be stopped and searched.

Proponents of the deterrent view argue for robust enforcement measures such as the extensive and random use of stop and search against those in society seen as proximate causes of crime and disorder on the streets: groups of youths, alcoholics, drug users and the homeless, for example. This policing strategy reflects the 'broken windows thesis' (Wilson and Kelling, 1982), which postulates that diligent policing of low-level crime and disorder such as vandalism, prostitution, anti-social behaviour and marijuana possession will deter individuals within society from committing more serious crime (Geller and Fagan, 2010). It is also linked to a belief that is prevalent among police worldwide, that the primary function of street patrol is the 'rigid and unrelenting enforcement of the law...to prevent and control crime' (Brown, 1981: 198). This belief was found to be common to some (but not all) police in South Africa (Marks, 2012) and England (Parmar, 2011; Quinton, 2011), and is uniformly held in New South Wales, Australia (Weber, 2012). Those who put forward the deterrent justification advocate general and widespread use of stop and search powers, and, as such, this negates the need for any reasonable suspicion or probable cause requirement.

In New York, the utilisation of 'Terry stops' in the context of Order Maintenance Policing speaks of this deterrent justification (Geller and Fagan, 2010). The aggressive use of police stop, question and frisk measures are central to strategic Order Maintenance Policing, popular in the city since the early 1990s. Although the effectiveness of these measures has been questioned by empirical research (see Bowling, 1999), to date this policing strategy has survived both strong criticism and civil litigation (Geller and Fagan, 2010). While 'Terry stops' are justified by police officers on investigative grounds and to protect officer safety, the low rate of weapons discovery and its place within the Order Maintenance Strategy suggest that stop and search in New York is defended not just on an investigative basis but also on the basis of deterrence.

In the UK, powers such as Section 60 of the Criminal Justice and Public Order Act 1994 and Section 44 of the Terrorism Act 2000 (recently repealed and replaced with Section 47A) have no individual reasonable suspicion requirement. Section 60 can be used to stop people in an explicitly authorised area, even where a police officer has no grounds to suspect that the person is in possession of dangerous items. Similar deterrent powers exist in other countries. In the Netherlands, the Municipalities Act 2002 and the Weapons and Ammunitions Act 2002 introduced 'preventative searches', allowing the mayor to designate 'security-risk zones' within which police may stop and search anyone without the requirement of reasonable suspicion (van der Leun and van der Woude, 2012). In Denmark, Section 6 of the Police Activities Act 2004 provides for the establishment of 'stop and search zones' where the police may carry out searches not grounded in suspicion for the purpose of discovering weapons (Futtrup and Jacobsen, 2011).

There are several problems with the deterrent justification for stop and search, both principled and practical. The first objection is based on the Kantian principle that no person should be used merely as a means to an end and not as an end in themselves. The investigative function – if it is carried out properly – does not in itself conflict with this principle, as it requires that a search be based on reasonable suspicion that the person stopped is involved in wrongdoing. The situations in which the state can act are, therefore, limited to those in which the individuals stopped are themselves the person intended to be affected. In contrast, the deterrent justification – if accepted – would permit people to be stopped and searched at random for the benefit of general deterrence, with the population at large the target of the measure's effect. This instrumental and utilitarian justification means that stop and search could be carried out at random, or based on profiling, and need not be based on any individualised suspicion at all. Stops justified in this way, therefore, designate the person stopped merely as a means to an end. Despite doubts about the basis for reasonable suspicion, it is nevertheless an important safeguard against the arbitrary use of police power. Evidence suggests that, under an unrestrained deterrent programme, members of poor and unpopular social groups are those most likely to find themselves subject to police harassment.

Second, there is very little evidence of the deterrent effect of stop and search. It is almost impossible to measure the deterrent effect of extensive use of stop and search, whether deployed randomly or targeted at specific groups; what evidence we do have is far from compelling (see Chapter 5). Third, the use of stop and search varies widely both within and between countries: in some places it is used widely and in others very sparingly. It is striking that in England the use of stop and search powers varies widely between police force areas with similar demographic characteristics and crime rates. For example, London police use the power far more extensively than their colleagues in Birmingham, Britain's second city. At one point, Humberside police conducted 17 times fewer searches per thousand population than neighbouring Cleveland, despite having similar policing problems (Bowling, 2007). Furthermore, recent reports by the UK Equality and Human Rights Commission (2013) and the Open Society Justice Initiative (Delsol, 2009b) have demonstrated that, with sufficient focus on police accountability in terms of establishing reasonable grounds for searches, overall use of the power can fall while 'hit-rates' increase, improving efficiency, fairness and legitimacy and reducing the extent of arbitrary stop and search. In some cases, where these programmes have been implemented they have been accompanied by falling crime rates (Equalities and Human Rights Commission, 2013). This supports the contention that the deterrent effect of stop and search is minimal.

The people who are stopped: Targeting the 'usual suspects'

Historically, the power to stop and search has been used as a tool for controlling poor or minority populations. Early instances of the power appear in the North American 'Black Codes' prohibiting slaves from travelling without a ticket or in the Pass Laws that existed under the South African apartheid regime. Earlier still, the power is found in laws aimed at controlling the movement of gypsy and traveller populations of 17th-century Europe. In the UK, as in many other parts of the world, stop and search powers first appeared in laws aimed at controlling vagrancy (Weber and Bowling, 2008). It is from these laws, constructed around the notion of 'the other', a racially defined concept (Hall et al., 1978) and necessarily discriminatory, that modern stop and search powers have evolved (Weber and Bowling, 2008).

The earliest manifestations of stop and search powers targeted already marginalised communities, and in practice in many parts of the world this has not changed. There is evidence of specific targeting of racially or culturally defined 'others' within many societies. In many countries the police have been criticised not only for using the power to stop and search too frequently and without sufficient justification, but also for using it disproportionately against specific groups. There is evidence that in several jurisdictions stop and search is used more frequently and more aggressively against young, urban males from economically marginalised, poor and ethnic minority communities.

In many places, stop and search is targeted more or less explicitly at migrant populations. To support this targeting, in most European and many other jurisdictions worldwide, including Australia, Russia and Japan, identity checks are legally empowered and routinely conducted (Weber and Bowling, 2012), either generally or for specific groups of people. Article 78.1 of the French Code of Criminal Procedure legally sanctions police ID checks (Goris et al., 2009), and in Moscow Article 11(2) of the Law on Police grants the police power to check citizens' ID papers where they have grounds for suspicion of criminal activity or administrative violations (Adjami, 2006).

In some jurisdictions, laws place positive duties on the police to stop and question or ID check individuals in certain situations. For example, in Japan, in executing the Five Year Plan to Halve the Number of

Illegal Immigrants in 2003, law-makers appear to have left officers little choice but to ID check those of foreign appearance without any suspicion of a crime having been committed, simply to establish sufficient grounds to suspect an immigration violation. It has been argued that the implementation of this Action Plan has 'de-facto justified illegal police stop and account' with no prior objective basis for suspicion (Namba, 2012: 82). The result of Japan's aggressive use of police ID checks and huge increase in police activity, combined with other measures, was the almost complete achievement of the Plan (Namba, 2012).

In Arizona, Mexican immigrants are most frequently the targets of police stop and search. Researchers attribute this to the redrawing of national borders with Mexico in the 19th century. Current legislation appears to legally sanction racially motivated stops (Provine and Sanchez, 2012). The Arizona state law SB1070 requires that officers ascertain the immigration status of all persons suspected of having no legal right to remain in the state. The law provides that failure to comply with its requirements may result in civil action against an individual officer by any Arizonian citizen. This unique focus on officer accountability to the citizen places an onus on officers to stop and question those of foreign appearance whether or not they have objective 'probable cause' required by the Fourth Amendment to suspect a crime or immigration violation.

In respect of effectiveness of ID checks, Australian police report a 13 per cent rate of success in identifying those with no legal residency status when carrying out immigration checks (Weber, 2012). Identity checks in Hungary yield a 3 per cent arrest rate and result in the instigation of petty offence procedures in 18 per cent of cases (Tóth and Kádár, 2012). In Stockholm, abandoned deportation project REVA yielded results in only 1 in 10 stops (*The Local*, 2013). In the Moscow metro, only 3 per cent of ID checks result in the discovery of document violations (Adjami, 2006), and a recent report into Greece's aggressive immigration enforcement operation Xeniou Zeus found that, of roughly 85,000 stops recorded over a six month period, 4,811 resulted in the discovery of illegal immigrants and only 59 resulted in arrest on criminal charges (Cossé, 2013).

Enduring animosity towards the Roma communities in Hungary makes them frequent targets for identity checks (Tóth and Kádár, 2012), and the history of oppressive colonial policing against Aboriginal communities in Australia seems to underpin and justify the constant harassment and surveillance of non-citizens (Weber, 2012). A risk management strategy in the Netherlands, inspired by a political backlash against multiculturalism, includes express generalisations about specific ethnic groups; in this context, racial characteristics can form the express basis for police stops, a clear example of state-sanctioned racial profiling (van der Leun and van der Woude, 2012). In Greece, a recent review of police ID checks uncovered conclusive evidence of racial profiling and widespread rights abuses, including the use of disproportionate violence against ethnic minority groups (Cossé, 2013). This is taking place against the backdrop of an immigration crisis in Greece, which is the entry country for 90 per cent of immigrants into the European Union.

The term 'racial profiling', a practice deeply entrenched in law enforcement for many years, emerged as a named concept in the US in the 1990s, referring to the basis on which African Americans were more frequently stopped, especially when travelling between states, because of an explicit suspect profile. Currently the term is used to describe situations in which ethnic or racial groups are targeted on that basis alone, irrespective of whether this is a deliberate policy of targeted stop and search or simply routine practices more aptly described as 'institutional racism' (Bowling and Phillips, 2007).

There are countless examples of these practices globally; in England, a former Home Office minister endorsed the practice of racial profiling by stating that, in the wake of Islamist terrorist attacks, British Muslim communities must face the 'reality' that they will be the main targets of counter-terrorist measures including, but not limited to, stop and search (Dodd and Travis, 2005). There is evidence that police in London now feel specifically justified in targeting young male Muslims, with damaging effects on their perceptions of the police (Parmar, 2011). The statistics demonstrate that members of Asian communities are twice as likely to be stopped as their white counterparts, and people from black communities seven times more likely (Her Majesty's Inspectorate of Constabulary, 2013). So in England there is evidence of both explicit targeting policy and ingrained police practices that amount to 'institutional racism' (Bowling and Phillips, 2007). Black communities also remain the 'usual suspects' in Toronto, Canada, and there is clear evidence of racial profiling (Wortley and Owusu-Bempah, 2012). In New York, the statistics point to the existence of racial profiling in police stop and search, with blacks and Hispanics up to nine times more likely to be stopped than their white counterparts (Center on Race, Crime and Justice, 2010). There is also evidence that these groups are more likely to be subjected to 'stop and frisk', searches or the use of force; this is despite the fact that white New Yorkers are more likely to be in possession of contraband or non-firearm weapons (Center on Race, Crime and Justice, 2010).

In several other jurisdictions studies have uncovered evidence of the disproportionate effect of stop and search, with non-Slavs 22 times more likely than Slavs to be searched on the Moscow Metro (Adjami, 2006) and blacks and Arabs more likely to be the targets of stops in Paris (Goris et al., 2009). In parts of Spain, Moroccans and Romanians were respectively seven and 10 times more likely to be stopped than ethnic Spanish, and these groups are also more likely to be subjected to more intrusive measures such as searches of their belongings (Delsol, 2009b).

In South Africa (Marks, 2012) and India (Belur, 2012), the boundaries of suspicion seem to be drawn in more subtle ways, less clearly aligned with racial or cultural categories, but there is evidence that youth are specifically targeted; police at Mumbai roadblocks are particularly likely to search 'young men on a two wheeler, of a certain age and build, generally carrying a backpack' (Belur, 2012: 73). In England, the tendency of police to use stop and search to disperse groups of youths means that young men from poor and ethnic minority communities are disproportionately affected. This is also reflected in Brazil, where young people are most likely to be the targets of police stops (Ramos and Musumeci, 2004).

Targeted groups have differing capacities to resist and draw attention to their disproportionate treatment. The outrage among established expatriate Mexican communities, and their supporters in Arizona, at being targeted for immigration checks by local police (Provine and Sanchez, 2012) stands in stark contrast to both the normalisation and the invisibility of immigration checking in Australia (Weber, 2012) and the open policies of removal of illegal immigrants in Japan (Namba, 2012). Roma, unfairly targeted for police attention in Hungary (Tóth and Kádár, 2012), seem to have fewer resources at their disposal to draw attention to this injustice than either black Torontonians (Wortley and Owusu-Bempah, 2012) or British Muslims (Parmar, 2011), which is not to say that the impact of unfair treatment would be any less acute. In Stockholm, public outrage in response to evidence of racial profiling during project REVA resulted in the abandonment of the project (*The Local*, 2013) but in jurisdictions such as Greece, the Netherlands and Arizona legislative sanctioning of racially motivated stop and search appears to be reinforcing and fuelling racial tensions. In Japan, Arizona and Greece, policy-makers have declared 'war on illegal immigrants' practically, if not legally, sanctioning police to stop and question those people perceived to be non-nationals.

Negative effects on individuals and society

Being stopped by a police officer is often the first and sometimes the only encounter an individual has with the coercive arms of the state. It is certainly the most frequent encounter for many people. The search may appear to be random in its application, as with roadblocks or other generalised stops. More often, though, stop and searches appear to affect specific individuals, and, where based on reasonable suspicion, however well founded, have the effect of labelling the individual as a suspect. The fact of being identified as a suspect is rarely welcomed, and the intrusion by officers into a person's right to go about their business unfettered is experienced as a coercive and non-negotiable exertion of power over the individual. Undergoing a search in a public place is an intrusion of privacy and often an embarrassing event. The feelings of resentment generated by this experience resonate with contract theorists and the idea that intrusion by state actors must be justified to be legitimate.

The unfair targeting and ineffective deployment of stop and search has a hugely negative impact on police legitimacy and community trust in law enforcement agencies. It can have a negative impact on voluntary compliance with the law and encourage witnesses and victims to disengage from police (Tyler, 1990; see Chapters 5 and 6). Without the consent or support of the community, stop and search can be hazardous and ineffective. Willis (1983: 23) argues that the use of coercive police power 'needs constantly to be reassessed not merely in relation to arrests or clear up rates, but also in the light of the effect on the community as a whole'. The satisfactory exercise of these powers 'depends crucially in the long term on police action being perceived by individuals and groups as acceptably fair and rational' (Willis, 1983: 23). No policing practice can survive in a democratic society without community consent; in the most extreme cases, inappropriate targeting of stop and search can provoke confrontations between police and communities and is a potential trigger for public disorder.

The unfair targeting of stop and search has been a political issue in both the US (Delsol, 2009b) and the UK for a long time (Institute of Race Relations, 1979). The overuse of the power in specific ethnic minority communities at the end of the 1970s and during Operation Swamp in 1981 was identified as one of the causes of the Brixton riots (Scarman, 1981). More recently, a 'catastrophic breakdown in trust in the police among young people' has been identified as one cause of the 2011 summer riots in the UK (Lewis et al., 2011). Disproportionate and aggressive use of stop and search has also formed part of the backdrop for civil unrest in other jurisdictions, including riots in Paris in 2005 (Goris et al., 2009) and in Copenhagen in 2008 and 2009 (Delsol, 2012). Over-zealous enforcement measures, particularly when aimed at specific social groups, can lead to increased criminal victimisation and community dissatisfaction, while having no effect on the perception or fear of crime and disorder (Sherman, 1993; see also Skogan and Frydl, 2004). They also run the risk of disrupting existing social cohesion and control, and enforcing racial prejudice within society (Bradford and Jackson, 2010). Policing that relies on coercion and force risks depleting its own legitimacy and alienating communities by failing to establish long-term order and failing to develop and utilise non-coercive methods of achieving this end (Muir, 1977). In a democracy, the function of policing relies heavily on legitimacy derived from the consent of the community; perception of disproportionate or unfair use of power threatens the consent to, and therefore the legitimacy of, the use of power, so it is essential that mechanisms exist to hold the authorities to account.

The problem with justification is that, no matter how rational the basis for a stop and search, people who are wrongly targeted experience stigmatisation, embarrassment and intrusion to no tangible end. Furthermore, those who are repeatedly targeted, as many young black men are in London, Toronto and New York, experience gradually building resentment and distrust of law enforcement as well as corrosion of their identity as legitimate and accepted members of their communities (Bradford, 2010). Even when stop and searches are justified (bearing in mind that the majority are fruitless), the markedly disproportionate impact on minority communities still creates the experience of being unjustly targeted. Tyler and Wakslak (2004: 254) argue that the subjective experience of feeling profiled may be as damaging to confidence in the police as the objective fact of being profiled.

Accountability for stop and search

It is implicit in the nature of democratic governance that the state must justify its interference with individual rights. It must be demonstrated that any intrusion occurs for the attainment of a legitimate end and that mechanisms exist through which institutional actors can be held to account. All discussions about police power should start and end with the issue of accountability, and the power to stop and search is no exception. Its coercive nature and the frequency with which it is invoked worldwide demand that mechanisms exist to ensure it is used accountably, transparently and at all times with respect for the human rights with which it interferes. This includes addressing questions about the purpose of the power and systematic assessment of the extent to which these purposes are achieved.

Aside from the need for a reasonable suspicion requirement, accurate recording and reporting of details relating to every stop and search is an essential starting point for any accountability system. The very nature of stop and search power – its deployment on the streets against marginal communities – means that it often happens in circumstances of low visibility. Often it is only the police and the person stopped who are aware of what has occurred. In most jurisdictions, recording is not required or is not completed in a form that allows any assessment of fairness or effectiveness of practice. Globally, the inconsistency in recording practice poses a serious obstacle to methodical research: practices range from the recording of all police encounters, including stop and account measures in the London Metropolitan Police District, to no recording requirements whatsoever in cities such as Rio de Janeiro (Ramos and Musumeci, 2004) and Moscow (Adjami, 2006). In the US, where state authorities dictate recording practices, an estimated 70 per cent of stops are recorded in New York City, while in Boston no records of police stops are compiled (Centre on Race, Crime and Justice, 2010).

Even in countries where some recording of police stops takes place, many jurisdictions, including Canada (Wortley and Owusu-Bempah, 2012), the Netherlands (van der Leun and van der Woude, 2012), Hungary (Tóth and Kádár, 2012) and France (Goris et al., 2009), have banned the recording of data pertaining to ethnicity, making the monitoring of racial disproportionality and racial-profiling practices impossible. The motivation for the ban on the collection of ethnicity data is the protection of ethnic minorities, inspired by events in Nazi Germany leading up to the Holocaust. Furthermore, many countries have interpreted data protection rules as precluding the collection of this data, but, as Tóth and Kádár (2012) rightly point out, these rules do not necessarily protect minority communities; rather, they shield discriminating parties by preventing the collection of statistical evidence that would illuminate patterns of unequal treatment. It would be possible to collect the quantitative data necessary to monitor racial disproportionality without linking this to individuals stopped, thereby negating fears surrounding the processing of sensitive personal data (Tóth and Kádár, 2012).

However, in most jurisdictions nationality or race is still considered – by at least some advocates within police forces – as a justifiable basis for a stop and search, both domestically and at borders (Weber and Bowling, 2012). The extent of racial disproportionality in many contexts is undeniable, and there is considerable evidence that ethnic and racial difference is used as grounds for suspicion and sufficient to invoke coercive and intrusive policing methods (Bowling and Phillips, 2007; Weber and Bowling, 2012). There is also evidence that in many societies the ironic situation has arisen that systems and structures put in place to monitor and combat discrimination are now being used to anticipate and control the perceived threat of growing minority communities. The political mainstream in many European countries has seemingly condemned multiculturalism as a failure, apparently oblivious to the social and cultural realities of mass migration, human difference and diversity in the contemporary global metropolis (Bowling, 2013). It is unclear where these political ideas are currently taking us, but, in a climate of political unrest surrounding the integration of communities, the accountability of the state becomes all the more important.

Only if accurate records of stops, the reasons for the stop and their results, and essential details about the people stopped are made and collated can any effective check on the use of the power take place. With detailed information about how police use the power in practice, it is possible to make general assessments of whether its use is fair and equitable or discriminatory and vexatious. Record-keeping also serves an important normative function, making officers aware that their individual decisions can be scrutinised and encouraging responsible and thoughtful decision-making, or at least the formation of clear justification for the use of power.

Towards a comparative and transnational approach to the study of stop and search in the global context

Police have always monitored and controlled 'suspect populations' defined on the basis of their economic status, class position, race or ethnicity and their presumed 'dangerousness' (Weber and Bowling, 2008). The historical origins of stop and search powers clearly demonstrate that. But there are new and renewed fears about suspect populations that are rooted in the instability caused by rapid global change, the events of globalisation and the emergence of international terrorism. In this context, the secretary general of Interpol has spoken of his 'visionary model' of global policing whereby Interpol will provide operational support to domestic police, including access to global databases on the ground, so that when domestic police stop someone they have worldwide information on whom they are stopping (Bowling and Sheptycki, 2011). Advance passenger information systems, the posting of overseas liaison officers, biometric data requirements for foreign nationals, and immigration status databases all demonstrate the move towards globally integrated security policing that will unite immigration control and counter-terrorism with domestic street policing, and the practice of stop and search (Bowling, 2013).

Crucial to this development is the emergence of what has been described as a 'crimmigration' control system (Stumpf, 2006; Bowling, 2013). This refers to the convergence of criminal law and immigration law and the gradual intertwining of the institutions of immigration control and domestic criminal justice. It is clear in many contexts that, as border infractions such as unlawful entry, failure to register as an 'alien' or working illegally have become criminal offences, ordinary street policing and migration policing are being integrated and the lines between enforcement agencies and their internal or external enforcement jurisdiction are blurring. Immigration authorities, with their power to arrest and detain, operate extensively within domestic spaces (Weber and Bowling, 2004, 2008). At the same time, policing is becoming increasingly globalised (Bowling and Sheptycki, 2011). This raises the concern that we are witnessing the creation of globalised suspect populations in which a person's transnational or migratory status is taken as the basis for their suspiciousness and information on this state of suspiciousness is shared among police agencies around the world. In the 'risk society', police agents seek to sort the tourist from the vagabond (Weber and Bowling, 2008). New notions of 'immigration crime' and 'crimmigration' speak to this process.

The manifest justification for the globalisation of crime control is the presumed growth of transnational organised crime and terrorism. But this is also part of a broader reconfiguration of the state, as governments attempt to manage the contradictions stemming from the fact that national boundaries are no longer the constraints that they once were (Bowling and Sheptycki, 2011). In the face of neoliberal global governance, police organisation has undergone a number of shifts that can be brought under the broad headings of pluralisation, militarisation, transnationalisation and securitisation (Bowling and Newburn, 2006). This development is also linked to the extent of hybridisation of agency functions across the local, national, regional and international spheres. These are critical sites for analysis, particularly in relation to the role of counter-terrorism (Bowling, 2008). Security policing, therefore, has an important transnational dimension, which has not been subject to extensive research (Bowling, 2010).

The key point is that policing is not just done by the police, nor is it tied exclusively to the boundaries of the nation state. It obviously still includes 'blue uniformed police', but must also include customs, immigration, military and civil agencies, private police, security guards and a range of other state and private actors (Bowling, 2010). An important focus is to examine the policing of border crossings, and the policing of peoples in ways that connect local, national and transnational mechanisms of security policing (Weber and Bowling, 2004). These developments mean that a shift in research methods to encompass comparative and transnational approaches is needed to gain a better understanding of stop and search in the global context.

A comparative approach involves comparing and contrasting practices and experiences in different jurisdictions, drawing on worldwide knowledge and data, to develop richer theories with stronger external validity and wider applicability (Sheptycki and Wardak, 2005; Larsen and Smandych, 2008; Nelken, 2009). Comparative research in the area of stop and search would use comparative survey methods, case studies or ethnography to identify and explore differing policing practices and enforcement regimes and seek to explain and contrast different patterns in stop and search. Comparative research brings with it the possibility of developing more widely applicable theories by the collection of wide and rich data from different jurisdictions. A systematic comparative study of stop and search on a global scale would greatly enrich the knowledge available regarding global police practice. There is much that can be learned from comparing police practice in different countries, drawing on both similarities and differences. For example, what can be learned from jurisdictions that use stop and search powers very sparingly about the theory that aggressive and wide use of the power helps to maintain social order? A comparative approach might also seek to explore questions such as: What kinds of justifications are put forward, what specific stop and search practices are used, how extensively, how effectively and in what circumstances? What contribution does stop and search make to public safety in those places where it is used? Why are there such wide variations? How effective are legal, democratic and political means to hold the police use of stop and search to account in different contexts?

The transnational approach moves beyond the comparative study of different jurisdictions and focuses on policing practices that transcend national boundaries and therefore need to be understood through the study of linkages between places. Held and McGrew (2002) note that recent years have involved global events that clearly demonstrate the effect that what happens in one part of the world can have on another. Transnational research into stop and search focuses on how practices are linked across time and space: how events in one part of the world affect practice in others. Transnational criminology investigates the emergence of international legal regimes and enforcement strategies, such as the 'visionary' Interpol-backed global police force and the sharing of information between national police forces or the worldwide understanding of zero-tolerance policies, which have the aggressive use of stop and search powers at their core.

A transnational approach requires detailed research into and knowledge of different geographical areas and the processes of transnational power and knowledge-sharing. It requires methodological flexibility and a complex theoretical approach in order to facilitate the leap required to connect experiences around the globe. In the area of stop and search, a transnational body of research could add considerably to our understanding of the policing of national borders, spaces that are by definition transnational (Bowling, 2010). Research in this area could also contribute to the study of national policing of 'suspect communities' or those racially defined as 'others' within a society. Just as policing, intelligence and immigration policies have become internationally entwined, so too have the perceived threats of insecurity, particularly following the terror attacks in New York in 2001. Existing evidence indicates that both border control and street policing are focused on those who are ethnically different from the majority population (see Chapters 3 and 7). Much of the research that has been referred to clearly demonstrates that this is not a domestically contained issue. The issues identified relating to the inconsistency of recording in police stops globally are also relevant to border control. The lack of oversight and available data in the area of police stops and immigration control, which have become increasingly linked, directly inhibits comparative and transnational research and should be addressed urgently, as required by international human rights jurisprudence.

Conclusion

The power to stop and search is one the widest and most unfettered police powers in the domestic and transnational spheres. It is, perhaps, the widest and least constrained of all the coercive powers of government. It therefore requires the highest degree of critical scrutiny and public accountability, and deserves to be a much greater priority for researchers in political science, police studies and criminology.

Evidence on the use of use of stop and search powers from many jurisdictions shows that it is highly problematic in practice. It interferes with liberty and privacy and facilitates unlawful racial discrimination while offering little or nothing in terms of public protection. It is often synonymous with police harassment and abuse. Nonetheless, in our view, the idea that the police should have the power to stop someone who is genuinely suspected of wrongdoing, and to interview or search them without the need for arresting them and taking them to a police station, seems sensible *in principle*. From a security perspective, it seems preferable to doing nothing when genuine suspicions are aroused. From the perspective of liberty, it seems preferable to permitting the police to exercise powers of arrest based on mere suspicion.

Crucially, however, we must hold in mind the burden that stop and search imposes. The police act of stopping someone is an infringement of liberty and should be considered a form of detention, consistent with the notion of a deprivation of liberty. The act of searching a person or their belongings is an infringement of the right to privacy. State intrusion into the rights to liberty, privacy and freedom of movement require proper safeguards and mechanisms for accountability, review and redress. These powers are often used in conditions of low visibility against marginalised groups, and in many jurisdictions there is clear evidence of racism and discrimination in terms of both the process of using the power and its impact on minority communities. In practice, the power to stop and search is frequently used for reasons other than investigation, including for general deterrence, intelligence-gathering, harassment and discouraging public protest. None of these goals can be justified in a democracy.

The case that stop and search makes a significant contribution to public safety has not been made. In our view, stop and search practice in the jurisdiction from which we have evidence is simply not 'good enough' (Bowling, 2007). At best, it can be argued that the power brings very limited benefits in terms of crime control and order maintenance, and then only if it is used in narrowly circumscribed contexts. On the other hand, it is evident that stop and search has far-reaching iatrogenic effects – such as criminalisation, undermining police legitimacy, and the potential to trigger conflict. Police agencies can, and should, function with a much less extensive use of the power. 'Suspicionless searches' are justifiable in certain very narrowly defined and specific circumstances – such as boarding aircraft – but can never be justified in the general policing of public space. The use of stop and search powers should be restricted to those circumstances where an officer justifiably needs to confirm or allay well-founded suspicions of serious criminal behaviour and to those instances where the conditions of legality, proportionality, necessity and parsimony are satisfied (Bowling and Phillips, 2007).

Much of the debate in this area has been restricted to domestic policing in the UK and the US, with a gradually growing body of research in other contexts (Weber and Bowling, 2012). Inconsistency in global recording practices and the lack of oversight of police, border control and private actors around the world directly hampers research in this area and inhibits understanding of global stop and search practices, which are both directly comparable and interrelated. The limited international evidence that we have suggests that similar patterns of the use of stop and search, and similar controversies surrounding the power, are emerging in various different contexts. The overall picture is that the power is open to abuse if it is not carefully regulated and if the police are not held robustly to account.

It is clear that policing is rapidly globalising and that this is bringing new challenges to the study and control of police power (Bowling and Sheptycki, 2011). Police officers are sharing information, developing new hybrid practices that link domestic policing with immigration and counter-terrorist policing in various locations. The ambition among at least some leading police officials is for intrusive and coercive police powers – including the power to stop and search – to be globally connected. In order to understand the development of stop and search powers in the domestic context and beyond, police researchers must develop a transnational and comparative approach. Systematic research on this most controversial of state powers is essential to the task of ensuring that its use is transparent, accountable and consistent with the protection of fundamental human rights.

Note

1. Most notably in the landmark judgements of Sir Edward Coke in Semayne's Case (1604) and Lord Camden in Entick v Carrington [1765] EWHC KB J98.

10
Conclusion

Rebekah Delsol and Michael Shiner

The New York Roundtable that gave rise to this edited collection was a sobering experience for the British delegation. We left for New York on 9 August 2011, less than a week after police shot and killed Mark Duggan, whom they suspected of being a prominent gang member – a claim that has been disputed by his family (Moore, 2014). The riots that ensued provided a distant backdrop to our meeting, but lent the proceedings an eerie sense of urgency. While it was abundantly clear that all was not well at home, many of us were struck by how polarised the situation was in the US. We were told that several representatives from local community groups had refused to attend the event because the host institution had a history of training police officers; those community members who did attend talked about regular armed patrols in their neighbourhoods and spoke of the police as an occupying force, intent on harassment and intimidation; and we visited a Brooklyn-based community project that regularly took to the streets to film the police as a means of 'empowering communities, ending police misconduct, unprofessional behavior, and discrimination' (CopWatchNYC, 2013). Three years later, as we sit down to write this conclusion, it is the US that is picking up the pieces after rioting sparked by the fatal police shooting of a young black man – 18-year-old Michael Brown. A few weeks after Brown was shot, a peaceful demonstration was held in New York City in protest at the death of another African American: 43-year-old Eric Garner was intercepted by police for allegedly selling loose cigarettes and died after being placed in an apparent chokehold by an officer in what the Medical Examiner's Office ruled to be a homicide (CBS New York, 2014; Roberts et al., 2014). On average, police in America use lethal force on one person per day (*The Economist*, 2014), while 'police, and a smaller number of security guards and self-appointed vigilantes' do so on one black person every 28 hours (Malcolm X Grass Roots Movement, 2013; Johnson et al., 2014).

A member of our delegation came face-to-face with the euphemistic nature of New York's 'quality of life' policing during the visit. Chris, a member of the StopWatch youth group, was sitting in Times Square watching a street performance when several officers from the New York Police Department intervened to move the performer on, pushing their way through the assembled audience and kicking over his drum. The performer objected and produced documentation that he claimed was a permit, authorising his performance at that time and place, but the officers were unimpressed and insisted he move on. As the dispute showed signs of escalating and members of the crowd began to intervene in support of the performer, another group of officers arrived, creating a protective ring around their colleagues and the performer. When Chris tried to speak up in support of the performer, one of the officers pushed him back and told him to disperse. As he issued this instruction, the officer patted his holstered gun.

We arrived back in London to headlines that Bill Bratton, one of the chief architects of New York's quality of life policing, was being considered for the post of commissioner of the Metropolitan Police Service and was being courted by Prime Minister David Cameron, who was calling for a 'zero-tolerance' approach to crime (Dodd and Stratton, 2011; Eaton, 2011). In the event, Bratton, 'America's most fearsome policeman', did not get the job, though he was appointed as a government advisor on crime and gangs (*Daily Mail*, 2011). The post of commissioner was given to Bernard Hogan-Howe, who was billed as a 'gang buster' with a reputation for 'zero-tolerance' tactics (Davenport, 2011). During his first week in the job, Commissioner Hogan-Howe promised a 'war on crime' to 'put fear back in the minds of criminals', saying that 'no tactic – if it works – will be considered out of bounds' providing it is 'legal, ethical and done in good faith' (Godfrey, 2011; Whelan, 2011).

Our worst fears about where this might lead have not materialised. The politics of stop and search has taken an unexpected turn, and the trend towards greater use of the powers with less accountability has faltered. For the first time in almost a decade, the number of stop-searches is falling, and use of these powers is under more scrutiny now than at any other time since the Stephen Lawrence Inquiry. All 43 territorial police forces in England and Wales have recently signed up to the 'Best Use of Stop and Search Scheme', agreeing to a series of measures that increase police accountability, including the reintroduction of some of the recording requirements that were removed in 2011 (Home Office,

2014a; Rush, 2014). To some extent it feels as though we have come full circle, as the new scheme undoes part of what led to the formation of StopWatch. This does not mean StopWatch has become redundant, however, as levels of stop and search remain high; black and minority ethnic groups continue to be stopped and searched at disproportionately high rates; a large proportion of stop-searches continue to be carried out for minor drug possession offences; arrest rates remain low; there is no national requirement for the police to record stop and account; and 'exceptional' powers that do not require reasonable suspicion are still in place. Politically, moreover, the pull of New York 'zero-tolerance' style policing remains strong. The Metropolitan Police Service, with the support of the London Mayor Boris Johnson, recently launched a six-month trial of high-visibility patrols in London's West End, based on the New York Police Department's model for Times Square (BBC, 2014b).

Given this underlying continuity, StopWatch's central strategy remains unchanged, though the specifics of our work programme are evolving. Over the next year we will be working actively with impacted communities to advocate for stop and search reform in the lead up to the general election. Our youth-oriented work has come to include a sharper focus on child protection and safeguarding. Many stop-searches are of young people below the age of 18 years and some are of children below the age of 10, yet there are no specific regulations in place addressing the particular vulnerabilities of minors. This seems anomalous given that 'juveniles' cannot be questioned or subject to intimate searches in a police station without the presence of an appropriate adult (Home Office, 2013h). We have also broadened our focus to include areas that are allied to stop and search, including traffic stops and strip search, which are not covered by the recording requirement laid down by the Police and Criminal Evidence Act 1984 and are not subject to meaningful public scrutiny. Both these activities, we believe, should be recorded and monitored as part of the general requirement under Section 95 of the Criminal Justice Act 1991 that the secretary of state shall publish such information as s/he 'considers expedient' for the purpose of avoiding discrimination on the ground of race or sex or any other improper grounds (Ministry of Justice, 2013: 4).

We are acutely aware that 'well-intentioned' efforts at police reform often involve a 'systematic failure to confront the nature of policing' (Reiner, 2010: 253). As noted in the Introduction, policing necessarily involves the exercise of discretion and the ability to use coercive force, even though most incidents are resolved without it. We accept, and have been schooled in, critiques that warn against 'circumlocutions' and readily acknowledge that reform will always come up against the messy realities of everyday policing. We accept the point that, in an egoistic, anomic, divided society dominated by the interests of capital, much of what the police have to deal with is not of their own making. We also accept the corollary argument that the ability of the police to deliver a legitimate and effective service depends on the development of more inclusive social and economic policies. But we are wary of the potential fatalism involved in these arguments, which may be (mis)read as: policing requires discretion and violence, so let it be discretionary and violent. We maintain it is possible to accept that police discretion and the ability to use force are regrettable necessities without giving them free rein. Policing can be done more or less well, based on more or less proportionate responses, which are distributed more or less fairly. Stop and search is an important part of this equation and should be discussed as part of a broader conversation about the kind of police service we want.

References

M. Adjami (2006) *Ethnic Profiling in the Moscow Metro* (New York: Open Society Institute).

M. Ainsworth (2011) *Are Police-Initiated Stop Powers Effective?* Paper Delivered to UK/USA Roundtable on Current Debates, Research Agendas, and Strategies to Address Racial Disparities in Police Initiated Stops (New York: John Jay College), http://www.jjay.cuny.edu/centers/race_crime_justice/4788.php [accessed 25 August 2013].

A. Akwagyiram (2012) 'Stop and Search Use and Alternative Police Tactics', *BBC News*, 17 January, http://www.bbc.co.uk/news/uk-16552489 [accessed 27 August 2013].

C. Alexander (2000) *The Asian Gang: Ethnicity, Identity, Masculinity* (Oxford: Berg).

M. Alexander (2010) *The New Jim Crow: Mass Incarceration in the Age of Colorblindness* (New York: New Press).

American Psychological Association (2001) *Letter to U.S. House in Support of the End Racial Profiling Act, H.R. 2074*, 9 August 2001, http://www.apa.org/monitor/nov01/ppup.aspx [accessed 12 March 2014].

D. Anderson (2011) *Report on the Operation in 2010 of the Terrorism Act 2000 and of Part 1 of the Terrorism Act 2006* (London: The Stationery Office).

D. Anderson (2012) *The Terrorism Acts in 2011: Report of the Independent Reviewer on the Operation of the Terrorism Act 2000 and Part 1 of the Terrorism Act 2006* (London: The Stationery Office).

D. Anderson (2013) *The Terrorism Acts in 2012: Report of the Independent Reviewer on the Operation of the Terrorism Act 2000 and Part 1 of the Terrorism Act 2006* (London: Stationery Office).

D. Anderson (2014) 'Independent Review of Terrorism Laws: Searchlight or Veil?', *Social Science Research Network*, http://papers.ssrn.com/sol3/papers.cfm?abstract_id=2400656 [accessed 28 June 2014].

R. Aust and N. Smith (2003) *Ethnicity and Drug Use: Key Findings from the 2001/2002 British Crime Survey* (London: Home Office).

I. Awan (2012) 'The Impact of Policing British Muslims: A Qualitative Exploration', *Journal of Policing, Intelligence and Counter Terrorism*, 7(1): 22–35.

I. Ayres and J. Braithwaite (1992) *Responsive Regulation: Transcending the Deregulation Debate* (Oxford: Oxford University Press).

J. Ball and M. Taylor (2011) 'Theresa May to Review Stop and Search in Wake of Reading the Riots Study', *The Guardian*, 14 December 2011, http://www.theguardian.com/uk/2011/dec/14/theresa-may-stop-search-review [accessed 1 September 2013].

M. Banton (1964) *The Policeman in the Community* (London: Tavistock).

G. Barwell (2013) 'Tories Must Urgently Listen to Complaints About Stop and Search', *The Telegraph*, 3 July 2013, http://www.telegraph.co.uk/news/uknews/law-and-order/10157151/Why-Tories-must-urgently-listen-to-complaints-about-stop-and-search.html [accessed 1 September 2013].

G. Bazemore and C. Griffiths (2003) 'Police Reform, Restorative Justice and Restorative Policing', *Police Practice and Research: An International Journal*, 4(3): 335–346.
BBC (2014a) '"Regressive Attitudes" Hold Up Stop and Search Changes', *BBC NEWS UK*, 6 March 2014, http://www.bbc.co.uk/news/uk-26462039 [accessed 24 June 2014].
BBC (2014b) 'London West End "Cops" to Mimic New York Policing', *BBC NEWS London*, 28 July 2014, http://www.bbc.co.uk/news/uk-england-london-28525627 [accessed 26 August 2014].
H.S. Becker (1963) *Outsiders: Studies in the Sociology of Deviance* (New York: The Free Press).
J. Belur (2012) 'Police Stop and Search in India: Mumbai Nakabandi', in L. Weber and B. Bowling (eds.) *Stop and Search: Police Power in Global Context* (London: Routledge).
J. Bennetto (2009) *Police and Racism: What Has Been Achieved 10 Years After the Stephen Lawrence Inquiry Report* (London: Equality and Human Rights Commission).
T. Bingham (2011) *The Rule of Law* (London: Penguin Books).
E. Bittner (1970) *The Functions of Police in Modern Society* (Washington, DC: National Institute of Mental Health).
E. Bittner (1974) 'Florence Nightingale in Pursuit of Willie Sutton: A Theory of the Police', reprinted in T. Newburn (ed.) (2004) *Policing: Key Readings* (Cullompton: Willan).
D. Black (1998) *The Social Structure of Right and Wrong* (San Diego: Academic Press).
L. Blackwood, N. Hopkins, and S. Reicher (2012a) '"I know Who I Am, But Who Do They Think I Am?" Muslim Perspectives on Encounters With Airport Authorities', *Ethnic and Racial Studies*, 36(6): 1090–1108.
L. Blackwood, N. Hopkins, and S.D. Reicher (2012b) 'Divided by a Common Language? Conceptualizing Identity, Discrimination, and Alienation', in K.J. Jonas and T.A. Morton (eds.) *Restoring Civil Societies: The Psychology of Intervention and Engagement Following Crisis* (West Sussex: John Wiley and Sons).
N. Bland, J. Miller, and P. Quinton (2000a) *Upping the PACE? An Evaluation of the Stephen Lawrence Inquiry Recommendations on Stops and Searches* (London: Home Office).
N. Bland, J. Miller, and P. Quinton (2000b) *Managing the Use and Impact of Searches: A Review of Force Interventions* (London: Home Office).
D. Bonner (2007) *Executive Measures, Terrorism and National Security: Have the Rules of the Game Changed?* (Aldershot: Ashgate Publishing).
P. Bourdieu (1998) *On Television* (New York: New Press).
W.H. Bovey and A. Hede (2001) 'Resistance to Organisational Change: The Role of Defence Mechanisms', *Journal of Managerial Psychology*, 16(7): 534–548.
B. Bowling (1999) 'The Rise and Fall of New York Murder', *British Journal of Criminology*, 39(4): 531–554.
B. Bowling (2007) 'Fair and Effective Police Methods: Towards "Good Enough" Policing', *Scandinavian Studies in Criminology and Crime Prevention*, 8(1): 17–23.
B. Bowling (2008) 'Transnational Policing: The Globalisation Thesis, a Typology and a Research Agenda', *Policing: A Journal of Policy & Practice*, 3: 149–160.

B. Bowling (2010) *Policing the Caribbean: Transnational Security Cooperation in Practice* (Oxford: OUP).
B. Bowling (2013) 'The Borders of Punishment: Towards a Criminology of Mobility', in K.F. Aas and M. Bosworth (eds.) *Migration and Punishment: Citizenship, Crime Control, and Social Exclusion* (Oxford: OUP).
B. Bowling, A. Parmar, and C. Phillips (2008) 'Policing Ethnic Minority Communities', in T. Newburn (ed.) *The Handbook of Policing* (Cullompton: Willan).
B. Bowling and C. Phillips (2002) *Racism, Crime and Justice* (Harlow: Pearson).
B. Bowling and C. Phillips (2003) 'Policing Ethnic Minority Communities', in T. Newburn (ed.) *Handbook of Policing* (Cullompton: Willan).
B. Bowling and T. Newburn (2006) 'Policing and National Security', Paper presented at the London-Columbia Police, Community and Rule of Law Workshop, London 16–17 March 2006.
B. Bowling and C. Phillips (2007) 'Disproportionate and Discriminatory: Reviewing the Evidence on Stop and Search', *Modern Law Review*, 70(6): 936–961.
B. Bowling and J. Sheptycki (2011) 'Policing Globopolis', *Social Justice*, 38: 1–2.
B. Bowling and L. Weber (2013) *Stop and Search: Police Power in Global Context* (Oxford: Routledge).
B. Bradford (2013) *Disproportionality and the Effectiveness of Stop and Search: Evidence From Police Force Area Level Data* (London: StopWatch).
B. Bradford (2014) 'Policing and Social Identity: Procedural Justice, Inclusion and Cooperation Between Police and Public', *Policing and Society*, 24(1): 22–43.
B. Bradford and J. Jackson (2010) 'Cooperating With the Police: Social Control and the Reproduction of Police Legitimacy', *Social Science Research Network*, http://papers.ssrn.com/sol3/papers.cfm?abstract_id=1640958 [accessed 29 August 2013].
B. Bradford and J. Jackson (2011) 'When Trust Is Lost: The British and Their Police After the Tottenham Riots', *Books and Ideas.Net*, http://www.booksandideas.net/When-Trust-is-Lost.html [accessed 14 March 2014].
B. Bradford, J. Jackson, and M. Hough (2013) 'Police Futures and Legitimacy: Redefining Good Policing', in J. Brown (ed.) *The Future of Policing* (Oxford: Routledge).
B. Bradford, J. Jackson, and E.A. Stanko (2009) 'Contact and Confidence: Revisiting Asymmetry in the Impact of Encounters With the Police', *Policing and Society*, 19(1): 20–46.
A. Braga, A. Papachristos, and D. Hureau (2012) *Hot Spots Policing Effects on Crime* (Oslo: Campbell Collaboration).
A.A. Braga and B.J. Bond (2008) 'Policing Crime and Disorder Hot Spots: A Randomized, Controlled Trial', *Criminology*, 46: 577–607.
A.A. Braga, D.L. Weisburd, E.J. Waring, L.G. Mazerolle, W. Spelman, and F. Gajewski (1999) 'Problem-Oriented Policing in Violent Crime Places: A Randomized Controlled Experiment', *Criminology*, 37(3): 541–579.
J. Braithwaite (2002) *Restorative Justice and Responsive Regulation* (Oxford: Oxford University Press).
L. Bridges, M. Shiner, R. Delsol, and K. Gill (2011) *StopWatch Statement on Police Stop and Account, 21 December 2011* (London: StopWatch).
A. Brogden (1981) ' "Sus" Is Dead: But What About "Sas"?' *New Community*, 9(1): 44–52.

F. Brookman and M. Maguire (2003) *Reducing Homicide: A Review of the Possibilities* (London: Home Office).

M.K. Brown (1981) *Policing the Street: Discretion and the Dilemmas of Reform* (New York: The Russell Sage Foundation).

R. Camber (2011) ' "We Don't Do Water Cannon, We Rely on Consent": May Rules Out Tough Action as Vigilantes Are Forced to Defend Shops', *Daily Mail*, 9 August 2011, http://www.dailymail.co.uk/news/article-2023932/London-riots-2011-Theresa-May-rules-tough-action-vigilantes-defend-shops.html [accessed 1 September 2013].

A. Carlile (2009) *Report on the Operation in 2008 of the Terrorism Act 2000 and of Part 1 of the Terrorism Act 2006* (London: Stationery Office).

A. Carlile (2010) *Report on the Operation in 2009 of the Terrorism Act 2000 and Part 1 of the Terrorism Act 2006* (London: The Stationery Office).

CBS New York (2014) *City Council Holds Hearing on Proposed Changes to NYPD Training in Wake of Eric Garner Case*, 8 September 2014, http://newyork.cbslocal.com/2014/09/08/city-council-to-hold-hearing-on-proposed-changes-to-nypd-training-in-wake-of-eric-garner-case/ [accessed 8 September 2014].

S. Cemlyn, M. Greenfields, S. Burnett, Z. Matthews, and C. Whitwell (2009) *Inequalities Experienced by Gypsy and Traveller Communities: A Review* (London: Equalities and Human Rights Commission).

Center on Race, Crime and Justice (2010) *Stop, Question and Frisk Policing Practices in New York City: A Primer* (New York: John Jay College of Criminal Justice).

S. Chainey and I. Macdonald (2012) *Stop and Search, the Use of Intelligence and Geographic Targeting: Findings from Case Study Research* (London: NPIA).

J.M. Chanin (2014) Examining the Sustainability of Pattern or Practice Police Misconduct Reform, Police Quarterly, doi: 10.1177/1098611114561305.

S. Choongh (1997) *Policing as Social Discipline* (Oxford: OUP).

T. Choudhury and H. Fenwick (2011) *The Impact of Counter-Terrorism Measures on Muslim Communities* (London: Equalities and Human Rights Commission).

J. Churcher (2012) 'Met Chief Vows to Uncover Truth About "Plebgate" Row', *The Independent*, 23 December 2012, http://www.independent.co.uk/news/uk/politics/met-chief-vows-to-uncover-truth-about-plebgate-row-8430371.html [accessed 1 September 2013].

A. Clancy, M. Hough, R. Aust, and C. Kershaw (2001) *Crime, Policing and Justice: The Experience of Ethnic Minorities – Findings from the 2000 British Crime Survey* (London: Home Office).

T. Cockcroft (2013) *Police Culture: Themes and Concepts* (Abingdon: Routledge).

T. Cockcroft and I. Beattie (2009) 'Shifting Cultures: Managerialism and the Rise of "Performance" Policing', *An International Journal of Police Strategies and Management*, 32(3): 526–540.

D. Cole (2003a) 'Security and Freedom – Are the Governments' Efforts to Deal with Terrorism Violative of Our Freedoms?' *Canada-United States Law Journal*, 29(1): 339–349.

D. Cole (2003b) 'Their Liberties, Our Security: Democracy and Double Standards', *International Journal of Legal Information*, 31(1): 290–311.

D. Cole and J. Dempsey (2006) *Terrorism and the Constitution* (New York: New Press).

Y. Cooper (2014) 'Statement to Parliament on Stop and Search', *Hansard*, 30 April 2014, Column: 831–847.

CopWatchNYC (2013) *CopWatchNYC.Org – Getting Started*, http://copwatchnyc.org/getting-started/ [accessed 26 August 2014].
E. Cossé (2013) *Unwelcome Guests – Greek Police Abuses of Migrants in Athens* (London: Human Rights Watch).
Daily Mail (2011) *Taking on Our Gangs: Man Who Cleaned Up New York Taken on as Cameron's Adviser*, 12 August 2011, http://www.dailymail.co.uk/news/article-2024946/UK-riots-Bill-Bratton-advise-David-Cameron-gang-warfare.html [accessed 25 August 2014].
J. Davenport (2011) 'New Met Chief Is Gang Buster Bernard Hogan-Howe', *Evening Standard*, 12 September 2011, http://www.standard.co.uk/news/new-met-chief-is-gang-buster-bernard-hoganhowe-6442565.html [accessed 25 August 2014].
J. Davenport (2012) 'Police Stop and Search Slashed', *London Evening Standard*, 12 January 2012, http://www.standard.co.uk/news/police-stop-and-search-slashed-7307091.html [accessed 1 September 2013].
R. Delsol (2009a) 'Racial Profiling', in A. Wakefield and J. Fleming (eds.) *The SAGE Dictionary of Policing* (London: Sage).
R. Delsol (2009b) *Addressing Ethnic Profiling by Police. A Report on the Strategics for Effective Police Stop and Search Project* (New York: Open Society Institute).
R. Delsol (2010) 'Section 60 Stop and Search Powers', in K.P. Sveinsson (ed.) *Ethnic Profiling: The Use of 'Race' in UK Law Enforcement* (London: Runnymede).
R. Delsol (2012) 'London's Police Rethink Stop and Search Tactics', *Open Society Foundations*, http://www.opensocietyfoundations.org/voices/london-s-police-rethinks-stop-and-search-tactics [accessed 3 March 2013].
R. Delsol and M. Shiner (2006) 'Regulating Stop and Search: A Challenge for Police and Community Relations in England and Wales', *Critical Criminology*, 14: 241–263.
Z. Derfoufi (2012) 'West Midland's PCC Candidates Pledge to Review Stop and Search', *StopWatch News and Comment* (London: StopWatch), http://www.stop-watch.org/news-comment/story/west-midlands-pcc-candidates-pledge-to-review-stop-and-search [accessed 1 September 2013].
B. Dickson (2009) 'The Detention of Suspected Terrorists in Northern Ireland and Great Britain', *University of Richmond Law Review*, 43(1): 927–965.
D. Dixon (1997) *Law in Policing: Legal Regulation and Police Practices* (Oxford: Clarendon).
D. Dixon (2008) 'Authorise and Regulate: A Comparative Perspective on the Rise and Fall of a Regulatory Strategy', in E. Cape and R. Young (eds.) *Regulating Policing* (Oxford: Hart).
V. Dodd (2005) 'Asian Men Targeted in Stop and Search', *The Guardian*, 17 August 2005, http://www.theguardian.com/uk/2005/aug/17/race.july7 [accessed 21 August 2013].
V. Dodd (2011) '"Racist" Stop-and-Search Powers to Be Challenged', *The Guardian*, 8 July 2011, http://www.theguardian.com/law/2011/jul/08/racist-stop-search-powers-challenge [accessed 29 August 2013].
V. Dodd (2012) 'Metropolitan Police to Scale Back Stop and Search Operation', *The Guardian*, 12 January 2012, http://www.theguardian.com/uk/2012/jan/12/met-police-stop-search-suspicion [accessed 12 June 2013].
V. Dodd and A. Stratton (2011) 'Bill Bratton Says He Can Lead Police Out of "Crisis" Despite Budget Cuts', *The Guardian*, 14 August 2011, http://

www.theguardian.com/uk/2011/aug/14/bill-bratton-police-crisis-cuts [accessed 25 August 2014].
V. Dodd and A. Travis (2005) 'Muslims Face Increased Stop and Search', *The Guardian*, 2 March 2005, http://www.theguardian.com/politics/2005/mar/02/terrorism.immigrationpolicy1 [accessed 29 August 2013].
J.F. Dovidio, P. Glick, and L. Rudman (2005) *On the Nature of Prejudice: Fifty Years After Allport* (Malden, MA: Blackwell).
M.D. Dubber (2005) *The Police Power: Patriarchy and the Foundations of American Government* (New York: Columbia University Press).
N. Eastwood, M. Shiner, and D. Bear (2013) *The Numbers in Black and White: Ethnic Disparities in the Policing and Prosecution of Drug Offences in England and Wales* (London: Release).
G. Eaton (2011) 'What Bill Bratton Really Thinks About "Zero Tolerance"', *The New Statesman*, 16 August 2011, http://www.newstatesman.com/blogs/the-staggers/2011/08/zero-tolerance-cameron-bratton [accessed 25 August 2014].
M. Ellis (2014) 'Statement to Parliament on Stop and Search', *Hansard*, 30 April 2014, Column: 831–847.
C. Emsley (2014) 'Peel's Principles, Police Principles', in J. Brown (ed.) *The Future of Policing* (Abingdon: Routledge), pp. 11–22.
C.R. Epp (2009) *Making Rights Real: Activists, Bureaucrats, and the Creation of the Legalistic State* (Chicago: The University of Chicago Press).
Equality and Human Rights Commission (2010) *Stop and Think: A Critical Review of the Use of Stop and Search Powers in England and Wales* (London: Equalities and Human Rights Commission).
Equalities and Human Rights Commission (2012) *Race Disproportionality in Stops and Searches Under Section 60 of the Criminal Justice and Public Order Act 1994* (London: Equalities and Human Rights Commission).
Equality and Human Rights Commission (2013) *Stop and Think Again: Towards Race Equality in Police PACE Stop and Search* (London: Equalities and Human Rights Commission).
R. Ericson (1975) *Criminal Reactions: The Labelling Perspective* (London: Ashgate).
J.A. Eterno and E.B. Silverman (2012) *The Crime Numbers Game: Management by Manipulation* (New York: CRC Press).
European Court of Human Rights (2010) *Gillan and Quinton v. the United Kingdom*, Application no. 4158/05, Judgement of 12 January 2010.
C. Falconer (2013) 'The Detention of David Miranda Was an Unlawful Use of the Terrorism Act', *The Guardian*, 21 August 2013.
D.P. Farrington (1977) 'The Effects of Public Labelling', *British Journal of Criminology*, 17: 112–125.
D.P. Farrington, S.G. Osborn, and D.J. West (1978) 'The Persistence of Labelling Effects', *British Journal of Criminology*, 18: 277–284.
V. Felbab-Brown (2013) *Focused Deterrence, Selective Targeting, Drug Trafficking and Organised Crime: Concepts and Practicalities* (London: International Drug Police Consortium).
A. Field (2009) 'The "New Terrorism": Revolution or Evolution?' *Political Studies Review*, 7(2): 195–207.
N. Fielding (1991) *The Police and Conflict: Rhetoric and Reality* (London: The Athlone Press).

M. FitzGerald (1999) *Searches in London Under Section 1 of the Police and Criminal Evidence Act* (London: Metropolitan Police Service).
M. FitzGerald (2010a) *Background Note: Analyses of MPS Knife Crime Data and the Use of S60 Searches*, Unpublished Briefing Note.
M. FitzGerald (2010b) 'A Confidence Trick?' *Policing: A Journal of Policy and Practice*, 4(3): 298–301.
M. FitzGerald, M. Hough, I. Joseph, and T. Quereshi (2002) *Policing for London* (Cullompton: Willan Publishing).
M. FitzGerald and R. Sibbitt (1997) *Ethnic Monitoring in Police Forces: A Beginning* (London: Home Office).
R. Flanegan (2007) *The Review of Policing: Interim Report* (London: Home Office).
C. Flood-Page, S. Campbell, V. Harrington, and J. Miller (2000) *Youth Crime: Findings from the 1998/1999 Youth Lifestyles Survey* (London: Home Office).
J. Foster, T. Newburn, and A. Souhami (2005) *Assessing the Impact of the Stephen Lawrence Inquiry* (London: Home Office).
R. Fuller (2014) 'Statement to Parliament on Stop and Search', *Hansard*, 30 April 2014, Column: 831–847.
M. Futtrup and B.C. Jacobsen (2011) *Ethnic Profiling in Denmark – Legal Safeguards Within the Field of Work of the Police* (Copenhagen: Danish Institute of Human Rights).
D. Garland (2001) *The Culture of Control* (Oxford: Oxford University).
C. Gearty (1999) 'Terrorism and Human Rights: A Case Study in Impending Legal Realities' *Legal Studies*, 19(3): 367–379.
A. Geller and J. Fagan (2010) 'Pot as Pretext: Marijuana, Race and New Disorder in New York City Street Policing', *Journal of Empirical Legal Studies*, 7(4), 591–633.
K. Gill (2012) 'Stop and Search Your PCC – ISCRE's Stephanie Palmer Meets the PCC Candidates for Suffolk', *StopWatch News and Comment*, http://www.stop-watch.org/news-comment/story/stop-and-search-your-pcc-iscres-stephanie-palmer-meets-the-pcc-candidates-f [accessed 1 September 2013].
P. Gilroy (1987) 'The Myth of Black Criminality', in P. Scraton (ed.) *Law, Order and the Authoritarian State* (Milton Keynes: Open University Press).
B. Glassner (1980) *Essential Interactionism: On the Intelligibility of Prejudice* (London: Routledge and Paul Kegan).
H. Godfrey (2011) 'New Met Police Chief Bernard Hogan-Howe Promises "War on Crime" ', *The Guardian*, 14 September 2011, http://www.theguardian.com/uk/2011/sep/14/met-police-hogan-howe-crime [accessed 26 July 2013].
J. Goldstein (2013) 'Judge Rejects New York's Stop-and-Frisk Policy', *New York Times*, 12 August 2013, http://www.nytimes.com/2013/08/13/nyregion/stop-and-frisk-practice-violated-rights-judge-rules.html?ref=nyregion&_r=1& [accessed 27 August 2013].
J. Goodey (2006) 'Ethnic Profiling, Criminal (In)Justice and Minority Populations', *Critical Criminology*, 14: 207–212.
I. Goris, F. Jobard, and R. Lévy (2009) *Profiling Minorities: A Study of Stop-and-Search Practices in Paris* (New York: Open Society Institute).
J. Graham and B. Bowling (1995) *Young People and Crime* (London: Home Office).
J. Graham and J. Karn (2013) *Policing Young Adults: A Scoping Study* (London: The Police Foundation).
R. Grimshaw and A. Jefferson (1987) *Interpreting Policework* (London: Unwin).

C. Hales, C. Nevill, S. Pudney, and S. Tipping (2009) *Longitudinal Analysis of the Offending, Crime and Justice Survey 2003–06* (London: Home Office).

S. Hall, C. Critcher, T. Jefferson, J.N. Clarke, and B. Roberts (1978) *Policing the Crisis: Mugging, the State and Law and Order* (London: Palgrave Macmillan).

S. Hallsworth (2006) 'Racial Targeting and Social Control: Looking Behind the Police', *Critical Criminology*, 14(3): 293–311.

B. Harcourt (2004) 'Rethinking Racial Profiling: A Critique of the Economics, Civil Liberties, and Constitutional Literature, and of Criminal Profiling More Generally', *The University of Chicago Law Review*, 71(4): 1329–1330.

B.E. Harcourt (2007) *Against Prediction: Profiling, Policing, and Punishing in an Actuarial Age* (Chicago: University of Chicago Press).

D.A. Harris (2007) 'The Importance of Research on Race and Policing: Making Race Salient to Individuals and Institutions Within Criminal Justice', *Criminology and Public Policy*, 6: 5–24.

D. Harris (2013) 'Across the Hudson: Taking the Stop and Frisk Debate Beyond New York City', *Legislation and Public Policy*, 16: 853–882.

K. Hawkins (2003) 'Order, Rationality and Silence: Some Reflections on Criminal Justice Decision-Making', in L. Gelsthorpe and N. Padfield (eds.) *Exercising Discretion: Decision-Making in the Criminal Justice System* (Cullompton: Willan).

A. Heath and J. Martin (2013) 'Can Religious Affiliation Explain "Ethnic" Inequalities in the Labour Market?' *Ethnic and Racial Studies*, 36(6): 1005–1027.

D. Held and A. McGrew (2002) *The Global Transformation Reader: An Introduction to the Globalization Debate* (Cambridge: Polity).

N. Herbert (2010) 'PACE (Stop and Search)', *Hansard*, 1 December 2010: 298WH, http://www.publications.parliament.uk/pa/cm201011/cmhansrd/cm101201/halltext/101201h0001.htm#10120146000001 [accessed 31 August 2013].

Her Majesty's Government (1974) *Prevention of Terrorism (Temporary Provisions) Act 1974* (London: Stationery Office).

Her Majesty's Government (2000) *The Terrorism Act 2000* (London: The Stationery Office).

Her Majesty's Government (2014) *Anti-Social Behaviour, Crime and Policing Act 2014* (London: Her Majesty's Stationery Office).

Her Majesty's Inspectorate of Constabulary (1999) *Winning the Race (Revisited): Policing Plural Communities* (London: Home Office).

Her Majesty's Inspectorate of Constabulary (2013) *Stop and Search Powers: Are the Police Using Them Effectively and Fairly?* (London: HMIC).

M.J. Hickman, L. Thomas, S. Silvestri, and H. Nickels (2011) *'Suspect Communities'? Counter-Terrorism Policy, the Press, and the Impact on Irish and Muslim communities in Britain* (London: London Metropolitan University).

High Court of Justice (2013) *Elosta v Commissioner of Police for the Metropolis*, [2013] EWHC 3397 (QB) (London: Royal Courts of Justice), http://www.judiciary.gov.uk/wp-content/uploads/JCO/Documents/Judgments/elosta-judgment.pdf [accessed 24 July 2014].

J. Hills, M. Brewer, S. Jenkins, R. Lister, R. Lupton, S. Machin, C. Mills, T. Modood, T. Rees, and S. Riddell (2010) *An Anatomy of Economic Inequality in the UK: Report of the National Equality Panel* (London: Government Equalities Office).

P. Hillyard (1993) *Suspect Community: People's Experience of the Prevention of Terrorism Acts in Britain* (London: Pluto Press).

S. Holdaway (1983) *Inside the British Police* (Oxford: Blackwell).

References 205

L. Holloway (2013) *Power of the Black Vote in 2015: The Changing Face of England and Wales* (London: Operation Black Vote).
Home Affairs Select Committee (2005) *Terrorism and Community Relations, Sixth Report* (London: House of Commons).
Home Affairs Select Committee (2007) *Young Black People and the Criminal Justice System* (London: Houses of Parliament).
Home Office (1999) *Statistics on Race and the Criminal Justice System 1999* (London: Home Office).
Home Office (2002) *Statistics on Race and the Criminal Justice System 2002* (London: Home Office).
Home Office (2003) *Statistics on Race and the Criminal Justice System 2003* (London: Home Office).
Home Office (2004) *Statistics on Race and the Criminal Justice System 2004* (London: Home Office).
Home Office (2006) *Statistics on Race and the Criminal Justice System 2005* (London: Home Office).
Home Office (2009a) *Police Powers and Procedures England and Wales 2007/08* (London: Home Office).
Home Office (2009b) *Statistics on Race and the Criminal Justice System 2007/8* (London: Home Office).
Home Office (2010a) *Police Workforce, England and Wales, March 2010* (London: Home Office).
Home Office (2010b) *Statistics on Race and the Criminal Justice System 2008/9* (London: Home Office).
Home Office (2010c) *Policing in the 21st Century: Reconnecting Police and People*. Cm 7925, July, www.homeoffice.gov.uk/publications/consultations/policing-21st-century [accessed 22 September 2014].
Home Office (2011a) *Terrorism Act 2000: Code of Practice (England, Wales and Scotland) for the Authorisation and Exercise of Stop and Search Powers Relating to Section 47A of Schedule 6B to the Terrorism Act 2000* (London: Home Office).
Home Office (2011b) *Police and Criminal Evidence Act 1984 Codes of Practice, Code A* (London: Home Office).
Home Office (2011c) *Police Powers and Procedures England and Wales 2009/10* (London: Home Office).
Home Office (2012a) *Review of the Operation of Schedule 7: A Public Consultation* (London, Home Office).
Home Office (2012b) *Police Powers and Procedures England and Wales 2010/11* (London: Home Office).
Home Office (2012c) *Offences Recorded by the Police in England and Wales by Offence and Police Force Area, 1990 to 2011–12* (London: Home Office).
Home Office (2012d) *Drug Misuse Declared: Findings From the 2011/12 Crime Survey for England and Wales* (London: Home Office).
Home Office (2013a) *Police and Criminal Evidence Act 1984 (PACE) Codes of Practice, Code A* (London: Home Office).
Home Office (2013b) *A Consultation on Police Powers of Stop and Search* (London: Home Office).
Home Office (2013c) 'Home Secretary Launches Consultation into Stop and Search', *Home Office News Story*, 2 July 2013, https://www.gov.uk/government/

news/home-secretary-launches-consultation-into-stop-and-search [accessed 29 August 2013].

Home Office (2013d) *Police Powers and Procedures England and Wales 2011–2012* (London: Home Office).

Home Office (2013e) *Police Workforce, England and Wales–2013* (London: Home Office).

Home Office (2013f) *Operation of Police Powers Under the Terrorism Act 2000 and Subsequent Legislation, Quarterly Update to September 2012 (Great Britain)* (London: Home Office).

Home Office (2013g) *Drug Misuse Declared: Findings From the 2012/13 Crime Survey for England and Wales* (London: Home Office).

Home Office (2013h) *Police and Criminal Evidence Act 1984 (PACE) Codes of Practice, Code C* (London: Home Office).

Home Office (2014a) *Best Use of Stop and Search Scheme* (London: Home Office).

Home Office (2014b) *Police Powers and Procedures England and Wales 2012/2013* (London: Home Office).

Home Office (2014c) 'Launch of Government's Best Use of Stop and Search Scheme', *Home Office News Story*, 1 December 2014, https://www.gov.uk/government/news/launch-of-governments-best-use-of-stop-and-search-scheme [accessed 10 January 2015].

Home Office (2014d) *Schedule 7: Background Information* (London: Home Office).

N. Hopkins (2011) 'Dual Identities and Their Recognition: Minority Group Members' Perspectives', *Political Psychology*, 32(2): 251–270.

M. Hough, J. Jackson, B. Bradford, A. Myhill, and P. Quinton (2010) 'Procedural Justice, Trust, and Institutional Legitimacy', *Policing: A Journal of Policy and Practice*, 4(3): 203–210.

C. Hoyle and R. Young (2003) 'Restorative Justice, Victims and the Police', in T. Newburn (ed.) *Handbook of Policing* (Cullompton: Willan).

E.C. Hughes (1962) 'Good People and Dirty Work', *Social Problems*, 10(1) (Summer, 1962): 3–11.

D. Huizinga, K. Schuman, B. Ehret, and A. Elliot (2003) *The Effects of Juvenile Justice Processing on Subsequent Delinquent and Criminal Behaviour: A Cross-National Study* (Washington, DC: Final Report to the National Institute of Justice).

A.Z. Huq, T.R. Tyler, and S.J. Schulhofer (2011) 'Why Does the Public Cooperate with Law Enforcement? The Influence of the Purposes and Targets of Policing', *Psychology, Public Policy, and Law*, 17(3): 419–450.

B. Hurst (2014) 'Crime Commissioner: Police Used Stop and Search Just 8 Times in Last Year', *Birmingham Mail*; http://www.birminghammail.co.uk/news/midlands-news/police-used-stop-search-powers-6649793 [accessed 3 May 2014].

Independent Police Complaints Commission (IPCC) (2012) *Police Complaints: Statistics for England and Wales – 2011/12* (London: IPCC).

M. Innes (2006) 'Policing Uncertainty: Countering Terror Through Community Intelligence and Democratic Policing', *The ANNALS of the American Academy of Political and Social Science*, 605: 222–241.

M. Innes and D. Thiel (2008) 'Policing Terror', in T. Newburn (ed.) *Handbook of Policing* (Collumpton: Willan).

Institute of Race Relations (1979) *Policing Against Black People* (London: Institute of Race Relations).

Institute of Race Relations (1987) *Policing Against Black People* (London: Institute of Race Relations).
J. Jackson and B. Bradford (2009) 'Crime, Policing and Social Order: On the Expressive Nature of Public Confidence in Policing', *British Journal of Sociology*, 60(3): 493–521.
J. Jackson, B. Bradford, M. Hough, A. Myhill, P. Quinton, and T.R. Tyler (2012a) 'Why Do People Comply with the Law?: Legitimacy and the Influence of Legal Institutions', *British Journal of Criminology*, 52(6): 1051–1071.
J. Jackson, B. Bradford, E.A. Stanko, and K. Hohl (2012b) *Just Authority? Trust in the Police in England and Wales* (London: Routledge).
J. Jackson, A. Huq, B. Bradford, and T.R. Tyler (2013) 'Monopolizing force?: Police Legitimacy and Public Attitudes Toward Private Violence', *Psychology, Public Policy, and Law*, 19(4): 479–497.
J. Jackson, T.R. Tyler, B. Bradford, D. Taylor, and M. Shiner (2010) 'Structured Communications in Prison: A Project to Achieve More Consistent Performance and Fairer Outcomes for Staff and Prisoners', *Prison Service Journal*, 191: 24–26.
K. Johnson, H. Meghan and B. Heath (2014) 'Local Police Involved in 400 Killings Per Year', *USA TODAY*, 15 August 2014; http://www.usatoday.com/story/news/nation/2014/08/14/police-killings-data/14060357/ [accessed 30 August 2014].
P. Johnson (2005) 'The Police Must End Their Abuse of Anti-Terror Legislation', *The Telegraph*, 3 October 2005, http://www.telegraph.co.uk/comment/personal-view/3620110/The-police-must-end-their-abuse-of-anti-terror-legislation.html [accessed 26 August 2013]
T. Jones (2003) 'The Governance and Accountability of Policing', in T. Newburn (ed.) *Handbook of Policing* (Cullompton: Willan).
T. Jones and T. Newburn (2007) *Policy Transfer and Criminal Justice* (Maidenhead: Open University Press).
J. Karn (2013) *Policing and Crime Reduction: The Evidence and Its Implications for Practice* (London: Police Foundation).
H.C. Kelman and V.L. Hamilton (1989) *Crimes of Obedience* (New Haven, CT: Yale University Press).
M. Khalid (2011) 'Gender, Orientalism and Representations of the "Other" in the War on Terror', *Global Change, Peace and Security*, 23(1): 15–29.
D. S. Kirk and M. Matsuda (2011) 'Legal Cynicism, Collective Efficacy, and the Ecology of Arrest', *Criminology*, 49(2): 443-472.
J. Kleinig (1996) *The Ethics of Policing* (Cambridge: Cambridge University Press).
C.B. Klockars (1988) 'The Rhetoric of Community Policing', in J.R. Greene and S. Mastrofski (eds.) *Community Policing: Rhetoric or Reality?* (New York: Praeger).
C. Koper (1995) 'Just Enough Police Presence: Reducing Crime and Disorderly Behavior by Optimizing Patrol Time in Crime Hotspots', *Justice Quarterly*, 12(4): 649–672.
A. Kundnani (2009) *Spooked: How Not to Prevent Violent Extremism* (London: Institute of Race Relations).
N. Lacey (1988) *State Punishment: Political Principles and Community Values* (Oxford: Routledge).
N. Larsen and R. Smandych (2008) *Global Criminology and Criminal Justice: Current Issues and Perspectives* (Ontario: Broadview Press).
S. Laville (2014) 'Plebgate Row: Police Officer Sacked Over Leaks to the Press', *The Guardian*, April 30 2014; http://www.theguardian.com/uk-news/2014/apr/30/plebgate-row-police-officer-sacked-leaks-press [accessed 3 May 2014].

J. Lea (2000) 'The Macpherson Report and the Question of Institutional Racism', *The Howard Journal*, 39(3): 219–233.
J. Lea and J. Young (1984) *What Is to Be Done About Law and Order?* (Harmondsworth: Penguin Books).
M. Lee (2007) *Inventing Fear of Crime: Criminology and the Politics of Anxiety* (London: Routledge).
L.H. Leigh (1981) 'The Royal Commission on Criminal Procedure', *The Modern Law Review*, 44(3): 296–308.
R. Levitas, C. Pantazis, E. Fahmy, D. Gordon, E. Lloyd, and D. Patsios (2007) *The Multi-Dimensional Analysis of Social Exclusion* (Bristol: University of Bristol).
P. Lewis, T. Newburn, M. Taylor, C. McGillivray, A. Greenhill, H. Frayman, and R. Proctor (2011) *Reading the Riots: Investigating England's Summer of Disorder* (London: LSE and *The Guardian*).
I. Loader and A. Mulcahy (2003) *Policing and the Condition of England* (Oxford: Oxford University Press).
I. Loader and R. Sparks (2011) *Public Criminology?* (London: Routledge).
B. Loftus (2009) *Police Culture in a Changing World* (Oxford: Oxford University Press).
V. Lowe (2005) 'Clear and Present Danger: Responses to Terrorism', *International and Comparative Law Quarterly*, 54(1): 185–196.
L. Lustgarten (2002) 'The Future of Stop and Search', *Criminal Law Review*, 603–618.
C. Mackey (2012) 'Section 60 Criminal Justice and Public Order Act 1994', *The Guardian*, 12 January 2012, http://www.theguardian.com/law/2012/jan/12/craig-mackey-letter-chief-constables [accessed 12 June 2013].
W. Macpherson (1999) *Inquiry into the Matters Arising from the Death of Stephen Lawrence* (London: The Stationery Office).
M. Maguire (2008) 'Criminal Investigation and Crime Control', in T. Newburn (ed.) *Handbook of Policing* (Cullompton: Willan).
Malcolm X Grass Roots Movement (2013) *Operation Ghetto Storm: 2012 Annual Report on the Extrajudicial Killing of Black People*, https://mxgm.org/wp-content/uploads/2013/04/operation_ghetto_storm_updated_october_2013.pdf [accessed 14 June 2014].
P. Manning (2003) *Policing Contingencies* (Chicago: University of Chicago Press).
O. Marenin (1983) 'Parking Tickets and Class Repression: The Concept of Policing in Critical Theories of Criminal Justice', *Contemporary Crises*, 6(2): 241–66.
A. Margalit (1996) *The Decent Society* (Cambridge, MA: Harvard University Press).
M. Marks (2012) 'The Fantastical World of South Africa's Roadblocks: Dilemmas of a Ubiquitous Police Strategy', in L. Weber and B. Bowling (eds.) *Stop and Search: Police Power in Global Context* (London: Routledge).
G. Marshall (1978) 'Police Accountability Revisited', in D. Butler and A.H. Halsey (ed.) *Policy and Politics* (London: Macmillan).
G.T. Marx (2001) 'Police and Democracy', in M. Amir and S. Einstein (eds.) *Policing, Security and Democracy* (Chicago: Office of International Criminal Justice).
D. Matza (1964) *Delinquency and Drift* (New York: Wiley).
T. May (2014) 'Statement to Parliament on Stop and Search', *Hansard*, 30 April 2014, Column: 831–847.

T. May, T. Gyateng, and M. Hough with the assistance of B. Bhardwa, I. Boyce, and J.C. Oyanedel (2010) *Differential Treatment in the Youth Justice System* (London: Equalities and Human Rights Commission).

L. Mazerolle, S. Bennett, E. Antrobus, and E. Eggins (2012) 'Procedural Justice, Routine Encounters and Citizen Perceptions of Police: Main Findings from the Queensland Community Engagement Trial (QCET)', *Journal of Experimental Criminology*, 8(4): 343–367.

L. Mazerolle, D. Soole, and S. Rombouts (2007) 'Drug Law Enforcement: A Review of the Evaluation Literature', *Police Quarterly*, 10(2): 115–153.

L. McAra and S. McVie (2005) 'The Usual Suspects? Street-Life, Young People and the Police', *Criminal Justice*, 5(1): 5–36.

L. McAra and S. McVie (2007) 'Youth Justice?: The Impact of System Contact on Patterns of Desistance from Offending', *European Journal of Criminology*, 4(3). 315–345.

L. McAra and S. McVie (2012) 'Negotiated Order: Towards a Theory of Pathways Into and Out of Offending', *Criminology and Criminal Justice*, 12(4): 347–376.

M. McGovern (2010) *Countering Terror or Counter-Productive? Comparing Irish and British Muslim Experiences of Counter-Insurgency Law and Policy* (Ormskirk: Edge Hill University).

E. McLaughlin (2007) 'Diversity or Anarchy? The Post-Macpherson Blues', in M. Rowe (ed.) *Policing Beyond Macpherson: Issues in Policing, Race and Society* (Cullompton: Willan).

J.J. Medina Ariza (2013) 'Police-Initiated Contacts: Young People, Ethnicity and the "Usual Suspects" ', *Policing and Society*, 23 (4): 1–16.

Metropolitan Police Authority (2004) *Report of the MPA Scrutiny on MPS Stop and Search Practice* (London: Metropolitan Police Authority).

Metropolitan Police Authority (2008) *Operation Blunt 2* (London: Metropolitan Police Authority), http://www.mpa.gov.uk/committees/mpa/2008/080529-agm/06/ [accessed 18 April 2012].

Metropolitan Police Federation (2014) *The Consequences of a Target Driven Culture Within Policing: From the Voices of Metropolitan Police Officers* (London: MPF).

Metropolitan Police Service (2014) 'Stop and Search', *Metropolitan Police Website*, http://content.met.police.uk/Site/stopandsearch [accessed 20 April 2014].

J. Miller (2010) 'Stop and Search in England: A Reformed Tactic or Business as Usual?' *British Journal of Criminology*, 50(5): 954–974.

J. Miller, N. Bland, and P. Quinton (2000) *The Impact of Stops and Searches on Crime and the Community Police* (London: Home Office).

Ministry of Justice (2008) *Statistics on Race and the Criminal Justice System 2006/7* (London: Ministry of Justice).

Ministry of Justice (2009) *Statistics on Race and the Criminal Justice System 2007/08* (London: Ministry of Justice).

Ministry of Justice (2010) *Statistics on Race and the Criminal Justice System 2008/09* (London: Ministry of Justice).

Ministry of Justice (2011) *Statistics on Race and the Criminal Justice System 2009/10* (London: Ministry of Justice).

Ministry of Justice (2013) *Statistics on Race and the Criminal Justice System 2012* (London: Ministry of Justice).

D. Moon, J. Flatley, J. Parfrement-Hopkins, P. Hall, J. Hoare, I. Lau, and J. Innes (2011) *Perceptions of Crime, Engagement with the Police, Authorities Dealing with Antisocial Behaviour and Community Payback: Findings from the 2010/11 British Crime Survey* (London: Home Office).

S. Moore (2014) 'Mark Duggan Inquest: Gang Lieutenant or Respected, Popular Father? A Divided Portrait', *Tottenham and Wood Green Journal*, 8 January 2014, http://www.tottenhamjournal.co.uk/news/crime-court/mark_duggan_inquest_gang_lieutenant_or_respected_popular_father_a_divided_portrait_tmd_1_3187834 [accessed 4 August 2014].

R. Morgan and T. Newburn (2012) 'Youth Crime and Justice: Rediscovering Devolution, Discretion, and Diversion?' in M. Maguire, R. Morgan, and R. Reiner (eds.) *The Oxford Handbook of Criminology* (Oxford: Oxford University Press).

W.K. Muir (1977) *Police: Streetcorner Politicians* (London: University of Chicago Press).

K. Murji (1997) 'White Lines: Culture, "Race" and Drugs', in N. South (ed.) *Drugs: Cultures, Controls and Everyday Life* (London: Sage).

MVA and J. Miller (2000) *Profiling Populations Available for Stops and Searches* (London: Home Office).

A. Myhill and B. Bradford (2012) 'Can Police Enhance Public Confidence by Improving Quality of Service? Results from Two Surveys in England and Wales', *Policing and Society*, 22(4): 397–425.

A. Myhill, P. Quinton, B. Bradford, A. Poole, and G. Sims (2011) 'It Depends What You Mean by "Confident": Operationalizing Measures of Public Confidence and the Role of Performance Indicators', *Policing: A Journal of Policy and Practice*, 5(2): 114–124.

G. Mythen, S. Walklate, and F. Khan (2009) ' "I'm a Muslim, But I'm Not a Terrorist": Victimization, Risky Identities and the Performance of Safety', *British Journal of Criminology*, 49(6): 736–754.

NACRO (1997) *Policing Local Communities: The Tottenham Experiment* (London: NACRO).

M. Namba (2012) ' "War on Illegal Immigrants", National Narratives, and Globalisation: Japanese Policy and Practice of Police Stop and Question in Global Perspective', in L. Weber and B. Bowling (eds.) *Stop and Search: Police Power in Global Context* (London: Routledge).

S. Neal (2003) 'The Scarman Report, the Macpherson Report and the Media: How Newspapers Respond to Race-Centred Social Policy Interventions', *Journal of Social Policy*, 32(1): 55–74.

D. Nelken (2009) 'Comparative Criminal Justice: Beyond Ethnocentrism and Relativism', *European Journal of Criminology*, 6(4): 291–311.

T. Newburn (2007) ' "Tough on Crime": Penal Policy in England and Wales', in M. Tonry (ed.) *Crime, Punishment and Politics in Comparative Perspectives* (Chicago: University of Chicago Press).

C. Norris, C. Kemp, J. Fielding, and N. Fielding (1992) 'Black and Blue: An Analysis of the Effect of Race on Police Stops', *British Journal of Sociology*, 43(2): 207–224.

Office for National Statistics (2012) *Key Statistics for Local Authorities in England and Wales* (London: Office of National Statistics).

Office for National Statistics (2013a) *Crime in England and Wales, Year Ending March 2013: Statistical Bulletin* (London: Office for National Statistics).

Office for National Statistics (2013b) *Detailed Characteristics for England and Wales, March 2011* (London: Office for National Statistics).

P. O'Flynn (2013) 'Cutting Back on Stop and Search Is Folly', *The Express*, 6 July 2013, http://www.express.co.uk/comment/columnists/patrick-o-flynn/412912/Cutting-back-on-stop-and-search-is-folly?comments=show-all [accessed 5 September 2013].

Open Society Justice Initiative (2011) *Addressing Ethnic Profiling in the European Union: A Good Practice Handbook* (London: Open Society Justice Initiative).

N. Padfield, R. Morgan, and M. Maguire (2012) 'Out of Court, Out of Sight? Criminal Sanctions and Non-Judicial Decision-Making', in M. Maguire, R. Morgan, and R. Reiner (eds.) *The Oxford Handbook of Criminology* (Oxford: Oxford University Press).

C. Pantazis and S. Pemberton (2009) 'From the "Old" to the "New" Suspect Community: Examining the Impacts of Recent UK Counter-Terrorist Legislation', *British Journal of Criminology*, 49(5): 646–666.

C. Pantazis and S. Pemberton (2011) 'Restating the Case for the "Suspect Community": A Reply to Greer', *British Journal of Criminology*, 51(6): 1054–1062.

Parliament of the United Kingdom (1824) *The Vagrancy Act* (London: Parliament of the United Kingdom), http://www.legislation.gov.uk/ukpga/Geo4/5/83 [accessed 5 June 2013].

A. Parmar (2007) *Crime and 'The Asian Community': Disentangling Perceptions and Reality*, unpublished doctoral thesis (Cambridge: University of Cambridge).

A. Parmar (2011) 'Stop and Search in London: Counter-Terrorist or Counter-Productive?' *Policing and Society*, 21(4): 369–382.

P. Peachey (2012) 'Theresa May Faces Calls to Resign After Being Booed Offstage at Police Federation Address', *The Independent*, 16 May 2012, http://www.independent.co.uk/news/uk/politics/theresa-may-faces-calls-to-resign-after-being-booed-offstage-at-police-federation-address-7757366.html [accessed 2 September 2013].

J. Penzer (1999) *Reported Crime and PACE Stop and Search Activity: An Investigation of the Possible Relationship* (Unpublished paper).

C. Phillips and D. Brown (1998) *Entry Into the Criminal Justice System: A Survey of Police Arrests and Their Outcomes* (London: Home Office).

Population Estimates by Ethnic Group (PEEGs) Team (2011a) *Population Estimates by Ethnic Group: Methodology Paper* (London: Office of National Statistics).

Population Estimates by Ethnic Group (PEEGs) Team (2011b) *Population Estimates by Ethnic Group: Important Note on Reliability of Estimates for Subnational Areas* (London: Office of National Statistics).

R. Prasad (2011) 'English Riots Were "A Sort of Revenge" Against the Police', *The Guardian*, 5 December 2011, http://www.theguardian.com/uk/2011/dec/05/riots-revenge-against-police [accessed 12 August 2013].

M. Provine and G. Sanchez (2012) 'Suspecting Immigrants: Exploring Links Between Racialised Anxieties and Expanded Police Powers in Arizona', in L. Weber and B. Bowling (eds.) *Stop and Search: Police Power in Global Context* (London: Routledge).

P. Quinton (2011) 'The Formation of Suspicions: Police Stop and Search Practices in England and Wales', *Policing and Society*, 21 (4), 357–368.
P. Quinton, N. Bland, and J. Miller (2000) *Police Stops, Decision-Making and Practice* (London: Home Office).
P. Quinton and J. Olagundoye (2004) *An Evaluation of the Phased Implementation of the Recording of Police Stops* (London: Home Office).
D.A. Ramirez, J. Hoopes, and T.L. Quinlan (2003) 'Defining Racial Profiling in a Post-September 11 World', *American Criminal Law Review*, 40: 1195.
D. Ramirez and S. Woldenberg (2005) 'Balancing Security and Liberty in a Post-September 11th World: The Search for Common Sense in Domestic Counter-Terrorism Policy', *Temple Political and Civil Rights Law Review*, 14(1): 495–515.
S. Ramos and L. Musumeci (2004) *Police Stops, Suspects and Discrimination in the City of Rio de Janeiro* (Rio de Janeiro: Centro de Estudos de Segurança e Cidadania).
J.H. Ratcliffe (2008) *Intelligence-Led Policing* (Cullompton: Willan).
J.H. Ratcliffe and M. McCullagh (2001) 'Chasing Ghosts? Police Perception of High Crime Areas', *British Journal of Criminology*, 41 (2): 330–341.
J.H. Ratcliffe, T. Taniguchi, E.R. Groff, and J.D. Wood (2011) 'The Philadelphia Foot Patrol Experiment: A Randomized Controlled Trial of Police Patrol Effectiveness in Violent Crime Hotspots', *Criminology*, 49(3): 795–831.
G.L. Ream, B.D. Johnson, E. Dunlap, and E. Benoit (2010) 'The Role of Marijuana Use Etiquette in Avoiding Targeted Police Enforcement', *Drugs: Education, Prevention and Policy*, 17(6): 689–706.
R. Reiner (1985) *The Politics of the Police*, 1st edition (London: Wheatsheaf).
R. Reiner (2000) *The Politics of the Police*, 3rd edition (Oxford: Oxford University Press).
R. Reiner (2007) *Law and Order: An Honest Citizen's Guide to Crime and Control* (Cambridge: Polity).
R. Reiner (2010) *The Politics of the Police*, 4th edition (Oxford: Oxford University Press).
A. Reiss (1971) *The Police and the Public* (London: Yale University Press).
C. Reith (1956) *A New Study of Police History* (London: Oliver & Boyd).
M. Riddell (2000) 'The New Statesman Interview – Sir William Macpherson', *The New Statesman*, 21 February 2000, http://www.newstatesman.com/node/136908 [accessed 24 June 2013].
Riots, Communities and Victims Panel (2011) *5 Days in August: An Interim Report on the 2011 English Riots* (London: Riots Communities and Victims Panel).
Riots, Communities and Victims Panel (2012) *After the Riots: The Final Report of the Riots Communities and Victims Panel* (London: Riots Communities and Victims Panel).
K. Roach (2011) *The 9/11 Effect: Comparative Counter-Terrorism* (Cambridge: Cambridge University Press).
G. Roberts, S. Cohen, A. Short, and L. Italiano (2014) 'Thousands March to Protest Police Death of Eric Garner', *New York Post*, 23 August 2014, http://nypost.com/2014/08/23/thousands-march-to-protest-police-death-of-eric-garner/ [accessed 10 January 2015].
J.V. Roberts and M. Hough (2005) *Understanding Public Attitudes to Criminal Justice* (Maidenhead: Open University Press).

P. Rock (1979) *The Making of Symbolic Interactionism* (London: Macmillan).
N. Rollock (2009) *The Stephen Lawrence Inquiry – Ten Years On: A Review of the Literature* (London: Runnymede Trust).
J. Rush (2014) 'Police Sign Up to New Code of Conduct for Stop and Search Powers Including Recording Every Outcome', MailOnline; http://www.dailymail.co.uk/news/article-2734403/Police-sign-new-code-conduct-stop-search-powers-including-recording-outcome.html#ixzz3RpXfcjvi, August 26 2014 [accessed 24 August 2014].
J. Rowe (1994) *Report on the Operation in 1994 of the Prevention of Terrorism (Temporary Provisions) Act 1989* (London: Stationery Office).
M. Rowe (2004) *Policing, Race and Racism* (Cullompton: Willan).
Royal Commission on Criminal Procedure (1981) *Report of the Royal Commission on Criminal Procedure, Cmnd 8092* (London: HMSO).
J. Rubinstein (1973) *City Police* (New York: Farrar, Straus and Giroux).
R. Sampson and J. Cohen (1988) 'Deterrent Effects of the Police on Crime: A Replication and Theoretical Extension', *Law and Society Review*, 22: 163–169.
A. Sanders and R. Young (2007) *Criminal Justice* (London: Oxford University Press).
A. Sanders, R. Young, and M. Burton (2010) *Criminal Justice* (Oxford: Oxford University Press).
S. Savage (2003) 'Tackling Tradition: Reform and Modernization of the British Police', *Contemporary Politics*, 9(2). 171–184.
L.G. Scarman (1981) *Scarman Report: The Brixton Disorders, 10–12 April 2001* (London: HMSO).
A. Schutz (1970) *On Phenomenology and Social Relations* (Chicago and London: The University of Chicago Press).
H. Sergeant (2008) *The Public and the Police* (London: Civitas).
C. Sharp and T. Budd (2005) *Minority Ethnic Groups and Crime: Findings from the Offending, Crime and Justice Survey 2003* (London: Home Office).
D. Sharp and S. Atherton (2007) 'To Serve and Protect? The Experiences of Policing in the Community of Young People From Black and Other Ethnic Minority Groups', *British Journal of Criminology*, 47(5): 746–763.
J. Sheptycki and A. Wardak (2005) *Transnational and Comparative Criminology* (London: Glasshouse).
L. Sherman (1983) 'After the Riots: Police and Minorities in the US 1970–1980', in N. Glazer and
L. Sherman (1993) 'Defiance, Deterrence, and Irrelevance: A Theory of the Criminal Sanction', *Journal of Research in Crime and Delinquency*, 30: 445–473.
L.W. Sherman and H. Strang (2007) *Restorative Justice: The Evidence* (London: The Smith Institute).
L.W. Sherman and D. Weisburd (1995) 'General Deterrent Effects of Police Patrol in Crime "Hot Spots": A Randomized, Controlled Trial', *Justice Quarterly*, 12: 625–648.
M. Shiner (2006) *National Implementation of the Recording of Police Stops* (London: Home Office).
M. Shiner (2010) 'Post-Lawrence Policing in England and Wales: Guilt, Innocence and the Defence of Organisational Ego', *British Journal of Criminology*, 50(5): 935–953.

M. Shiner (2012) *Report on the Use of Section 60 of the Criminal Justice and Public Order Act 1994 by the Police*, Expert Witness Statement for Bhatt Murphy Solicitors, Unpublished.
J. Sim (1982) 'Scarman: The Police Counter-Attack', *Socialist Register* (London: Merlin).
L. Singer (2013) 'London Riots: Searching for a Stop', *Policing*, 7(1): 32–41.
W. Skogan (2006) 'Asymmetry in the Impact of Encounters with the Police', *Policing and Society*, 16(2): 99–126.
W. Skogan and K. Frydl (2004) *Fairness and Effectiveness in Policing: The Evidence, Committee to Review Research on Police Policy and Practices, National Research Council* (Washington, DC: National Academy of Sciences).
D.J. Smith (1983) *Police and People in London 1: A Survey of Londoners* (London: Policy Studies Institute).
D.J. Smith (1997) 'Ethnic Origins, Crime, Criminal Justice', in M. Maguire, R. Morgan, and R. Reiner (eds.) *The Oxford Handbook of Criminology* (Oxford: Clarendon).
D.J. Smith and J. Gray (1985) *Police and People in London* (Aldershot: Avebury).
J. Smith (2003) *The Nature of Personal Robbery* (London: Home Office).
A. Souhami (2007) 'Understanding Institutional Racism: The Stephen Lawrence Inquiry and the Police Service Reaction', in M. Rowe (ed.) *Policing Beyond Macpherson: Issues in Policing, Race and Society* (Cullompton: Willan).
B. Spalek (2010) 'Community Policing, Trust, and Muslim Communities in Relation to "New Terrorism" ', *Politics and Policy*, 38(4): 789–815.
B. Spalek, S. El Awa, and L. McDonald (2009) *Police-Muslim Engagement and Partnerships for the Purposes of Counter-Terrorism: An Examination* (Birmingham: University of Birmingham).
B. Spalek and R. Lambert (2008) 'Muslim Communities, Counter-Terrorism and Counter-Radicalisation: A Critically Reflective Approach to Engagement', *International Journal of Law, Crime and Justice*, 36: 257–270.
D. Spiegelhalter and A. Barnett (2009) 'London Murders: A Predictable Pattern', *Significance*, 6(1): 5–8.
StopWatch (2010) *Response to the Proposed Changes to the Police and Criminal Evidence Act 1984 (PACE) Code of Practice A: Revisions Proposed 20th September 2010* (London: StopWatch), http://www.stop-watch.org/news-comment/story/stopwatch-responds-to-the-pace-code-of-practice [accessed 31 July 2013].
StopWatch (2011) *'Carry on Recording': Why Police Stops Should Still Be Recorded* (London: StopWatch), http://www.stop-watch.org/get-informed/research/carry-on-recording [accessed 29 August 2013].
StopWatch (2012) *Section 60: Stop and Search Facts and Figures* (London: StopWatch), http://www.stop-watch.org/uploads/documents/Factsheet_-_Section_60.pdf [accessed 14 May 2014].
StopWatch (2013) *Appeal Granted to Challenge Discriminatory Section 60 Stop and Search* (London: StopWatch), https://www.facebook.com/StopWatchUK/posts/552443354776351 [accessed 31 July 2013].
StopWatch and the Open Society Justice Initiative (2013) *Viewed with Suspicion: The Human Cost of Stop and Search in England and Wales* (New York: Open Society Foundations).
J.P. Stumpf (2006) 'The Crimmigration Crisis: Immigrants, Crime, and Sovereign Power', *American University Law Review*, 56: 367.

J. Sunshine and T.R. Tyler (2003) 'The Role of Procedural Justice and Legitimacy in Public Support for Policing', *Law and Society Review*, 37(3): 513–548.

J. Tankebe (2013) 'Viewing Things Differently: The Dimensions of Public Perceptions of Police Legitimacy', *Criminology*, 51(1): 103–135.

B. Taylor, C. Koper, and D. Woods (2011) 'A Randomized Controlled Trial of Different Policing Strategies at Hot Spots of Violent Crime', *Journal of Experimental Criminology*, 7: 149–181.

G. Tendayi Viki, M.J. Culmer, A. Eller, and D. Abrams (2006) 'Race and Willingness to Cooperate with the Police: The Roles of Quality of Contact, Attitudes Toward the Behaviour and Subjective Norms', *British Journal of Social Psychology*, 45: 285–302.

The Economist (2014) *The Ferguson Riots – Overkill: Police in a Missouri Suburb Demonstrate How Not to Quell a Riot*, 23 August 2014, http://www.independent.co.uk/news/world/americas/michael-brown-shooting-us-to-review-militarisation-of-police-in-aftermath-of-ferguson-riots-9688633.html [accessed 25 August 2014].

The Guardian (2014a) *Court of Appeal Rejects Challenge Over Legality of Stop-and-Search Powers*, 4 February 2014, http://www.theguardian.com/law/2014/feb/04/court-of-appeal-rejects-challenge-race-stop-and-search-powers [accessed 5 May 2014].

The Guardian (2014b) *Muslim Man Stopped by Police Was Wrongly Refused Access to Solicitor*, 20 February 2014, http://www.theguardian.com/uk-news/2014/feb/20/muslim-man-stopped-police-wrongly-schedule-7 [accessed 15 May 2014].

The Local (2013) 'Police Deportation Sting Fails in Nine of Ten Cases', *The Local*, 16 February 2013, http://www.thelocal.se/20130225/46386 [accessed 29 August 2013].

The Police Foundation (2012) *Stop and Search* (London: The Police Foundation).

T.P. Thornberry and M.D. Krohn (2000) 'The Self-Report Method for Measuring Delinquency and Crime', in D. Duffee, R.D. Crutchfield, S. Mastrofski, L. Mazerolle, D. McDowall, and B. Ostrom (eds.) *Innovations in Measurement and Analysis* (Washington, DC: National Institute of Justice).

A. Tomkins (2002) 'Legislating Against Terror: The Anti-Terrorism, Crime and Security Act 2001', *Public Law*, Summer: 205–220.

B. Tóth and A. Kádár (2012) 'Ethnic Profiling in ID Checks by the Hungarian Police', in L. Weber and B. Bowling (eds.) *Stop and Search: Police Power in Global Context* (London: Routledge).

M. Townsend (2010) 'Black People Are 26 Times More Likely Than Whites to Face Stop and Search', *The Guardian*, 17 October 2010, http://www.theguardian.com/uk/2010/oct/17/stop-and-search-race-figures [accessed 12 June 2013].

M. Townsend (2012) 'Stop and Search "Racial Profiling" by Police on the Increase, Claims Study', *The Observer*, 14 January 2012, http://www.theguardian.com/law/2012/jan/14/stop-search-racial-profiling-police [accessed 12 June 2013].

P.E. Tracey and K. Kempf-Leonard (1996) *Continuity and Discontinuity in Criminal Careers* (New York: Plenum).

M. Tran (2008) 'Ray Mallon Profile: Middlesbrough's Robocop', *The Guardian*, 17 July 2008, http://www.theguardian.com/politics/2008/jul/17/police.localgovernment1 [accessed 26 July 2013].

A. Travis (2000) 'How Hague Mugged Macpherson', *The Guardian*, 15 December 2000, http://www.theguardian.com/uk/2000/dec/15/lawrence.ukcrime [accessed 29 August 2013].

A. Travis (2009) 'Terror Law Used to Stop Thousands "Just to Balance Racial Statistics" ', *The Guardian*, June 17 2009; http://www.theguardian.com/uk/2009/jun/17/stop-search-terror-law-met [accessed 12 June 2012]

A. Travis (2013a) 'Stop and Search Needs to Be Scaled Back, Theresa May to Tell MPs', *The Guardian*, 2 July 2013, http://www.theguardian.com/society/2013/jul/02/police-scale-back-stop-and-search [accessed 30 July 2013].

A. Travis (2013b) 'Stop and Search: Home Secretary Launches Consultation on Police Powers', *The Guardian*, 2 July 2013, http://www.theguardian.com/law/2013/jul/02/stop-search-theresa-may-police-powers [accessed 29 August 2013].

T.R. Tyler (1990) *Why People Obey the Law* (Princeton: Princeton University Press).

T.R. Tyler (2006a) *Why People Obey the Law* (New Haven: Yale University Press).

T.R. Tyler (2006b) 'Psychological Perspectives on Legitimacy and Legitimation', *Annual Review of Psychology*, 57: 375–400.

T.R. Tyler (2011) 'Trust and Legitimacy: Policing in the USA and Europe', *European Journal of Criminology*, 8(4): 254–266.

T.R. Tyler and S. Blader (2003) 'Procedural Justice, Social Identity, and Cooperative Behavior', *Personality and Social Psychology Review*, 7: 349–361.

T.R. Tyler and J. Fagan (2008) 'Legitimacy and Cooperation: Why Do People Help the Police Fight Crime in Their Communities?' *Ohio State Journal of Criminal Law*, 6: 231–276.

T.R. Tyler and Y.J. Huo (2002) *Trust in the Law: Encouraging Public Cooperation with the Police and Courts* (New York: Russell Sage Foundation).

T.R. Tyler and C. Wakslak (2004) 'Profiling and Police Legitimacy: Procedural Justice, Attributions of Motive, and Acceptance of Police Authority', *Criminology*, 41(2): 253–281.

J. van der Leun and M. van der Woude (2012) 'Ethnic Profiling in the Netherlands? A Reflection on Expanding Preventive Powers, Ethnic Profiling and a Changing Social and Political Context', in L. Weber and B. Bowling (eds.) *Stop and Search: Police Power in Global Context* (London: Routledge).

K. Vaz (2014) 'Statement to Parliament on Stop and Search', *Hansard*, 30 April 2014, Column: 831–847.

S. Vertigans (2010) 'British Muslims and the UK Government's "War on Terror" Within: Evidence of a Clash of Civilizations or Emergent De-Civilising Processes?' *British Journal of Sociology*, 61(1): 26–44.

A. Von Hirsch, A.E. Bottoms, E. Burney, and P. Wikstrom (1999) *Criminal Deterrence and Sentence Severity: An Analysis of Recent Research* (London: Hart).

P.A.J. Waddington (1999) *Policing Citizens: Authority and Rights* (London: University College Press).

P.A.J. Waddington, K. Stenson, and D. Don (2004) 'In Proportion: Race and Police Stop and Search', *British Journal of Criminology*, 44(6): 889–914.

A. Walker, J. Flatley, C. Kershaw, and D. Moon (2009) *Crime in England and Wales 2008/09* (London: Home Office).

C. Walker (2008) 'Know Thine Enemy as Thyself: Discerning Friend From Foe Under Anti-Terrorism Laws', *Melbourne University Law Review*, 32(1): 275–301.

L. Ward and A. Diamond (2009) *Tackling Knives Action Plan (TKAP) Phase I: Overview of Key Trends from a Monitoring Programme* (London: Home Office).

L. Ward, S. Nicholas, and M. Willoughby (2011) *An Assessment of the Tackling Knives and Serious Youth Violence Action Programme (TKAP) – Phase II* (London: Home Office).

L. Weber (2012) 'It Sounds Like They Shouldn't Be Here': Immigration Checks on the Streets of Sydney', in L. Weber and B. Bowling (eds.) *Stop and Search: Police Power in Global Context* (London: Routledge).

L. Weber and B. Bowling (2004) 'Policing Migration: A Framework for Investigating the Regulation of Global Mobility', *Policing & Society*, 14(3): 195–212.

L. Weber and B. Bowling (2008) 'Valiant Beggars and Global Vagabonds: Select, Eject, Immobilize', *Theoretical Criminology*, 12(3): 355–375.

L. Weber and B. Bowling (2012) *Stop and Search: Police Power in Global Context* (London: Routledge).

Webster, C. (2007) *Understanding Race and Crime*. Maidenhead, UK: Open University Press.

D. Weisburd and J. Eck (2004) 'What Can Police Do to Reduce Crime, Disorder and Fear?' *The Annals of the American Academy of Political and Social Science*, 593: 42–65.

R. Weitzer and S. Tuch (2002) 'Perceptions of Racial Profiling: Race, Class, and Personal Experience', *Criminology*, 40(2): 435–456.

D. Werb., G. Rowell., G. Guyatt, T. Kerr, J. Montener, and E. Wood (2011) 'Effect of Drug Law Enforcement on Drug market Violence: A Systematic Review', *International Journal of Drug Policy*, 22: 87–94.

D. Werb, E. Wood, W. Small, S. Strathdee, K. Li, J. Montaner, and T. Kerr (2008) 'Effects of Police Confiscation of Illicit Drugs and Syringes Among Injection Drug Users in Vancouver', *International Journal of Drug Policy*, 19(4): 332–338.

A. Whelan (2011) 'The "Genteel" Boy Who Grew Up to Become Scotland Yard's "Zero Tolerance" Eliot Ness', *Daily Mail*, 18 September 2011; http://www.dailymail.co.uk/news/article-2038733/Bernard-Hogan-Howe-The-boy-Scotland-Yards-zero-tolerance-Eliot-Ness.html#ixzz3BPaZA55D [accessed 25 August 2014].

J. Whitfield (2004) *Unhappy Dialogue: The Metropolitan Police and Black Londoners in Post-War Britain* (Cullompton: Willan).

J. Whitfield (2009) 'Stop and Search: What Can We Learn from History?', *Historyextra.com*, 12 August, http://www.historyextra.com/feature/stop-and-search-what-can-we-learn-history [accessed 10 January 2015].

S.A. Wiley and F.-A. Esbensen (2013) 'The Effect of Police Contact: Does Official Intervention Result in Deviance Amplification?' *Crime and Delinquency*, published online 12 July 2013.

C.F. Willis (1983) *The Use, Effectiveness and Impact of Police Stop and Search Powers* (London: Home Office).

G. Wilson, R. Dunham, and G. Alpert (2004) 'Prejudice in Police Profiling: Assessing an Overlooked Aspect in Prior Research', *American Behavioral Scientist*, 47: 896–909.

J.Q. Wilson and G.L. Kelling (1982) 'Broken Windows', *Atlantic Monthly*, 249(3): 29–38.

S. Wortley and A. Owusu-Bempah (2012) 'The Usual Suspects: Police Stop and Search Practices in Canada', in L. Weber and B. Bowling (eds.) *Stop and Search: Police Power in Global Context* (London: Routledge).
J. Young (1994) *Policing the Streets: Stops and Search in North London* (London: Islington Council).
K. Young (1983) 'Ethnic Pluralism and the Policy Agenda in Great Britain', in N. Glazer and K. Young (eds.) *Ethnic Pluralism and Public Policy* (London: Heinemann), 287–300.
L. Zedner (2007) 'Pre-Crime and Post-Criminology?' *Theoretical Criminology*, 11(2): 261–281.
L. Zedner (2009) *Security* (Abingdon: Routledge).

Index

Note: Locators followed by letter 'n' refer to notes.

Adjami, M., 176, 180, 181, 183, 186
adversarial contact, 1, 47, 80
African-Americans, 94, 130, 182
Ainsworth, M., 100
Akwagyiram, A., 40
Alexander, C., 130, 131
al Qaeda-inspired attacks, 123–4, 128–9, 142
al-Shabaab terror group, 142
Anderson, D. (Lord), 20, 23, 24, 39, 123, 125, 126, 127, 128, 129, 136, 137, 138, 139, 141, 142, 143, 144
anti-social behaviour, 5, 24, 71, 131, 174, 178
Anti-social Behaviour, Crime and Policing Act 2014, 24
Anti-terrorism, Crime and Security Act 2001, 129
Arizona state law SB1070, 181
'Asian crime' time bomb, 130
Atherton, S., 95, 107, 108
August 2011 riots, 161
Aust, R., 72
Awan, I., 142
Ayres, I., 169

Ball, J., 161
Banton, M., 1
Barnett, A., 39
Barwell, G., 164
Beattie, I., 99
Becker, H.S., 115
Belur, J., 171, 172, 183
Bennetto, J., 153
Bingham, T., 174
Birmingham Six, 124
Bittner, E., 1, 2
Black, D., 111
black and minority ethnic (BME) groups, 57, 60–1, 64, 70, 73–4, 76–7, 103, 108, 117, 122n.2

Blackwood, L., 143
Blader, S., 107
Bland, N., 58, 63, 164
Bond, B.J., 98
Bonner, D., 124, 125, 126, 128, 129
Bovey, W.H., 159, 165
Bowling, B., 8, 18, 35, 52, 53, 55, 57, 61, 67, 72, 79, 80, 91, 95, 102, 104, 108, 121, 130, 131, 139, 152, 153, 170, 171, 172, 173, 174, 177, 178, 179, 180, 182, 186, 187, 188, 189, 190, 191, 192
Bradford, B., 7, 44, 97, 102, 103, 105, 106, 108, 110, 111, 114, 121, 130, 185
Braga, A.A., 83, 98
Braithwaite, J., 147, 165, 166, 167, 168, 169
Bridges, L., 6, 7, 9, 26, 54, 63
British Crime Survey, 47
British Muslims, 115, 131, 183
Brixton 'riots,' 3, 4, 6, 10,16, 34, 96, 98, 99, 149, 150, 184
Brogden, A., 99
Brown, D., 86
Brown, M.K., 178
Budd, T., 53

Camber, R., 161
Cameron, David (Prime Minister), 194
Carlile, A. (Lord), 38, 131, 132, 133, 134, 136, 141, 142
Cemlyn, S., 49
Chainey, S., 55, 61, 62, 91, 92
Chanin, J.M., 148
Choongh, S., 99, 175
Choudhury, T., 24, 131, 136, 142, 143
Churcher, J., 163
civil agencies, 189
Civil Rights Act 1964 (USA), 147
Clancy, A., 47, 67

219

Cockcroft, T., 99, 146
Cohen, J., 82
Cole, D., 123, 128, 140
Conservative government
  attack on law and order (Labour government), 33
  Lawrence Inquiry, 35, 160
  misuse of stop and search', 162, 164
  PACE, 10, 22
  police vs, 163
contract theory, 173–5
Cooper, Y., 163
Cossé, E., 181, 182
Countering International Terrorism (CONTEST), 129
counter-terrorism policing, 8, 115, 139, 142
  al Qaeda-inspired attacks, 123–4, 128–9
  bombings in Birmingham city, 124–5
  2001 bombings of New York and Washington (9/11), 123, 128, 129
  conflict in Northern Ireland, 131
  false negatives, 140–2
  false positives, 140–2
  intelligence-led stop and searches, 139
  portrayals of British Asians, 130–1
  racial profiling, 130
  Schedule 7, use of, 136–8, 141, 144
  stop and search, 123–7, 131, 135–6, 139, 141–4
  use of Section 43, 144
  use of Section 44, 131–6, 142–3
Crime and Disorder Act 1998, 39
crime control, 3, 6–7, 31, 33–4, 135, 144, 148, 154, 174, 188, 191
Criminal Justice Act 1991, 15
Criminal Justice and Public Order Act 1994, 16, 23, 25, 30n.4, 37, 39, 64, 81, 84, 154, 163, 171, 178
criminal justice system
  arrest rate, 53
  costs of stop and search, 94–5
  counter-terrorism policing, 8
  criminogenic effects, 115–18
  crimmigration control system, 188
  effectiveness of stop and search, 103, 105, 119, 121
  ethnic disproportionality, 102
  Lawrence, 156, 160
  police conduct, 146
  police legitimacy, 58
  political violence, 125
  post-PACE period, 16
  racial issues, 15, 73, 139
  reasonable suspicion, 11
  self-help violence, 111
  symbolic exclusion, 114–15
  terrorism and, 128
criminal law, 123–4, 128, 188

Davenport, J., 36, 93, 161, 194
Delsol, R., 1, 7, 31, 39, 52, 57, 64, 79, 81, 104, 119, 130, 140, 157, 165, 166, 176, 177, 179, 183, 184, 185, 193
Dempsey, J., 128
Derfoufi, Z., 8, 123, 164
deterrent effect, 19, 84, 89, 98, 115, 126, 177–80
Diamond, A., 85
Dickson, B., 126, 127
disproportionality
  available population, 53, 55
  BME residents, 64–5
  border control issues, 173
  calls from public, 65–7, 70
  causes and consequences, 57, 76, 78
  data collection, 186
  fairness issues, 104
  geographic targeting, 61
  intelligence-led stop and search, 18
  Lawrence Inquiry, impact on, 51, 54, 58
  police decision-making and, 52, 59, 77
  structural factors, 19, 62–3
  suspicion-based searches, 49–51, 69
  unconscious racial biases, 52
  unintended consequences, 102
  use of Section 60, 25
  see also racial profiling
Dixon, D., 60
Dodd, V., 40, 41, 139, 154, 182, 194
Dovidio, J.F., 52

drug offences, 41–2, 79, 93–4, 130
Dubber, M.D., 170
Duggan, Mark (killing of), 6, 193

Eastwood, N., 42, 53, 95, 100, 146, 165
Eaton, G., 194
Eck, J., 94
Edinburgh Study of Youth Transitions and Crime, 47
effectiveness of stop and search
  arrest rates, 83, 85–90
  costs (stop and searches), 94–9
  crime levels, 84
  deterrence, 81–82
  investigative power, 81–2
  police tactics, 83
  preventative power, 82, 139–43
  role of intelligence, 90–3
  seriousness of offences, 93–4
  Tackling Knives and Serious Youth Violence Action Programme (TKAP), 84
Ellis, M., 162
England and Wales
  arrest rates, 83–90
  'Best Use of Stop and Search Scheme,' 29, 162, 194
  BME voters, 164
  calls for service, 67
  criminal justice system, 103, 117
  disproportionality ratios, 136
  drug use, 41–2
  exceptional powers, 37
  formal regulation of stop and search, 149
  modes of regulation, 147–8
  Offending Crime and Justice Survey, 48
  police and public cooperation, 103, 109
  policing styles, 43–4, 178
  punishment for non-compliance, 171
  racial profiling, 182–3
  Section 44, 136, 140
  Section 1 PACE, 175
  self-report surveys, 53
  stop and search powers, 3–4, 6–8, 79, 83, 179
  suspicion-based stop-searches, 33, 42–3, 45, 50–1
  Terrorism Act 2000, 132, 134
Epp, C.R., 147, 148, 154
Equality Act 2010, 12, 151
Equality and Human Rights Commission (EHRC), 19, 24, 36, 103, 155, 179
Ericson, R., 115
Esbensen, F.-A., 117
Eterno, J.A., 34, 100
ethnic profiling
  definition, 130
  public information, 65
  structural factors, 19
  suspect description, 92
European Court of Human Rights
  Section 60 decision (2010), 21, 38, 127, 171
  see also Gillan decision

Fagan, J., 98, 105, 108, 109, 175, 178
Falconer, C., 25
Farrington, D.P., 116
Felbab-Brown, V., 82
Fenwick, H., 24, 131, 136, 142, 143
Field, A., 123, 124
Fielding, N., 33, 45
Firearms Act 1968, 11
FitzGerald, M., 39, 46, 65, 66, 73, 82, 85, 86, 92, 94, 108, 109, 122n. 4
Flanegan, R., 42
Flood-Page, C., 53
Foster, J., 46, 58, 63, 70, 153, 158, 159
Frydl, K., 185
Fuller, R., 162
Futtrup, M., 178

Garland, D., 33, 34
Gearty, C., 126
Geller, A., 175, 178
Gill, K., 164
Gillan section 60 decision, 21–3, 25, 38, 127
  See also European Court of Human Rights Section 60 decision
Gilroy, P., 52
Glassner, B., 71
Godfrey, H., 34, 194

Goldstein, J., 147
Goodey, J., 130
Goris, I., 177, 180, 183, 185, 186
Graham, J., 53, 72, 100
Gray, J., 70, 71, 73, 74
Grimshaw, R., 60
Guildford Four, 125
Gulf War, 130

Hales, C., 72
Hall, S., 180
Hallsworth, S., 135
Hamilton, V.L., 111
Harcourt, B.E., 94, 139, 140
Harris, D.A., 52, 147, 165
Hawkins, K., 60
Heath, A., 49, 135
Hede, A., 159, 165
Held, D., 189
Herbert, N., 160
Her Majesty's Inspectorate of Constabulary (HMIC), 3, 27–8, 41, 46, 52, 55, 152, 161, 164–5, 169
Hickman, M.J., 131, 142
Hills, J., 49
Hillyard, P., 124, 125
Hispanics, 130, 182
Hogan-Howe, Bernard, 34, 36, 93, 161, 194
Holdaway, S., 70, 73
Holloway, L., 164
Home Affairs Select Committee on Terrorism and Community Relations, 139
Home Affairs Select Committee on Young Black People and the Criminal Justice System, 111, 118
Hopkins, N., 143
Hough, M., 98, 105, 109, 111
Hoyle, C., 168
Hughes, E.C., 1
Huizinga, D., 116
Human Rights Act 1998, 21
Huo, Y.J., 102, 105, 106
Huq, A.Z., 143
Hurst, B., 164

immigration
 Arizona state law SB1070, 181
 'blue uniformed police,' 189
 disproportionate treatment, 183
 domestic criminal justice, 188, 192
 Greece crisis, 182
 law enforcement, 130
 officer, 20, 127
 rules, 129
 transnational approach, 190
 violation, 181
independent reviewer of terrorism
 complaints against police, 151
 legislation, 8, 38
 Carlile, A (Lord), 131, 136
 Lord Shackleton, 125
 Anderson, D. (Lord) (see Anderson, D.)
 Her Majesty's Inspectorate of Constabulary (HMIC), 3
 Scarman Report, 4
 Schedule 7 powers, 137, 142, 144
 Section 44, 143
 use of Section 60, 40
Innes, M., 123, 128
intelligence-led stop and searches
 crime-fighting benefits, 7, 82
 crime hot-spots, 62, 72
 independent evaluation, 90–3
 predictive law enforcement, 139
 reasonable suspicion, 12–13
 Stephen Lawrence Inquiry's conclusions, 18
 strategic approach, 29
 types of offence, 80
interactional discrimination, 59, 74, 76
investigative power, 41, 81, 129
Irish Republican Army (IRA), 125
Islamist terrorism, 72, 140, 143, 182

Jackson, J., 58, 78, 97, 103, 105, 106, 108, 109, 110, 111, 113, 118, 120, 185
Jacobsen, B.C., 178
Jefferson, A., 60
Jenkins, Roy, 125
Jenkins, S., 125

John Jay College of Criminal Justice, New York, 6
Johnson, Boris (London Mayor), 195
Johnson, K., 194
Johnson, P., 38, 154
Jones, T., 34, 157

Kádár, A., 171, 176, 181, 183, 186
Karn, J., 79, 90, 100
Kelling, G.L., 178
Kelman, H.C., 111
Kempf-Leonard, K., 116
Khalid, M., 131
Kirk, D.S., 110
Kleinig, J., 174
Klockars, C.B., 1, 2, 4
Knives Act 1997, 39, 84
Koper, C., 98
Krohn, M.D., 53
Kundnani, A., 142

labelling theory, 115–17
Labour administration, 22
Lacey, N., 82
Lambert, R., 115
Larsen, N., 189
Laville, S., 164
Lawrence, Stephen Inquiry
 arrest rate, 88
 Conservative politicians, 35
 exceptional powers, stop and searches, 37
 institutional racism, 52, 54, 58, 158–9, 165
 legitimacy of searches, 164
 levels of disproportionality, after, 62
 police power, misuse, 152–3
 publication of report, 9, 27, 36, 51, 54, 161
 recording of stop account, 25, 32, 194
 role of police, 7
 stop and search practice, impact on, 16–20
 'voluntary stops,' prohibition, 14
Lea, J., 52, 153, 155, 156, 157
Lee, M., 131

legal powers
 formal regulation of stop and search, 149
 Police and Criminal Evidence Act 1984 (PACE), 9
 Scarman Report, 10
Leigh, L.H., 10
Levitas, R., 113
Lewis, P., 75, 184
Liberal Democrat parties, 22
Loader, I., 6, 106, 113
Loftus, B., 46, 47, 52, 100, 172
Lowe, V., 128
Lustgarten, L., 41, 81

Macdonald, I., 55, 61, 62, 91, 92
Mackey, C., 40
Macpherson, W., 9, 17, 18, 19, 35, 54, 58, 101, 104, 149, 152, 153, 158, 159, 160
Macpherson Report, 153
Maguire, M., 90, 125
Maguire Seven, 125
Manning, P., 1
Margalit, A., 105
Marks, M., 8, 170, 172, 178, 183
Marshall, G., 157
Martin, J., 49, 135
Marx, G.T., 2, 146
Matza, D., 115
May, T., 24, 29, 39, 43, 46, 52, 53, 58, 59, 72, 75, 79, 95, 99, 104, 117, 118, 146, 161, 162, 163
May, Theresa (Home Secretary), 29, 36, 79, 161
Mazerolle, L.G., 99, 122n. 4
McAra, L., 47, 48, 107, 113, 116, 117
McCullagh, M., 62
McGovern, M., 130, 131
McGrew, A., 189
McLaughlin, E., 36, 158, 160
McVie, S., 47, 48, 107, 113, 116, 117
Medina Ariza, J.J., 48
Metropolitan Police Service (MPS), 34–6, 39–41, 79, 84, 93, 103, 138, 152, 158, 161, 164, 194–5
Miller, J., 16, 19, 32, 44, 49, 53, 54, 55, 60, 61, 63, 65, 77, 78, 82, 83, 84, 91, 94, 95, 104, 119, 154

Misuse of Drugs Act 1971, 11, 41, 80
Moon, D., 32, 56n. 2
Moore, S., 193
Morgan, R., 42
Muir, W.K., 185
Mulcahy, A., 106, 113
Municipalities Act 2002 (the Netherlands), 178
Murji, K., 62
Musumeci, L., 172, 177, 183, 186
Myhill, A., 97, 108, 109
Mythen, G., 131, 142

Namba, M., 181, 183
Neal, S., 149
Nelken, D., 189
Newburn, T., 32, 33, 34, 42, 188
9/11 attacks, 123, 128–31, 133, 136, 142
Norris, C., 74

O'Flynn, P., 164
Olagundoye, J., 58, 122n. 4
order maintenance, 55, 178, 191
Owusu-Bempah, A., 182, 183, 186

Padfield, N., 42
Pantazis, C., 130, 131
Parmar, A., 130, 131, 135, 142, 177, 178, 182, 183
Peachey, P., 163
Pemberton, S., 130, 131
Phillips, C., 18, 35, 52, 53, 55, 57, 61, 67, 72, 80, 86, 95, 102, 104, 108, 139, 152, 153, 177, 182, 187, 191
Police Activities Act 2004 (Denmark), 178
Police and Criminal Evidence Act (PACE), 26, 89, 121n.1
  changes to Code of Practices, 25–7, 162
  Code A 12–14, 80, 151
  Conservative Government, 10, 22
  crime fighting tactics, 56
  drug offenses, definition, 41
  HMIC on, 161
  introduction, 4–5
  limitations, 152–4, 156, 165, 169
  reasonable suspicion, 32–7
  recording of stop and search, 14–15, 160
  Section 1, 86
  Section 4, 81
  stop and search, prior to, 9–10
  symbolic and practical function, 151–2
police legitimacy
  community relations, 98
  in democratic societies, 2
  law enforcement agencies, 184
  and public's sense, 7, 111
  self-help violence, 112
  unfair damages, 110
  use of stop and search powers, 191
police officers
  anti-terrorism legislation, 20
  'Best Use of Stop and Search Scheme,' 162
  crime-fighting practices, 79, 83
  decision-making context, 58–9, 73
  disciplinary proceedings against, 11, 163–4
  disproportionality evidence, 77, 94, 101
  fair treatment, 107, 109
  intrusive and coercive powers, 192
  Lawrence Inquiry, impact on, 159
  legal powers, 1, 3, 148–9
  public cooperation, 166, 168
  Section 60 of the Criminal Justice and Public Order Act 1994, 16
  social exclusion and, 113
  structural inequalities, 155
  'Terry stops,' 178
  training, 193
  voluntary stops, 14, 18
Police Official Duties Execution Act 1948, 176
police powers
  adverse media attention, 154
  codifying, 2–3, 10
  coercive powers of government, 190, 192
  contract theory, 173–5
  in England, 4
  European Convention on Human Rights, 21, 23, 174
  PACE provisions, 5, 11

regulation and reforms, 8, 26, 166
Scarman Report, 158
stop and search, 31, 80, 174
terrorist threat, 124
in Wales, 4
police racism, 7, 17, 52, 155
police reform
  denial politics, 160–4
  organisational resistance, 157–60
  structural inequality, 155–7
  well-intentioned efforts, 195–6
Police Reform and Social Responsibility Act 2011, 26
policing
  adversarial style, 46
  among British Muslims, 115
  community initiatives, 4
  by consent, 3, 35
  crime control, 31, 34, 79
  different styles, 43–4
  disciplinary model, 48
  disproportionality, 78, 108
  ethnic disparities, 95–6
  fair and accountable, 5
  'fire brigade,' 65
  formal powers, 119
  fundamental principle, 1, 4
  government reforms, 28
  hotspot, 83, 98
  'institutional racism,' 17, 46, 59
  intelligence-led, 90–1
  nature of stops, 45
  1960s and 1970s, 9
  positive-sum relationship, 121
  proactive, 82–3, 117
  problem-oriented interventions, 83, 98–9
  procedural justice theories, 106
  public cooperation and, 103, 105
  Scarman's analysis, implications, 97
  social reality, 12
  street availability, 19
  unfair, 115
  urban, 10
  young people, 72, 100
  zero-tolerance, 34, 44
  see also counter-terrorism policing

Prasad, R., 6
Prevention of Terrorism Act 1974, 124–5, 127
private actors, 173, 189, 192
private police, 189
procedural justice theory, 7, 102, 109, 110–11
Protection of Freedom Act 2012, 30n.2
Provine, M., 181, 183
public safety, 24, 144, 174, 189, 191

Quinlan, T.L., 8, 123
Quinton, P., 7, 21, 38, 46, 57, 58, 64, 70, 71, 73, 74, 92, 122n. 4, 127, 152, 176, 178

racial profiling
  definition, 129
  disproportionality, 94, 186
  effects on victims, 95
  indirect, 147
  minorities in US, 130
  Muslim communities, 129
  REVA project, 183
  Section 44 and, 133
  state-sanctioned, 182
Ramirez, D.A., 130, 140
Ramos, S., 172, 177, 183, 186
Ratcliffe, J.H., 62, 91, 119
Ream, G.L., 93, 119
reasonable suspicion
  of criminality, 29
  exceptional powers, 81, 154
  Gillan decision, 22–3, 25
  intelligence-led stop and searches, 139
  investigative justification, 175–9
  labelling effect, 184
  new Code of Practice, 23–5
  non-random nature, 45
  notion of detention, 14
  number of searches, 88, 91
  under PACE, 32–7, 162
  police abuse, 96
  under Section 44, 22, 38–9
  under Section 60, 20
  slipperiness, 11–13, 152
  Terrorism Act 2000, 23

reasonable suspicion – *continued*
  types of encounter, 63–4
  usual requirements, 127, 132, 144, 164, 186, 195
reform barriers
  denial politics, 160–4
  organisational resistance, 157–60
  structural inequality, 155–7
regulation
  centralised reforms, 153–5
  corporate pyramid, example, 167
  institutional racism, 150
  internal performance management, 164–8
  Lawrence Inquiry, impact on, 153
  legal powers, 149
  modes, 147–9
  police tactics, 150
  rights of suspects, 149–50
  Scarman's recommendation, impact on, 150–1
  see also reform barriers; stop and search powers
Reiner, R., 1, 3, 4, 5, 32, 33, 34, 43, 45, 53, 55, 56, 59, 61, 65, 71, 74, 76, 77, 99, 106, 113, 146, 148, 149, 150, 151, 152, 153, 154, 155, 156, 157, 158, 159, 164, 165, 195
Reiss, A., 74
Reith, C., 4
Riddell, M., 35
Roach, K., 126, 128, 129
Road Traffic Act 1988, 11, 32, 81
Roberts, G., 193
Rock, P., 60
Rollock, N., 153
Rowe, J., 125
Rowe, M., 81, 149, 158
Royal Commission on Criminal Justice (1993), 125
Royal Commission on Criminal Procedure (1981), 9, 10, 31, 149
Rubinstein, J., 59, 60, 62, 69
rule of law, 2–3, 43, 131, 174
Rush, J., 162, 195

Sampson, R., 82
Sanchez, G., 181, 183
Sanders, A., 1, 11, 12, 31, 32, 33, 38, 39, 41, 46, 47, 54, 63, 64, 81, 92, 99, 127, 148, 149, 152, 153, 154
Savage, S., 157
Scarman, L.G. (Lord), 3, 4, 6, 10, 17, 34, 96, 97, 149, 150, 151, 153, 155, 156, 158, 159, 160, 168, 184
Scarman Report
  on police functions, 4
  publication, 9, 17
  on racism, 10, 153, 155–6, 158–9
  on stop and search operations, 18–19
Schutz, A., 71
security guards, 172–3, 189, 193–4
self-help violence, 7, 111–12
Sergeant, H., 42, 74
Serious Crime Act 2007, 39
7/7 bombings, 128–9, 131, 139, 142
Sharp, C., 53
Sharp, D., 95, 107, 108
Sheptycki, J., 187, 188, 189, 192
Sherman, L.W., 98, 120, 156, 167, 185
Shiner, M., 1, 7, 8, 31, 35, 36, 46, 52, 57, 58, 63, 64, 89, 92, 104, 146, 154, 157, 158, 159, 165, 166, 193
Shoe Bomber (Reid, Richard), 142
Sibbitt, R., 73
Silverman, E.B., 34, 100
Sim, J., 158, 160
Singer, L., 48, 97
situational discrimination, 59, 61, 64
Skogan, W., 77, 97, 108, 185
Smandych, R., 189
Smith, D.J., 45, 53, 66, 70, 71, 73, 74, 108
Smith, J., 72
Smith, N., 72
social class, 45, 47–8
social exclusion, 56, 103, 113, 118
social identities, 103
Souhami, A., 159
Spalek, B., 105, 115, 143
Sparks, R., 6
Spiegelhalter, D., 39
stop and search
  anti-terrorism legislation, 20–2
  2010 general election, impact on, 22–3

HMIC review on, 27–30
intelligence led, 18–20
legal challenges, 11–14
national regulation, 16–18
negative consequences, 101
PACE code of practice, 10–11, 25–7
police attitude, 70–2
prior to PACE, 9–10
racial differences, 57
recording, 14–15
Stephen Lawrence Inquiry, 16–18
targeted, 18–20
without reasonable suspicion, 16, 23–5
stop and search powers
accountability, 185–7
contract theory, 173–5
definition, 170–1
deterrent justification, 177–80
global context, 187–90
investigative justification, 175–7
negative effects on individual and society, 184–5
notion of detention, 171–2
police-like agencies, 172–3
theory and practice, 170
usual suspects, 180–3
StopWatch
on ethnic differences, 49, 95
formation, 195
New York's 'quality of life' policing, 194
objectives, 5–6
rebalancing of police powers, 154
on use of Section 60, 40
Strang, H., 167
Stratton, A., 194
Stumpf, J.P., 188
Sunshine, J., 97
'suspect communities', 24, 190
'Swamp 81,' 4, 10, 97, 150

Tackling Knives and Serious Youth Violence Action Programme (TKAP), 39, 84–5
Tankebe, J., 105
Taylor, B., 98
Taylor, M., 161

Terrorism Act 2000
amended version, 23
general police power, 11
overview, 126–8
Prevention of Terrorism Act vs, 126
Schedule 7, 24, 81, 136, 171
Section 43, 20, 138
Section 44, 16, 21, 37, 40, 81, 131–2, 134, 140, 154, 178
Section 60, 25, 37
Section 47A, 144
suspicionless' searches, 177
Terrorism Act 2006, 129
'the Troubles', 126, 131
Thiel, D., 128
Thornberry, T.P., 53
Tomkins, A., 129
Tóth, B., 171, 176, 181, 183, 186
Townsend, M., 40
Tracey, P.E., 116
traffic stops, 108, 130, 195
Tran, M., 34
transmitted discrimination, 59, 65
Travis, A., 38, 41, 160, 161, 182
Tuch, S., 143
Tyler, T.R., 78, 97, 98, 102, 105, 106, 107, 108, 109, 111, 118, 120, 143, 184, 185

'Underwear Bomber' (Abdulmutallah, Umar Farouk), 142
unintended consequences
drug offenses, 42
effectiveness of stop and search, 118–20
ethnic disproportionality, 102–4
fairness issues, 104–8
negative public confidence, 108–11
organisational policies, 150
policing reforms, 28
procedural justice theory, 7
self-help violence, 111–13
social exclusion, 113–18

Vagrancy Act 1824, xi, 9
van der Leun, J., 178, 182, 186
van der Woude, M., 178, 182, 186
Vaz, K., 163
Vertigans, S., 115

Violent Crime Control and Law Enforcement Act 1994, 148
Von Hirsch, A., 82

Waddington, P.A.J., 53, 60, 61, 104, 106, 113
Wakslak, C., 107, 143, 185
Walker, A., 108, 110
Walker, C., 126, 128
Ward, L., 39, 85
Wardak, A., 189
'war on crime,' 34, 194
'war on terror,' 128, 130
Weapons and Ammunitions Act 2002 (the Netherlands), 178
Weber, L., 79, 170, 172, 174, 177, 178, 180, 181, 183, 186, 187, 188, 189, 192
Webster, C., 130, 131
Weisburd, D.L., 98
Weisburg, D., 94
Weitzer, R., 143
Werb, D., 94
Whelan, A., 194
'White Widow' (Lewthwaite, Samantha), 142
Whitfield, J., 9, 31
Wiley, S.A., 117
Willis, C.F., 10, 97, 184
Wilson, G., 52
Wilson, J.Q., 178
Wortley, S., 182, 183, 186

Young, J., 52, 65, 66
Young, R., 39, 46, 54, 63, 64, 81, 92, 99, 168

Zedner, L., 123, 128
zero-tolerance, 34, 44, 190, 194–5

Printed and bound by CPI Group (UK) Ltd, Croydon, CR0 4YY